Vipers and Geckos

Defining Friend, Foe, and Truth in an Alien Land

Debra Pritchard

Contents

Foreword   V

Preface   VII

Epigraph   VIII

1. Chapter 1   1

2. Chapter 2   18

3. Chapter 3   30

4. Chapter 4   56

5. Chapter 5   78

6. Chapter 6   96

7. Chapter 7   118

8. Chapter 8   136

9. Chapter 9   150

10. Chapter 10   166

11. Chapter 11   182

12. Chapter 12   200

13. Chapter 13   220

14. Chapter 14   234

15. Chapter 15   248

16. Chapter 16   260

Epilogue   266

The Characters Now   272

Acknowledgements   274

Understanding Filipino Cultural Traits   276

Tagalog Glossary   280

Reading Guide Questions   286

About the Author   288

Foreword

In the pages of this book, the reader will embark on a transformative journey alongside Debra, a fellow traveler caught at the crossroads of cultures, navigating a maze of intricate human interactions, misunderstandings, and a profound journey of self-discovery.

I knew Deb through several of her recounted escapades and had fun reliving those. But I didn't know the extent of the ups and downs of her first years here on Palawan. Her candid narrative unravels the threads of truth and assumption that tether us to our upbringing, offering a heartfelt exploration into the complexities of belonging when immersed in the unfamiliar. Debra's story is neither a guidebook nor a critique; it is a genuine exploration into the ebb and flow of one woman's adjustment to a new culture, entering laden with good intentions and the earnest desire to connect, and then coping with the inevitable missteps accompanying cultural immersion.

At the age of 59, Debra leaves San Francisco for the Philippines and plunges headlong into the nuances of Filipino culture, particularly the complex provincial life of Palawan. Her journey unfolds with humility, humor, and an unyielding commitment to understanding, sharing moments of cultural clashes, language barriers, and the laughter that echoes through the journey of self-discovery.

This narrative is not a criticism; it is an invitation to appreciate the richness and diversity that defines Filipino culture. Debra's struggles, tears, laughter, and ultimate acceptance as an adopted Palaweña stand as a testament to humanity's capacity to adapt and connect across borders.

As you turn these pages, prepare to accompany Deb in moments of reflection, amusement, and a deeper understanding of the human experience. This is a cultural odyssey, a quest for belonging, and the revelation that acceptance often transcends language and customs.

Debra may not claim to comprehend every nuance of Filipino culture, but her journey offers a unique perspective—a narrative that calls readers to challenge assumptions, laugh at their own mistakes, and celebrate successes - even when they come little by little.

Kudos to Deb for taking a leap of faith at a crossroads in her life; for taking that risk of believing that we can embrace risk and the chance to bloom anew – at any age. And congratulations for surviving the obstacles and coming back for more and making such a big difference here in our island community.

Let this book serve as a reminder that the road to belonging is paved with curiosity, laughter, and an open heart willing to embrace the unfamiliar. May you enjoy this compelling and heartwarming account as much as I did, for within its pages lie lessons that resonate far beyond the shores of Palawan.

Ami Evangelista Swanepoel
Founding Executive Director, Ugat Ng Kalusugan
Roots of Health, Puerto Princesa, Palawan

Preface

This is a memoir of my first two years in the Philippines, serving as a 59-year-old Peace Corps volunteer, and attempting to acclimate to an alien culture without instruction and with a smile. While it is specific to the Philippines and the provincial culture of Palawan, the lessons learned apply to any new culture from your birth culture. Much of the content comes from the journal and blog I kept, but more of the stories are from my memory, as undependable as that might be. Each person has a different story, even if the characters are the very same people. This is my story as I recall it and there may be inconsistencies and outright mis-recollection for which I apologize.

It won't be the first or last time.

In Baclayon, Reading Levertov's "For Whom the Gods Love Less"
by Marjorie Evasco

Perhaps it is now the other way around,
and I have become an almost-perfect lover,
caring little that the Gods love poets less.
I am begun again, anew, listening
from the open window to the old *tambis* tree
drop red bells of fruit onto the grass and roof.
In this humid May afternoon in Baclayon,
the guava redolent on the branch meets the sunbird's praise, both scent and song passing through me,
as though I have turned into all-embracing air
in this keep of grace, Levertov's radiant wings
decanting shadows, urging the only way to let love.

Free Gift

Keep in touch with me by scanning the QR code to go to my website www.debrapritchard.com and get my my free recipe booklet, The Tastes of South Asia as a Thank You gift.

If you love the flavors of the Philippines and Southeast Asia like I do, click the **Tastes of SE Asia** tab to download my free recipe booklet from my time there: 'Deb's Travels.'

I also answer all my emails at www.debrapritchard805@gmail.com. I'd love to talk to any of you at a crossroads who might be inspired to take a leap into another culture - schedule a time to chat on my website.

Chapter 1

ADVENTURE - ROMANCE - LIFE - CHANGING ESCAPADES!

Paddle your own canoe
Isagwan mo ang iyong bangka
An American proverb meaning, 'Act independently and decide your own
fate.'

Paddle Your Own Canoe excerpt
Sarah Bolton, 1851
Voyager upon life's sea,
To yourself be true,
And whatever your lot may be,
Paddle your own canoe...

IT WAS TIME. MY PALM'S LIFELINE LOOKED SHORTER, and those familial ties that bind had been ripped away with obvious scars. The big door was closed, but that window was open, beckoning me. I was free in the Joplin definition - Janis, not Al. Nothing left to lose. Failure had led me here and while others judged me and might be happy to see me fail again, I needed to get back to Janis' feeling good, without the drugs. I returned full circle to the possibility of a childhood dream. Why not? It was time to leap.

The significance of partying with the Silicon Valley millennials hit me on my long, slightly inebriated drive home. My conundrum was how I could leave behind this life that I'd built, but now was crumbling. Visions of my daughters laced my foggy brain as I continued driving, cautious and alert, up a fairly deserted El Camino Real toward home. Where I'd had a family for 19 years in an affluent part of the San Francisco Bay Area, I now had a lovely home on the Peninsula, and lived alone, without even a pet, save the raccoons which came nightly to feast on my koi in my beloved pond in the back. Craving that water feature since my childhood had proved less ideal in reality than my reverie and was the scene of mayhem and blood – for the koi I mean - I didn't kill the raccoons but wanted to.

The divorce had rocked my life and the ensuing anger from my daughters was crumbling even that relationship which I thought unassailable. My insecurities and life newly focused on myself were causing a widening rift, yet I couldn't imagine how significant it would become. Wasn't the bond between mother and child durable and forever?

That night, these thoughts splashed in the background of the overarching message from the group of people I'd just met, those who had taken that leap of faith in their youth to serve for Peace in a far-off land. The bright, happy faces around the table cheered me on over our Thai sticky rice dessert.

"How did you decide? Why did you sign up?" I asked no one in particular as I looked down the long table.

One of the older men with graying hair and a paunch evident in his expensive suit, gave a loud laugh as he waved his empty bottle at the waiter.

"I was just out of college and an oppositional snot, primed for adventure."

Several of the youngers raised their cups in solidarity.

"My parents were terrified that I would die over in Cameroon, a place they'd never even heard of. I was so rebellious that their fear sealed the deal. Ah, the irony and folly of youth. Not only did those two years cure me of my rebellion and bring me back to my parents, but it set me on my life's mission - to eradicate cholera. I returned in 1982, got my medical degree, and have been with Stanford's Infectious Diseases department ever since."

"Inspiring stuff for the '80s," I said. But at the same time, I was thinking that from the looks of him, he hadn't wanted for anything for quite a while. I wondered if he still identified with the masses, or more with the elite doctors of famed medical schools.

"I put my marriage on hold and just left for two years," said a 40-something woman. "It changed my life, and our marriage, all for the better!" "What a change from my boring office job. Now I'm a web development consultant and commute between Palo Alto and Marrakech."

Well, that scenario sure wasn't me, but I started seeing opportunities for a drastic change.

"I craved the *chakery* when I was pregnant, and still miss it," giggled a woman who had gone to The Gambia five years prior. "I met my husband there and we lived in Banjul where my first child was born. We moved to Sunnyvale last year where my husband works for Google. As you can see, I'm expecting again and am salivating for that sweet pudding!"

Most of these folks were at least 20 years my junior, and many had served 20 or 30 years ago. Could they even understand my trepidation and how different it would be for a 60-year-old woman in 2010?

They accurately read my wrinkled forehead.

Three of them trumpeted, "Do It! Forget all the logistics and confusion you're feeling. Just Do It – Join the Peace Corps!" All glasses raised high in a toast as the waiter set down five more bottles of Singha.

Downing our beers, we all left for home, they reliving memories and me envisioning an unenvisionable future. With fragmented thoughts of possibilities and regrets, I turned onto Canyon Road and heard my undercarriage scrape the high curb into my circular driveway. Steering my trusty Honda CRV with Singha caution into the attached garage, I systematically closed both the car- and garage doors and unlocked the back entrance. Tripping on the top stair, I cursed as my already high-heel-sore toes kicked the old cat door, which I had blocked off to bar evening prowlers. Several nights, they had entered and eaten cereal in the pantry before scurrying out with their masked faces, and that was before they ate my koi.

But after midnight tonight, it was California winter cold, that crispness associated with the holidays, and only quiet and darkness welcomed me home. Kicking off my pointy shoes as I entered my warm home, I saw I'd forgotten to put away the feta cheese from lunch, and my stomach curdled at the smell. A quick pop of two ibuprofen and a slug of water to thwart the oncoming headache and I padded toward the stairs. The house was light and airy during the day from all the windows, but at night, the bright kitchen lights would illuminate me as the prime catch in a spotlighted fishbowl. I walked in the dark to turn on the softer interior hall lights, but still squinted in the glare, and headed upstairs, wishing only to flop into bed.

I turned right instead to my small octagonal office and its old desktop computer. The room was woodsy and comforting with its carved book-shelves filled with the likes of Beck's cognitive behavioral therapy, Vygot-sky's educational theory, *Chemistry* by Morrison and Boyd, and Larsson's *Girl with the Dragon Tattoo* series of mysteries. While books soothed me, the computer was one of my nemeses; keeping it up-to-date and virus-free was a chore for my low-tech brain.

I admit to having addictive personality traits, from chocolate to men to the internet. So, even at such a late hour, I compulsively turned on my HP Pavilion and it glowed in the dark, pulsating green, a metronome to my alcohol headache. I would check my emails...just in case.

...and there it was.

After soul-searching and months upon months of voluminous applications, intrusive medical check-ups, and invasive psychological histories, I had been interviewed by a 20-something recruiter in Oakland.

Interviewer: "Do you have any requests? Any medical needs?" as she prepared her final notes.

Me: "Well, I have the beginnings of arthritis and would love a warm climate. I can't speak Spanish, so I know South America's out, but someplace warm where I can swim - that's my request if you're asking."

Interviewer: "It's not likely that they'll send you someplace you'd hate, but I can't promise you a heated pool."

Me: "I always pictured myself in Madagascar teaching English. Or maybe in Dr. Livingone's Africa teaching students how to write in the jungle. Or somewhere near an oasis in the desert - have you ever seen the movie *The Wind and the Lion*?"

Interviewer: "No, but it sounds like you'll be fine wherever they send you. So, we've completed everything - you'll get an email in about three weeks that will tell you where and when."

End of the interview.

In those days, the Peace Corps assigned you to a country; nowadays, you can choose the region of the world you wish to serve. Back then, you were at the mercy of where they decided to place you. Thus, at 58, I was formally accepted into my childhood dream: the U.S. Peace Corps. Little did I know how unlike my dream the reality would be.

Adventure. Romance. Life-Changing Escapades! That was my childlike view of what it would be like. All that remained was to find out my assignment, which for some reason they kept secret. The interviewer told me to expect an emailed 'invitation' with my official departure and destination within three weeks. Now it was here, the answer, my future. Yet, my finger hesitated above the link, allowing time to remember how I got here.

When I was 12 years old, I said to my best friend, Liz, while we were doing homework together in the kitchen and petting Fraulein her shepherd,

"You know that peace club that Mr. D. talked about today that the President started? I'm going to go into it, wanna go with me?"

Liz usually followed me on my adventurous capers and probably thought this was but one more. She glanced at me and continued her algebra equation.

"Sure, when we get older, let's sign up," she said.

Liz still remembers, but I don't think she really had any intention of going.

I was crushed when the U.S. President who authorized the Peace Corps was assassinated only two years later. I remember sobbing with one politically precocious girlfriend on a grassy knoll of Traweek Middle School in West Covina, California. We learned about it at lunch. The Kennedy progressive schemes were staggering in scope: the space program to the moon, the Peace Corps, Civil Rights legislation, and his sister started the Special Olympics movement. What heady family times those Kennedys must have had sailing on the Cape, dreaming up such schemes. And we baby boomers bought into their Camelot. Certainly, it was a mythical time for me.

When I graduated from high school, the Peace Corps was still on my mind, but college loomed. I did mention it to Liz again during our freshman year, but she was otherwise occupied with a baby on the way and a wedding to plan. Then senior year, one of my addictions struck and I married my teaching assistant, quite another story, although rather short. Life kept intervening, from California to Texas to New Jersey and back to Texas in sales, then marketing for Shell Chemical. And back to California again with a new job, new husband, and quickly after, two babies. I went from making multi-million-dollar decisions in my job to deciding which park to go to and if I should make peanut butter or tuna sandwiches. The Peace Corps receded far to the back of my frenetic mind during the child-rearing years.

As a young adult, my cinematic vision of the Peace Corps was a cross between swashbuckling Indiana Jones, animal communication savant Dr. Doolittle, and the passionate Dr. Zhivago pining for Lara, a mixture that congealed somehow into one of my all-time favorite epics, *The Wind and the Lion*. In my prime, people said I looked like Candice Bergen, and I so loved fantasy and romance with that dash of Sean Connery's dry humor...it suited me well.

Much later, I read *Eat, Pray, Love*, and after sobbing at the opening chapter that so aligned with my own life, I decided that my time had come. I'd had similar experiences to Gilbert's through a 20-year marriage and now divorce. I was hoping for the same ending, LOVE.

Why the Peace Corps chose to send me the email invitation on a Saturday night just before Christmas, I didn't know, but there it was...all I had to do was open it. Deep breath. I clicked the link.

I read, "AZERBAIJAN, leaving in May 2010."

I was not a geography scholar to be sure, and nothing remotely familiar popped into my brain. So, of course, I Googled it.

Google's search engine ("About 428,000,000 results 0.67 seconds") prioritized the Lonely Planet site, and as they say, a picture is worth 1,000 words. I had only three screaming in my brain, and I won't repeat them here.

I could only liken the photo in that year's online travel guide to one summer experience flying into Anchorage, Alaska with two little girls screaming, "Look at all that snow!" Breathtaking snowy mountain ranges, as far as one could see. Tall white Azerbaijani mountains: The Greater Caucasus in the north and the Lesser in the south. In a country the size of Maine, how much warmth could be in-between those alpine mountain ranges? Not 'snow-capped,' but rather from foot to peak, the only color in the picture was white. Annoyed, I cursed the Peace Corps and more specifically, the recruiter I had interviewed with. More vexing than even the raccoons. I glared, leaning close to those mountains on the screen, fogging them.

"Are you deaf!? I asked for ONE thing: Warmth!"

My trepidation increased as I segued from the picture to the caption. "*The Caucasus includes the highest peak in Europe.*" What! Higher than the Matterhorn? Oh my. With an avalanche of muddy emotions, I snapped the computer off and stumbled to bed.

After aspirin the following morning, in bright daylight, I re-Googled multiple sites and my spirits fell further. It seemed that people in Azerbaijan were quite concerned with outward appearances and attire. Having clean and shiny leather shoes seemed to be a big deal, a task made quite difficult due to the oft-sludgy walkways filled with melting snow. Not my style at all, sigh.

Oh, for heaven's sake! Buck up! Adventure. Romance. Life-changing Escapades!

Flexibility was key, to roll with disappointments, I told myself. I regrouped and scribbled my Christmas Santa list. Santa's elves heard my need for a down jacket and alpine-grade bedroll. It was a warm and festive Christmas with *long* the operative word: long underwear, long puffy jacket, long-sleeved flannel shirts, and long-lasting thermal hand warmers. Liz sent both silky long underwear and flannel pajamas. She wasn't keen on joining me but cheered me on. My older daughter gave me my favorite jammies: small white polar bears on a sky-blue background, and I got fur-lined boots. Things were getting 'real.' In January, I took down my artificial Christmas tree for the last time and stuffed it in the back corner of the attic to wait for me.

I had purchased a home I loved the year before in the oak-studded, winding roads of the Emerald Hills part of Redwood City and had tried to make it my own. The attic was now finished and could provide space to stash my plethora of Christmas decorations and the silver tea service my favorite aunt insisted on giving me for a wedding present when I begged for a vacuum cleaner. Within five months, I had to get my property ready to rent out to strangers for two years while I was in Azerbaijan, and I was no handyman. Labor-intensive work like cleaning the gutters filled with redwood tree needles, raking up the cedar tree-lined backyard, and dredging the slimy and putrid algae from the pond now that the raccoons had annihilated the koi. De-cluttering the cluttered garage, chemically balancing the hot tub water, and making sure the roof rats were kept out of the landscaping shed. Lots of splinters and sore muscles later, the outside looked presentable.

It had taken me a while to find a home with the nooks and niches I wanted, with outdoor garden spaces and trees, and that cursed pond that I loved. It felt right and gave me solace, important since after leaving public education, I now worked out of my home assessing youth with learning differences. I wondered what my lodging would be like in the Caucasus but couldn't imagine. Visions of me in mukluks and a parka sipping hot tea in front of a fire were most prevalent. I just hoped I didn't have to forage for firewood.

Several years ago, I had gone back to school after the divorce and got a Master's in Special Education (SPED) and a certificate in Educational Therapy. I taught SPED in the Bay Area for two years at public middle schools, first in South San Francisco, which seemed a lot like West Side Story with all its gangs, but without the dance numbers. Parkway Heights

Middle School was smack in the middle with Surenos on one side of Grand Avenue and Nortenos on the other. Several of the dads were in prison.

"Yo, Ms. Pritchard."

"Hey Gabe - where are you guys off to?"

"Out to find some chicks and partay," he swaggered.

"Do you have condoms?" I asked my 13-year-old student.

"Yep - okay that we leave our stuff here?"

"Sure, just get it Monday morning and please be careful."

I loved my wannabe gangsta kids with their OG parents, and I considered all of us ill-fitted to the school. I didn't realize that clueless white male chauvinists still existed in 2008, but the MCP principal hated both my Latino students in Special Ed and me. I wasn't the typical detached teacher and bonded with several in my classes. The principal was appalled when the boys of the class refused to go with a male teacher for sex ed - they wanted to learn from me. I think I might have learned more from them that semester. That year provided an eye-opening and enriching experience with my students but was demoralizing for me professionally. I was used to being a stellar performer as a team leader in business and faced conflict with the principal-as-god administration.

I left the impoverished gangster school and moved to an affluent district farther south, closer to my home. This transition from business to teaching was tough going. Coming from twenty years of leading large teams of professionals with a bottom-line profit-and-benefit orientation didn't segue fluidly to a hierarchical and passive-aggressive environment with back-stabbing attacks and cliquish whispers. Naively I had thought teaching was a helping profession. Bay Area career administrators didn't like my independence, any divergence from a set routine, or my sticking up for my students. We parted ways, well, actually I was fired, I think with some glee on the administration's part.

When I left my classroom, I carted out a carload of textbooks and children's and young adult literature, purchased as most teachers do, with my meager salary. Immediately afterward, I started my own educational therapy business, accumulating diagnostic tools, research articles, and sensory materials to assess and report on learning issues and therapies for individual students. Where was I going to store all this stuff? My cherished

Asian antiques and furnishings weren't going to be tossed and needed protection. Somehow, I had to figure out where and how to stow all these belongings for two years.

And, at some point, I had to reflect on what the hell I was doing. I might have too much meta- and physical baggage to pull this off.

"Are you sure you want to do this?"

"Why don't you just stay and be happy here?"

"I don't understand how you are going to leave everything that you know!"

"Are you allowed to call us?"

"How far will you have to walk each day?"

"How can you learn a new language at your age?"

"Why are you really going?"

Responding to my friends' well-meaning worries really stressed me out, more than I already was.

Was I crazy? I didn't know the answer to their questions. I was between jobs, hated public education and it seemed like a good next step at the time.

Much easier to answer:

"Can I have this painting while you're gone?"

"What about the Cutco knives, shall I keep them for you?"

"I'll take the oriental rug."

"Can I have the bread maker?"

"How about your bike?"

My friends came one by one throughout the weeks and helped me divide piles in the garage. Ellen came and debated what I should take with me in a running monologue.

"I think this bra is too flashy and sexy," she said, nearly falling off the plastic chair in the garage. Howling with laughter, we drank chardonnay under the 100-year redwood tree that I would miss. She didn't need my end of the conversation and continued.

"...I assume you will have a washer and dryer, so let's not pack too much. But, you will need snow boots and warmer clothes than you have."

"...You have so much stuff. What are we posting on Craigslist? I'll take the breadmaker and that painting in the bedroom. I'll just keep a few things for you until you get back. I think you can give the rest of this pile to Goodwill.

...You'll come home for visits, right? Steve and I will visit you and you'll be back in no time..."

We prattled over the trivialities, with the big issues unspoken.

Another day, Laurie came to help, and Judy the next - the scenes were indistinguishable. My friends chatted, sorted discards for Goodwill, packed up cherishables, and posted items to Craigslist in flowery language. They chattered on, with me answering their redundant questions and getting more anxious as the time to depart drew closer. My friends, who still couldn't understand why I would do this, were rewarded with anything they wanted for themselves from my pile of leavings, from couches, a washer, and kitchen appliances to kids' books and area rugs.

I don't know if anyone noticed my spiraling angst. I cleaned cabinets and compartmentalized feelings, overcome with a bustle of frantic activity getting everything sold off or stored, packing up for two long years. Truly leaving life as I had known it. So many tasks to do, from powers of attorney to selling my car, to setting up a P.O. Box, and finding a renter. Daunted to get everything ready, my nerves were frazzled trying to cope with the details and deadlines of readying to sail into the unknown.

At the same time, I was preparing for my new culture. I searched free websites to attempt the language and learn about Azerbaijan's history of rather horrific genocides since 1918. It was hard to teach the old dog new phonetic sounds, but my guttural throat noises felt like I was making progress.

In early May, I received a phone call.

"Good day Ms. Pritchard. I am calling from Washington D.C. about your placement with the Peace Corps. Unfortunately, we are not able to access one of your medications in Azerbaijan. We have tried and it is just not available there. Would you mind if we changed your assignment to Asia?"

She sounded like that flat, prerecorded message you get when you dial the wrong number, maybe a little perkier. *Did I mind? Really?* I must admit that those nasty three words once again sprang into my head. Instead, I politely asked the bland-voiced woman, "Is the climate warm? And, is there water for me to swim?"

"There is a lot of water around, but I don't know if you can swim in it." Gadzooks! It sounded like a cesspool or toxic waste dump, or the arctic.

"Will it be warm? I only asked for a warm place."

"Yes, I think it will be warmer than Azerbaijan."

"What kind of food will I be eating? Will I be closer to Japan or India? What will I be required to wear?" I peppered her with questions, all meaning WHERE IS IT? hoping she would tell me something, anything.

She wouldn't tell me where I was going no matter how I tried, not even a hint. All I got was a continent.

"The country is in Asia, and you will now leave on July 16th.

This was only the beginning of the strange bureaucratic secrecy, red tape, condescension, and rigidity I would feel throughout my Peace Corps service. I stifled my irritation and respectfully thanked her for the call.

Then I hastily Googled, "U.S. Peace Corps departures July 16, 2010." Former library freak turned Google addict, I turned up several Asian destinations, but only one on the 16th: Manila, the Philippines. I thus amended my Good Evening greeting from *Axşamınız xeyir* to the Tagalog, *Magandang gabi*. Oh, my aching head.

I admit to being an ignorant American, although I was determined to never be the stereotypical Ugly American, that loud, shallow, and ethnocentric traveler. My parents were poor; I recall only three family vacations in my childhood, two driving for three days cross-country to visit my grandmother in our old Dodge station wagon, and me sleeping on blankets in the back. The first flight I took to another country was several years after college graduation. I grew up a loner, later termed more palatably an 'introvert,' and enjoyed reading, hikes with my dog, and solitude rather than heavy metal and parties. Hypersensitive to others like me who shied away from extroverts. I was ashamed of the many loud, clueless-yet-arrogant American tourists I met over the years when I vacationed overseas. Although I had traveled as an adult, I was far from worldly and had no cultural context, only my personal experiences. So, I was confused about my placement in the Philippines. Wasn't the Peace Corps supposed to work with 'developing' countries? The only Filipinos I knew in the U.S. were college-trained professionals, doctors, and nurses. My Google research showed me how ignorant I was:

The Philippines is composed of 7,100 islands (measured at high tide; at low tide, they count another 541 islands), although only 2,000 are inhabited. The average salary is about $3,300 per year. It ranks as the 25th worst country in the world for education, with 12% of the country completing only elementary school, 19% completing only high school, and 10% of school-aged children titled "out of school youth." The Filipinos I had met in the U.S. ranked in the top 1% of the nation.

The physical size of the Philippines is comparable to the state of Arizona, but the population is over 15 times that of Arizona's seven million residents. Over 105 million people, growing at the Catholic birth rate of 1.6% per year, or about 2 million additional bodies every year.

Wow. I needed to get up to speed on this country, I had a lot to learn. My immediate switch from Azerbaijani to Tagalog encountered tongue twister problems, everything came out garbled, like the notorious *ng* sounds. Still, I was determined to be able to say a few words upon arrival and have some knowledge of the country and culture. To not be an Ugly American.

I questioned anyone for facts about Filipinos. At a neighbor's pool party, I met a very tall and very white classmate of a friend who knew I was going to the Philippines. My friend beckoned to him to come to be introduced. He ambled over in his blue summer suit with a drink in his hand and an easy smile, looking the part of a playboy or the suave politician. Which, in fact, was his aspiration as the aide to Jerry Hill, the assemblyman for Daly City. Daly City is situated 10 miles south of San Francisco and is 40% Filipino. I asked him what 'they' were like. He winced and sipped his drink.

"They are short, and they lie," he responded to my very scrutable and shocked face.

It seemed that Ugly Americans weren't limited to those traveling abroad.

As part of my self-prescribed education, I frequented the library, reading books like *The Other Philippine History Textbook*, and *The Imperial Cruise*, which detailed the U.S. takeover of the Philippine islands in the early 1900s. President William McKinley and his Vice President, Teddy Roosevelt, compared Filipinos to Native Americans, calling them either "savage warriors" or "little brown brothers." At this point, I started re-learning American history from a radically different vantage.

I packed away the long underwear from Christmas and began shopping for lighter clothes, returning the down-filled sleeping bag purchased at REI and exchanging it for a mosquito net and bedsheet. We were only allowed forty pounds, so I was glad to shed the weight. Forty pounds for a two-year assignment; I felt like David Attenborough embarking on a jungle quest for birds of paradise in Papua New Guinea. But David knew a lot more about bird culture than I did about my destination.

Enlisting a local carpenter to build a secured storage unit in half of my garage, I piled my favorite furniture, wedding crystal, and antiques there out of harm's way, waterproofed as best I could, sold bulky furniture on Craigslist, and gave away loads more. It was almost time.

My nerves were frayed even before the property manager I had hired went AWOL two weeks before my departure, and one of the consequences was my daughter's birthday, a stressed-out cataclysmic failure. Another demerit to add to my growing pile. Our relationship was unraveling after the divorce, and not only had I been inept, but I was leaving for two years to a country 7,000 miles away without communication infrastructure and no anchor points for me. I was floundering.

Overwrought, I made it to the airport, vaccinated for everything from typhus to shingles to encephalitis, and flew from SFO to Detroit for staging with 199 other Peace Corps Volunteers (PCVs), most 30 years younger than I. What on earth was I doing here? My family was a wreck, I'd failed at my teaching jobs and shut the door on my old life. My house was rented out for two years and everything was sold off. I couldn't return now if I wanted to. Amid the chaos of excitement and trepidation, we bunked in Michigan one night, validated our new, no-fee passports for official government travel, and boarded our 12-hour flight to Nagoya, Japan, with another four hours to Manila. The plane landed after midnight when all 200 of us blearily boarded charter buses to Cavite, an hour south on the edge of Manila Bay.

We arrived before dawn at our two-week training location, the luxurious Island Cove resort...the last such luxury I would see for nearly two years. We were all spent from the long trip, but I was ready to learn about the culture and get tips I knew I would need. Which wasn't quite what happened.

MAP OF S.E.A

THE KOI POND

GIVING AWAY EVERYTHIN

PALAWAN IN PINK

TAKING OFF

Chapter 2

FIRST STEPS OF DISILLUSION

Mahirap gisingin ang nagtutulog-tulugan

It is hard to wake up someone who is pretending to be asleep

A Filipino proverb meaning, 'While it is easy to tell people something they do not know, it is much harder if they are willfully choosing not to see what is before them.'

Battle Hymn of the Republic, Updated excerpt
Mark Twain, 1900

Mine eyes have seen the orgy of the launching of the Sword;
He is searching out the hoardings where the stranger's wealth is stored;
He hath loosed his fateful lightning, and with woe and death has scored;
His lust is marching on

THIS WAS A FRAT PARTY nightmare, not my Dream. Our orientation at Island Cove sequestered us foreigners behind armed gates, for which residents of Cavite should be thankful. Spirits were high for all 200 volunteers, and with an average age of 27, cheap Philippine spirits were appreciated. The ubiquitous Tanduay rum and bottles of San Miguel beer were plentiful, with resulting couplings and liaisons in the first few days. These were the proud representatives of the U.S., the ambassadors of Peace to developing nations, nations that had petitioned the Peace Corps to send high-caliber college graduates to help with agriculture, ocean protection, English language instruction, and youth/family social work. It felt and smelled more like a frat party on Spring Break.

Days began early with the more appealing odors of yeast bread and coffee, a sumptuous breakfast buffet of whatever we craved. Fresh, sweet mangoes, bananas, pineapple, and masses of eggs, bacon, and pancakes, were a Western breakfast for us newbies. Alongside was laid the more typical Filipino *almusal* of *lamayo* (dried fish), *kanin* (rice), and the delicious sweet/spicy *longganisa* sausage. Breakfast was served any time before 7:00 AM with our first session an hour later. Each day you saw the early morning representatives of teetotalers (bright-eyed), athletic exercisers (sweaty and energized), and late sleepers (baggy eyes), some hungover, but all smiling in anticipation.

In class, we were given detailed schedules and lots of written information, but the notes I took felt trivial. We got detailed instructions about routine details, like which cellphone providers were best and where the 9-digit passcode was on the SIM card to load another $5. But, substance felt lacking. During the six hours of sitting in various white-walled square interior rooms, it didn't feel like I was learning much, or at least what I wanted to learn. I wondered if many of us had researched this country where we would be living, and I looked forward to a history lesson taught from the Filipino viewpoint. I never heard it.

It could have been that I was 30 years older than most and expected more, or just different. I wanted to hear about the history and societal mores, not cellphones and Tanduay. It could have been that we were being told a selective history, the whitewashed U.S. version of the truth. Maybe my pre-research made me suspicious of the canned history that we listened to. But then, it could be that our handlers' only intent was to allow us to acclimate to both the sweltering heat and the foreignness of this country, without taxing our minds. Whatever the intent, our sequestration worked well to protect Filipinos from the arrogance, ignorance, and entitlement of us myopic Americans.

The Peace Corps celebrated its 50th anniversary the following year, so I assumed that after 50 years they knew what they were doing. I had heard the jokes about the Peace Corps being undercover CIA and that volunteers infiltrated countries as spies. Still, it didn't occur to my idealistic head that we were fed only pro-American history in our training. I wanted the Peace Corps to be the objective, humanist organization that my pre-teen mythical brain and Camelot had conjured.

Only after orientation did I appreciate that a primary requirement of an organization's funding in the Philippines was to document that people were working (ironically, a significant amount of their cost and effort was in producing the documentation). So, itineraries and paperwork were crucial for the appearance of competence, and progress. Kill them with the details and keep the paychecks coming. I would find that most of our site assignments were heavily dependent on external money and even more concerned with that documentation. And that often, 'reality' was considerably augmented and improved with the flowery written documentation.

"Everyone in the Family and Youth group, stand over here," called one of the staff, waving at us. About 50 of us volunteers followed him. He positioned us against a wall of red bougainvillea as the backdrop for the photo.

"Now say Mabuhay!" as he pointed the camera at us.

We responded with a chorused cheer, some youthful arms pumping the air.

"Wait *lang*." said the staff person, "Another picture. Look up at the sky and point at the sun - everyone!"

We pointed enthusiastically.

"Now, look to your left. Over the shoulder of the person next to you. All together!"

Okay, aren't we done yet?

"One more - Whacky!"

It was pronounced 'wocky' and we all did something a little revolting for the cameras to capture.

The non-stop 'documentation' photo shoots of us happy volunteers during training prepared me for my later life in the Philippines. By then, it was no wonder to me that the Philippines consistently ranked in the top two countries in social media accounts per capita and topped the globe for the number of selfies. It seemed Filipinos had a thing for promoting personal beauty.

On one of our last nights at Island Cove, the staff announced that small groups would be allowed to take the classic and colorful local transport called *jeepneys* to shop at the local mall. We still had chaperones but were able to mingle with real people. This was August, in the torrential rainy season, and we experienced our first tropical storm with buckets of rain being hurled upon us. The jeepneys were sturdy, fit 20-30 people, and had windows, but it was so hot and humid that most of the steamy windows had to be cracked to let in oxygen. We slip-slid up the marble stairs in our sandals, squealing into an equally loud Philippine cacophony of wet masses. Most locals were dressed conservatively in jeans and summer dusters while we Americans wore tank tops and shorts, and like every nationality in the mall, we wore *tsinelas* (flip-flops).

From the outside, the mall looked like any mall in our neighborhoods back home. Inside, it was a labyrinth of innumerable stalls and kiosks, selling anything from watches and electronics to matches and hairpins, all tucked helter-skelter into narrow alleyways leading to other alleys, or dead ends. You could easily get lost in the maze, so we stayed together. Masses of humanity milled about, tall and thin, short and pudgy, bald or sporting man buns. Shopping, eating, and laughing in groups. Curious stares, hostile glares, and under-the-breath murmurings shortened our shopping spree, although many of us seemed oblivious. I hearkened back to the Ugly American syndrome, although it felt more than that. Our behavior felt judged, perhaps as provocatively dressed arrogant Americans, a differently defined generation of The Ugly American.

One of the older PCVs, Ryan, who had served two years in The Gambia, and must have faced diseases before, had a small cut on his big toe when we left for the mall. The next morning it had doubled in size and oozed pus, bright red with infection from the bacteria in the flooded streets; he couldn't even walk. A stick-in-the-eye lesson; I resolved to wash every inch of my body every night in this tropical land to make sure nothing grew on or in me the way his toe grew overnight.

Back in our training sessions, most of the speakers adopted the congenial tones of a buddy. "How many of you are comfortable drinking with your neighbors?" A slew of youthful hands shot up.

"You will need to be friendly with your community and get used to going to *piyestas* and drinking in a group. You heard me say *Piyestas* right? When you learn Tagalog, you will see that there is no "F" in Tagalog - it is Piyestas. We Pilipinos like our piyestas and you will be expected to be participants. Another Tagalog word you will hear a lot is *barkada*. It can be used to mean your group of friends, but it also means your drinking buddies. You women need to be careful. Don't give men the wrong idea. It's better to go with another volunteer or your host family if you are going out to drink."

"Do women have *barkadas*?" asked a young man.

"Oh yes, but they mostly shop," laughed the staff member in response.

Ah, yes, we weren't in San Francisco anymore, and my jaw tightened at his comment. Learning to be detached and only observe might not be as easy as I thought.

After the formal sessions, many of the speakers would have a poolside drink with volunteers before going to bed. But there was a line of hierarchy and decorum, the staff never got sloppy. Smiling and cordial, they knew that their big boss, the Country Director, was watching.

The Peace Corps organization designated the Country Director, and the Operations and Training directors as U.S. citizens, but all the other staff was from the country of residence, and as such, reflected the culture, although there was a subtle American overlay of caution and how to avoid being sacked. While many of the staff went out of their way to appear as 'one of the guys,' there was a sense that they abided by the rules and that their job was to make sure we did the same.

Arnel, who was the sector director of about fifty of us, spoke emotionally of his childhood on the streets, his providence, and his resulting passion to help his country. He was dedicated to the plight of street children who had been either orphaned, abandoned, or forced to steal so their families had food.

"We were so poor that we stole on the streets around del Pilar to bring home food and money for our family. It was me and my brother mostly. And once we got caught by a new priest when we went to hide in Malate Church."

Arnel told his story of petty thieving on the streets of Manila as a child until the priest caught him again. The second time the priest coerced him to either attend school or go to jail.

"The choice he forced me to make changed my life."

He told the story in a quiet and unemotional cadence, but a couple of times he had to regain his composure to remain dispassionate. Two minutes in, I had tears streaming down my cheeks.

"When I was a boy, I hated Americans for having so much money and freedom to do whatever they pleased; taking what they wanted from my country. After I saw how much good they could do for my country, I wanted to find out how to use that to help us. And that's why I joined the Peace Corps staff, to help Filipinos and our organizations get what they need."

As he spoke longer, I began to feel an undercurrent of dislike for Americans that, combined with his added power to gain funding and do his bidding, made me uncomfortable. In my still-glorified view of the Peace Corps, he was somehow off-putting. I glanced around as he finished and saw how many of the volunteers were visibly affected to the point of grasping his hand and almost consoling him. I wondered if his intent was to disarm us. I have been called an empath and pick up on nuances, even when I don't quite know what they mean. This man headed the division of the Youth and Family group where I would serve, and I was wary through my tears.

Island Cove maintained fantasy grounds cultivated for wealthy tourists, with botanical gardens and caged tropical birds arranged on the expansive green lawns in the front, a lovely diversion for newly arrived Americans and paying tourists. Showcasing formal grounds with prime specimens focused on appearances again, belying the reality behind the scenes.

The back enclosures, where they kept most of the animals were rather hellish: multiple turtles clambering over each other in a tiny concrete grotto of dirty water; an ostrich with barely any feathers standing alone and quiet, and smelly crocodiles packed in a small pit. But the domain that most guests saw was opulent and groomed.

The contrast with the surrounding residences outside the gates was stark. People living along the highway could be seen in the early morning and late afternoon cleaning their area. They swept the street with a *wallis tingting*, a broom made of stiff palm ribs. Each person swept only to the invisible edge of their property, never cleaning his neighbor's area so that there were patches of cleanliness bordered by mud and debris. Inside the gates of Island Cove, buildings and vegetation were manicured and white-glove clean, with workers meticulously trimming errant palm fronds in the hot sun.

During free time, when others were imbibing or liaising, I walked the back area, listening to the imploring sounds of native, caged wildlife like pangolins, civet cats, monitor lizards, and glorious birds of the rainforest. Their pleas begged me to free them, and scenes of *Free Willy* crossed my mind.

Floods from the monsoon rains necessitated planks to be laid down to be able to walk from cage to cage, and many of the animals were drenched and standing in several inches of water, pitiful. When we called attention to the caretakers, they looked at us like we were daft. With the poverty that so much of the population lived in, animals just weren't a priority; and, anyway didn't the bible say that man ruled all? Here, people quoted the first page of the bible, Genesis 1:26-28 to justify their treatment of animals:

God said, "Let us make humankind in our image, according to our likeness; and let them have dominion over the fish of the sea, and over the birds of the air, and over the cattle, and over all the wild animals of the earth, and over every creeping thing that creeps upon the earth."

I always thought that meant that man was supposed to take care of every living thing; this was the first time I heard an interpretation that we could do whatever we wanted to all living things, that we were the ruler, and not so benevolent at that.

The extreme temperatures and humidity, which would become commonplace to me later, made my walks short and sweaty, but also enticing with the native fauna and flora, even with the depressing conditions.

The birds were exotic to me, even molting or missing feathers, they were beautiful. The cage labeled "Bearcat" was small and dirty, barely housing the large lump of fur smelling strangely like popcorn; the animal moved his head slightly and I saw his long whiskers and recognized him as a binturong. He didn't look cared for or happy, just waiting to die. I commiserated with the turtles but didn't try to touch them or the crocodiles. It wasn't like their keepers had an affinity for them, and they looked ill-fed, so I didn't expect any of these animals would take kindly to being petted. Yet, nature has always been my solace and escape, and Island Cove provided this imperfect glimpse of nature as a buffer from one reality to the next.

Because the Philippines has over 7100 islands, and our main transport for the next 26 months would be boats that regularly capsized in rough weather, we all had to pass a water safety test at a location another hour south of Cavite in Manila Bay.

The hot morning sun reflected on the Bay which looked inviting from the boat. Wind and laughter on our faces and tooting ferry horns in our ears, we traveled to the middle of the sparkling waters. That was until the instructors issued directions over the hand-held megaphone:

"Keep your mouths closed at all times and close your eyes if you go underwater - best not to."

We ignorant Americans looked around confusedly and laughed.

"We aren't joking. Manila Bay is not clean. You will get parasites if you drink the water, and dysentery is NOT fun."

Thrown overboard in batches, we had to tread water, help others get back aboard, and then haul ourselves into the wooden boat without ladders or footholds. This was more of a transport boat like the interisland ferries use, so there were no outrigger pontoons to help us leverage ourselves aboard.

We had strict instructions that we had to wear life vests any time we traveled via water; not doing so would get us sent back to the U.S. Thus, we were buoyed today as we swam in dirty Manila Bay. While treading, I felt something slime around my legs and peeled off a long plastic wrapper with what looked to be meat scraps on it. I noticed other trash and dead matter floating in the water and clamped my lips tightly.

I love being in the water and am also fine in a boat - it's the in-between part where I fail. I'm a great swimmer, but bottom-heavy. And, life vests might hold you afloat, but they add girth and are cumbersome trying to boost oneself from the water and over the rail of a boat. After my third attempt, and failure, two small Filipinos jumped in the water to push my butt and two on board grabbed my arms, reeling me in. As I flopped aboard, humiliated and bloody, I hoped that my water-safety cuts and scrapes from that weathered boat wouldn't get infected like Ryan's big toe.

We dried off, coated with grunge and smelling like dead fish, and filed onto the bus. Back to the resort, we drove in the comfy double-decker bus, and I glimpsed a vantage hidden from tourists. An angled 10-foot-tall cement wall attempted to enclose a mountain of trash from a resort, only visible because of our height. The mound ebbed and flowed with the tide into the filthy bay.

Dreadful poverty all around, but beautiful fakery inside the resort walls. As our bus traveled forward with gay laughter inside, I wondered how many international resorts where I had vacationed as a privileged tourist also had walls obscuring reality so the paying tourist could enjoy the illusion. I startled at my obliviousness, which triggered an understanding of, and disgust for, "tourism" in developing countries. I would never look at luxury travel the same.

In some ways, I began to view the Filipinos I met as co-conspirators in perpetuating such delusions and the American-as-Savior myth. Workers seemed to accept their lot in life as dictated by outside forces and showed deference to white people. The deprecating "Good morning, Ma'am-Sir" bothered me, especially when it was delivered to shades of white and not to shades of brown. While I learned that it was taught and accepted as a measure of respect, something still felt wrong.

The hierarchy of society seemed almost like a caste system, which I hadn't foreseen. Food servers, landscapers, and masseuses were viewed as low-level workers, to serve those who had been to college, had office jobs, or whose family status could afford their services. Some volunteers and Peace Corps personnel hired masseuses to come to their rooms to knead out their stress after a hard day dealing with Peace Corps indoctrination. A masseuse came to the room with aromatic oils, gave a 60-minute massage in silence, received their $6 payment, and left. Similarly, food servers were not spoken to, they were simply there to place the food on your plate and to be ignored. The gardeners were dumbfounded if I spoke to them during my walks.

And, as I later found out first-hand, if one did not maintain that hierarchical detachment, one opened herself up to familiarity and was taken advantage of. Liberal egalitarianism did not work well here and everyone knew her place in the social hierarchy. The system facilitated the rich and powerful; first the colonial Spanish conquerors, then the imperialist white men from America, and now the Filipino political oligarchs - all who enjoyed their lives at the expense of others.

My pre-departure studies, in addition to my observations now that I had landed, were goading me to question the whole Peace Corps concept and to wonder if it had turned out quite as Kennedy and Sargent Shriver had envisioned 50 long years before. But we were about to find out where we would train for the next three months and that's what we all were waiting to hear.

PEACE CORPS WELCOME

PEACE CORPS KIT

OUT OF MANILA ON EDSA

OUR SMALL GROUP

Chapter 3

MEETING MY FAMILY

Habang maikli ang kumot, magtiis kang mamaluktot
If the blanket is short, learn to bend
A Filipino proverb meaning, 'Learn how to adapt to your environment
and be satisfied with what you have.'

Bend and Sway	
Ikalat ang iyong mga pakpak, mag-ingat ngayon	Spread your wings, careful now
Isipin mo munang at mamulaklak sa iyong bagong tahanan	Think first and blossom in your new home
Gumapang ang mga gagamba patungo sa iyo nang may pagtitiwala	Spiders crawl toward you in trust
Kung paano ka tumugon ay ang susi	How you respond is the key
Iangkop sa mga bagong paraan	Adapt to the new ways

ON OUR LAST NIGHT at Island Cove at our flashy farewell banquet, we were assigned to clusters of five volunteers to be located at small training sites throughout the country. We would spend a three-month stint together, learning the culture, the language, and our area of concentration. For me, with a Master's degree in Special Education, it was "Family and Youth" to be taught in Olongapo, about a four-hour drive from Manila.

That is once you were able to get out of Metro Manila, a population then of 12 million. The bus oozed through the many gridlocks of the famed EDSA (Epifanio de los Santos Avenue) where millions of people had gathered in protest of the Marcos regime in 1986 and drove the dictator and his family out of the country in the three-day-long People Power Revolution. As we sludged through the crowds with horn ablare, dodging cabs, pedestrians, potholes, and pushcarts, those millions still seemed to loiter, jamming the streets. Ant colonies of people overflowed the sidewalks where vendors sold food and necessities of life: flashlights, eyeglasses, flip-flops, paracetamol, and hot buttered corn along with pistols and *shabu* (methamphetamine) hidden from sight. Vehicles clogged the twelve lanes of EDSA, with two light-rail systems above. It took two hours to get out of Manila. Asphalt-to-sky humanity.

That first bus ride was on a plush, Peace Corps charter with aircon (aka 'AC,' or 'air conditioning'), and we were hermetically protected from the most visceral sights, sounds, and smells of Manila. Afterward, my transport was on the Victory Liner from Olongapo to the Cubao station, taking three to four hours, and once an agonizing eight. The fare, less than five dollars for that long trip, was the only thing going for it. Victory Liner was known for speediness, not safety, and locals joked about the body count of pedestrians hit that month. It was rather scary onboard, standing room only, the driver blaring his horn as the bus barreled through villages on narrow roads. Small children and beasts knew to scatter at the ear-piercing sound. This first trip was deceptively tame, coddling us newcomers.

In our first out-of-Manila view of the country, the congestion of EDSA gave way to agricultural fields of bright green tufts of rice, stalks of corn, and poles with green beans climbing them. Farther out, we saw our first carabao, the ubiquitous Filipino water buffalo, plowing the plots for planting. Rivers and streams crisscrossed the highway, looking cleaner and cleaner as we progressed into the countryside. Even the air cleared, and we chanced to open the windows to smell the trees and soil, wide-eyed in anticipation at this preview of our next two years.

Our bus had two stops to make for our three site locations, one for the Marine conservation volunteers in Morong near Bataan of WWII Death March notoriety, and our nearby neighbors, the group in Subic who would serve as English teachers. Those of us training in Olongapo with the Family and Youth sector would be last off. Slow to leave Manila, even slower to drop off volunteers and their luggage, the afternoon sun was slanting low as we neared the old U.S. military base of Subic Bay.

Continuing with their clever orientation games, the Peace Corps had given each volunteer half of a puzzle, a picture of hands. Brown and white; male and female, child and adult; each of our unique pictures matched the picture our host family had been given. We were the last four to get off the bus at dusk in a tiny village outside Olongapo, called Old Cabalan.

The charter stopped on the side of the rural road at the Petron gas station. Several host family members milled about, having waited an hour for our late arrival. They were expecting the quintessential American Peace Corps volunteer, a blonde-haired, blue-eyed, shapely, or brawny, 22-year-old. Only two of us, Annie and Chris, came close to fitting that Peace Corps icon. Objectionable for my age and non-petite size, I at least had blonde hair and blue eyes. One of the young volunteers, Paj, was a Hmong refugee who had lived in Minnesota as an American citizen since she was five years old, a very accomplished young woman. Both of us were rejected by our host families as not being acceptable.

"Good evening, *po*," I said to a smiling curly-haired woman. Showing her my puzzle piece of brown and white hands clasping, I said, "Yes, see, yours is the matching half; this is mine. I am your volunteer."

"No, no, this is not right. We were promised a Peace Corps volunteer!" and she hurried away. I watched her trying in vain to find her idea of an acceptable match.

My smile turned to panicked dismay as I was publicly rejected, and my eyes filled with tears as I looked around for help.

"She doesn't want me," I said to the Peace Corps facilitator.

"Oh, it's just a mistake. She didn't understand, I'm sure. Come with me, let's go find her again," said the young woman who would be my language instructor.

"*Magandang gabi, po*," she said to my host 'sister.' "*Opo*, Ma'am Joie, it is okay *po*, nothing to worry about. This is Miss Debra, yes *po*, she is your volunteer."

I didn't hear a "Harrumph!" but I felt it as Joie motioned me to follow her.

By the time we had arrived, been rejected, finally accepted, bags packed in the car, and the car started, night surrounded us. By now, I was somewhat used to the 7:00 AM dawn to 6:00 PM sunset range of light. In Old Cabalan, there were no streetlights, and we drove slowly, carefully to the family residence on Bennet Road, my eyes taking it all in. It was dark, but that's not to say there was no light. Vendors strung a single light bulb above their wares and hooked it up to an electrical post. Men and women were out in force walking on the street with flashlights and cellphones. Most were in same-sex groups, those close-knit *barkadas*, the gang you hang with, and the gang you drink with. Men walked with bottles of San Miguel or sat on the hill by the side of the street, talking, laughing, and watching *barkadas* of girls walk by arm-in-arm. Women gathered at the *sari sari* (variety) stores, picking up last-minute needs for dinner. Children, a lot of children, roamed close to their pregnant mothers, a lot of those too; it seemed a lively and vibrant community.

Smells of street food wafted into the windows - fried *isaw* (chicken intestines), strips of barbeque pork, and the sweet smell of caramelized banana cue. The smells mingled with laughter and the relentless jingle of the Selecta ice cream vendor pedaling his freezer cart. Immersed in first impressions, I thought I might like this a lot.

Our car talk on the way home was stranger-awkward, and Joie pointed out landmarks as we passed. "Behind those trees is the high school...the man there with the apron is the butcher...here is the elementary school. That is where we get fruits if we don't go into town." All said with a "just the facts ma'am" tone and eyes on the road.

"You will live in our family compound. This area is called Forestry. When you take a jeepney, just tell the driver to let you off at Forestry."

"Thank you, *po*."

"You don't need to call me *po*. *Po* is used for people older than you, not for someone younger."

"Okay, Miss Joie."

"You will live with my husband's mother. There are four family houses in our compound behind our gates. Our house is closest to you, and you can ask me for anything you need."

She felt so stiff; I was on pins and needles and so conscious of making a mistake, especially since she didn't want me to begin with. I mostly was quiet and thankfully, it was only a three-minute ride.

We arrived at the compound, our headlights illuminating tall, welded steel gates that were locked from the inside. Joie honked the horn three times and a silhouette unlocked them in the glare of the lights, as we turned left, inching into an uncovered and rocky patio area. She parked the car next to what looked like chicken coops covered with a sheet and another car alongside. Smiling, she introduced me to *Itim* and *Pula*, their Black and Red cars. From then on, we referred to them by name as if they were family members. We walked up the steps to the house where I would live, the only time I remember going in the front door.

"We're back!" Joie yelled.

I followed her up the stairs and felt like I had to stoop to enter because the door was a foot shorter than those in the U.S. This was my first experience being so close to people, and my size was gargantuan in comparison. Feeling my big-boned Norwegian heritage, clumsy alongside petite Joie, I entered twilight. Although all of the few interior lights were on, they weren't bright, and shapes were indistinct and shadowy. We stepped into an ample living room with basic furniture, a wooden sofa with blue cushions on the left and a hard rocking chair on the right. The floors were concrete, and the ceiling was high, with a tin roof and welded supports. It was open to the next room, where three forms were backlit by the kitchen light. I stopped.

Three people waited, stiff and silent, standing like the American Gothic painting without the pitchfork. There was a man about my height, a grandmotherly-looking woman a lot shorter than me, and a young boy. The boy gave me a half-smile, but the other two looked reserved and remained quiet, as still as the framed Gothic. Joie entered as a gust, threw her keys on the kitchen table, and said something curtly to the two adults in Tagalog.

"Great, we got the big, old one," she recounted years later.

Luckily, I knew very little Tagalog at the time.

Joie, a young, fiery Cebuana, and her husband, Joseph, had some sort of marital argument just before she picked me up, and the talk between them was short and tense. That was the last time I saw anger from her, at least directed at me. Joie was nothing if not passionate. And that first night, I was clueless, except for noting a tension in the air that could have been normal for all I knew.

Introductions began, first to my host and housemate, the matriarch of the compound. She wore red rectangle glasses, bright against her fair skin. Her hair was aging to pure white with some gray still around the crown, cropped short and shaggy to her face. She, as I, carried a few extra pounds, hers around her belly. The top of her head stopped below my clavicle, and she didn't smile; her brows knit slightly, and her lips formed a straight line. Her body posture seemed the opposite, soft and welcoming in her floral duster. And she greeted me.

"Hello *po*, I am Teresita, but people call me Tess."

I didn't know what to do, she still hadn't moved and didn't seem to want a hug. I didn't know how to hug such a short person anyway. But she didn't feel intimidating despite her stone face, so I took her hand, with a big smile. "I'm Debra or Deb."

"We call her Nanay," said the young boy.

"And what is your name?" I asked.

"Angelo," he replied.

Angelo was a name I had always associated with Italian, not Filipino lineage. I knew Nanay meant "mother" in Tagalog and was confused at their names but said nothing. It turned out that sons, neighbors, grandchildren, everyone, called her Nanay or mother, for being head of the family.

"You can call him Gelo like we do," said the man, grinning with bright white teeth that stood out against his handsome nut-brown face. He ruffled his son's hair. It seemed everyone and everything had a nickname here. "We will call you *Tita* Deb." Even adults seemed uncomfortable calling someone by their first name without a title in this culture; it was too familiar and lacked respect. Each person had a designation, not the Mr., Mrs., or Ms. of the West, but a relationship: *Tita* (auntie), *Tito* (uncle),

Nanay (mother), *Tatay* (father), *Ate* (older sister), or *Kuya* (older brother). It united everyone you knew in some way. So, I became *Tita* Deb.

Gelo was a bit shy, the antithesis of his dervish mother, although his face and hair looked a carbon copy of hers. His father, Joseph, was a rich brown color and Joie and Gelo were a little lighter, all in contrast to Tess's fair skin which was whiter than mine. Joie and Gelo shared a round face with dimpled cheeks, perfect for their many smiles. Nanay's face resembled theirs, also rounded, but lacking smiles, and Joseph's was a long rectangle, squared at the chin. A portrait of family contrasts and similarities.

'Tika was Nanay's fat, white and brown dog, an *askal*, or street dog, as most dogs are in the provinces. 'Tika was named for Latika in Slumdog Millionaire although I never found out if that was because she was a prized possession or just a miserable dog. She was collared in heavy chains outside the back door but wriggled with happiness having her humans nearby. The front door was locked and 'Tika stayed at the back so that she would still bark at intruders, but was hidden so no hungry thief in the neighborhood could steal her for food. She was clean and plump, and such tasty dogs often went missing around dinnertime.

She didn't bark at me long, but I was still wary due to the prevalence of rabies in the Philippines. Three hundred people die every year from the preventable disease and most dogs are not vaccinated. When we took 'Tika for rare walks, we carried long heavy sticks to defend ourselves from aggressive dogs in the neighborhood. But that first night, we let 'Tika come in, and, as tensions eased, we talked pleasantries. We started our Getting to Know You chitchat and celebrated our coming together with a liter of Coca-Cola, as was done for special occasions, drinking out of plastic glasses.

"Well, Deb, would you like to see where you will stay?" said Tess.

"I would love that. Thank you," as I picked up my backpack and duffle bag.

Tess led me to the bedroom adjacent to the living room and to the left of the CR, the Comfort Room, or bathroom. Nanay's room was on the other side of the CR, closest to the street. My room was at the back of the house, and I noticed that there were birdcages just outside my window with pigeons in them. Tess had painted my room a soft yellow and sewn ruffled floral curtains in lemon and lime, a larger and bolder print of her duster.

"We have used this room for when my son comes home. He works in Dubai most of the year, so I just leave his things in this box. Sometimes he comes home and stays here, but he hasn't been home in over a year. I don't know what he wants to keep, or I would have moved it out."

She didn't laugh or say more, just a statement of fact. The 'box' was a huge, dilapidated cardboard box filled with linens, clothing, electronics, and all his trappings that he had mailed from Dubai; a *balikbayan* box. *Balikbayan* boxes are sent "back to the homeland" from all over the world. Later, I tried to move it, but it was heavy and wouldn't budge without ripping, so it stayed where it was.

The room was spotless with the soft mattress on the floor as my bed, and I set up the last necessity, my mosquito netting, my *kulambo*. I told Tess I loved the room and curtains and was grateful to them all for letting me stay with them. Dragging my backpack and duffle bag inside, I took up residence, thanked them again, wished them goodnight, and fell asleep to the sound of pigeons cooing in their cages.

The next morning was Saturday with a tour of the *barangay* (the village) planned as an orientation by our instructors. I woke to an enormous downpour in the black morning and took out the silver locket my daughters had given me, inscribed, "*Whatever path you may choose, may our hearts be with you.*" I opened it, teary, and homesick for their smiling faces.

It was 6:00 AM, and Tess cooked us eggs scrambled with pieces of bright red hotdog for breakfast, and Ovaltine, made with water and powdered milk.

Our Peace Corps outing was cut short due to the flooded village and we returned before lunch. My family had fixed a whole fried tilapia and rice and waited for me to eat together. There was no silverware on the table, so I followed their lead and ate with my right hand.

"*Tita* Deb, like this," said Gelo as he demonstrated the move in slow motion.

"Why doesn't the rice stick to my hands? It just falls through," I lamented to their laughter.

"Do it like this *Tita*," he grinned and showed me again.

Gelo's tutelage cost me two hours of Monopoly. As Nanay and Joie cleaned up, throwing scraps to 'Tika and washing the dishes with cold water, Gelo skunked me in Monopoly at the dinner table. His mother finally called him off and told me to rest. I slept through dinner.

Joseph worked on weekends, so was gone even on Sundays. But this first Sunday was special, eight-year-old Gelo was being confirmed in the Mormon church.

There are less than a million Mormons in the Philippines, about six million Muslims, and 90 million Catholics. My family experiences were different from most other Peace Corps volunteers who lived with Catholics.

My family returned from the ceremony that day, full of smiles, and we ate lunch, me, rice only, as I had diarrhea. Even with filtering, little critters in the water disturbed my digestive tract, although I suspected yesterday's fried fish was the culprit. Nanay had fried it in the morning and had no refrigerator, so it sat out for hours, although it had been covered to keep off the flies. My discomfort didn't stop Gelo and me from playing more Monopoly while Joie finished laundry. As is Filipino custom, I wasn't allowed to do any work. I was the guest, and as much as I protested and tried to help with cooking or cleaning, it simply wasn't permitted. They saw their job as taking care of me.

"No *Tita*, you just sit and talk to me while I fry the fish."

"No *Tita*, Gelo will sweep the floor and feed 'Tika."

"No *Tita*, Joseph will go to the store on his way home, no need to worry."

"Rest lang, *po*." And we would chat while they worked.

"Why do you not yet speak Tagalog, *Tita*? All our missionaries arrive speaking fluent Tagalog," said Joie.

"That would have been nice, to be able to speak your language! The staff in Manila said that there are so many languages that they needed to figure out first where they would send us. Most of us will study Tagalog, but others will be placed in Samar or the Visayas and will need to learn Waray, Cebuano, or Hiligaynon. I just hope I can learn to speak Tagalog.

"Well, we can just speak English until you learn then." I heard her silent "Harrumph" and felt I was a dolt.

Joie introduced me to the families in the compound as she showed me around the property. The back of their lot abutted the Santa Rita River, which usually had a small stream of water flowing, but could flood up the 10-foot banks and into the yard during typhoon season. In later years, the water flooded six feet high inside their home, caking walls with mud and foul debris, and sweeping them off their feet with the current, but not this year. We hiked down the steep concreted banks to the river where discarded shopping carts and shoes littered the riverbed in a dirty trickle of water. Farther upstream, in the stifling heat, a woman scrubbed laundry in a small pool between the rocks.

Halfway up the property from the river was the small concrete house of Tess's sister-in-law. Her husband had died, and her son was working overseas, returning only occasionally. The auntie did not speak English well, was very shy, and kept to herself. She opened her screen door but hung back in the darkness, so I couldn't see her features, and I never got to know her well.

Across from the auntie was Joie and Joseph's house. The bottom floor was finished, with a living/dining room, indoor kitchen, and bedroom. Theirs was the only air conditioner, a window unit in the bedroom, where they all slept in one bed. Joseph was adding on two more stories as money permitted, currently, it was only concrete and rebar. The last two stories were waiting for more cement to be purchased, and the metallic bars stuck up like spiral lightning rods, reminiscent of the lightning hook Doc and Marty used in *Back to the Future*.

I laughed at Joseph's plan to build a double-decker pigeon condo with secure cages anchored to the third story at the back of the house. But, Joseph was quite serious.

＊＊＊＊＊＊＊＊

Joseph worked at the Subic water company and was a master welder, industrious and productive, always in motion working on projects. He had detailed plans for his *kalapati kondo* (pigeon condo) to shelter all his birds.

Joseph's pride and joy were his racing pigeons. His favorite and best money-maker was named Precious and he pampered her. I never told him that she looked like all the rest to me. Although he had a full-time, laborious job, and took care of the family, he, along with his brother Oliver, was passionate about winning races.

A pigeon could easily win its owner a month's salary if it was a good competitor, and much more if it was great. Precious was better than good and had the potential for great. Joseph had 20 females, and his brother had 10 males called cocks. Precious not only won races, but she also laid eggs and Joseph raised and trained her offspring to race. In addition to the cages outside my room, the big aviary in the front patio where the cars were parked was also for the pigeons, not chicken coops as I had thought. The brothers would convene there early in the morning at feeding time, sipping coffee and talking about an upcoming race; a camaraderie over birds.

At his lunch break, Joseph came home to tend the birds, and, in the evenings, he exercised them, letting all of them out to glide as a flock. Beautiful to watch the birds circling silently above with tall trees and mountains as the backdrop in the sunset, then knowing somehow to return single file through the pigeonhole to their quarters to sleep.

One of my favorite Saturdays was going with Joseph to the racing club in Olongapo as the pigeon "fanciers" assembled their pigeons for a long race. Men enclosed their precious birds in travel crates to protect them on their long ride to the starting point. We arrived at the club around 3 AM, long before the sun rose, and a swarm of men and cooing pigeons crowded the street. Each crate was stacked and secured onto a rig that would navigate far into the mountains for the premier race, over 300 kilometers long. Quiet chortling of the birds and men churned in the dark.

The club's truck would drive for more hours than the birds would fly due to the winding and poorly maintained mountain roads. When the driver arrived at the designated starting point, he would feed and water the pigeons for their long journey and count down to the release time. He then would free the birds all at once and start the clock that would announce the winner to receive a prize that could be equal to several months' wages.

The pigeons would fly their hearts out, arrive home and peck the electronic plate that registered the metal band on their leg for the official timing. That is, if they made it back. The danger to the racing birds in long-distance races was enormous, only one out of ten would make it home. There were predators along the way, hawks swooping down for a tasty morsel, cloudy weather to confuse the homing instinct, and torrential rains to douse or fell a bird. And worst, the human predator.

The date of the race was kept secret to prevent humans from setting up fishing nets in the mountains to capture the birds in flight. So, everything was done in the dark of early morning as they loaded the crates and watched the truck take off, wishing each other luck. Joseph drove us home, where I went back to sleep, and he prepared for work. Joseph worked his normal day shift and, at lunch, returned home to fill the trays with food for the returning, exhausted pigeons in case they arrived early. We waited, watching the skies, and Joseph worked, checking in with Joie to see if there had been any sightings. Almost at dusk, after he returned, we saw his birds circling above, all making it back safe and sound into their cages. Precious placed first. We drank Coke that night.

Nanay and I lived in the two-bedroom house next to Joseph's, close enough to be within shouting distance and shout they did. This norm of their communication reminded me of Alexander Graham Bell yelling into his first attempt at a telephone. "Joie?"

"Coming Nanay!"

"Gelo, come take this to Nay!"

"Joie, when are you coming over?"

"Coming now, Nanay!"

The *askal*, 'Tika, was kept busy monitoring a highway of food, laundry, and shouts between the two houses.

In front of, and just south of Nanay's front door, with grilled windows facing the street, was the house of her other son, Oliver. He lived there with his wife, Amor, and three little girls, whom I came to love. After I left, their *bunso* (youngest), a little boy, was added to their numbers. While I was there, the child of Amor's younger sister came to live with them, and they raised him for many years. Often Amor's elder sister, who worked in Malaysia, would come home to visit for a couple of months, bearing gifts for all and filling the house to the brim. On sunny days, their front door was open, with lots of giggles and activity floating outside.

Oliver was a sales manager for an international insurance firm, so with her two sons earning good salaries, Nanay's whole family seemed to be on a path forward. The other two sons, and a daughter in the U.S., sent money home to Nanay. I never knew how much, but every sibling helped out. In this poor country, where no one had a pension and older people struggled, parents relied on their children to sustain them in their later years.

Oliver had a corporate job and seemed to oversee his extended family, which kept growing. He and Joseph conferred about finances and constructed additions to their houses together. Still, the two who seemed to be in control of our part of the compound were Nanay and Joseph who had the moniker "Boss." Head of the clan was a normal family position in Filipino culture; heads of the family would often make decisions for everyone within the compound. In many cases, families chose to pool all their money to send one child to a good college in Manila or abroad with the expectation that s/he would get a high-paying job abroad and would fund the family. This collective responsibility is what kept people afloat, despite the poverty and hardships that threatened to pull them down.

My language instructor told me that Joseph was a typical and common-looking Filipino, but I found him strikingly handsome and charming and wondered if a similar-looking man had broken my instructor's heart for her to think that way. Joseph felt self-conscious about his English, but we were able to communicate ideas and had intense discussions with questions and laughter spattering the conversations from both sides. So English was our home language, my toddler Tagalog just wasn't good enough.

Nanay and Joseph had a close relationship, at times making me wonder if the roles of Nanay and Joie had been switched. Walking up the street or on our nights out, you would see Joseph and Nanay strolling arm-in-arm with Joie, Gelo, and me walking behind them. So bonded, yet so different. Joseph's easy, broad smile was at odds with Nanay's refusal to bend her lips upwards. And, to make things more confusing to my stranger-in-a-strange-land brain, was the seeming detachment of the other son's family, whose home was equidistant to Nanay's. The only interaction I saw was the back and forth of his three little girls, who might run over to show Nanay and me something they made at school or to draw with us for a while, but their parents didn't visit us; nor did we go there.

An exception was a full-fledged party at their house for Joseph's 40th birthday. The occasion called for Oliver to rent a huge karaoke machine and us to make plenty of birthday food. I bought Joseph his first birthday cake and helped in cooking the traditional Filipino birthday foods of spag (spaghetti) with bright red hotdogs, macaroni salad with canned tropical fruit, cassava cakes, and *ube*. It took us hours to grate three kilos of cassava roots into a big tin bucket; it looked like the same bucket used for doing laundry, but maybe not. My knuckles were scraped from the grating and then singed over the fire as we mixed that pile of cassava with sweetened evaporated milk, coconut milk, sugar, cream, and eggs. Pouring the smooth mixture into glass plates we baked it until it was almost translucent. We also grated bright purple yams and cooked them into sweet *ube* paste, constantly stirring the paste for 45 minutes and exhausting my arms as it got thicker and thicker. Everyone helped bring the platters of sweets to Oliver's; everything, even spaghetti and macaroni salad is sweet in the Philippines (diabetes anyone?).

Oliver's youngest daughter gyrated to Justin Bieber's popular *Baby, Baby, Baby Oh!* which was way too provocative for a four-year-old. Nanay and I practiced singing Paper Roses together. Karaoke is wildly fashionable at Filipino celebrations to my off-tune vocal consternation. You don't need to sing well, but you do have to sing. Refusing to sing could ruin any chance of my ability as a foreigner to connect with my hosts or the local community. So, I sang. I warned people I croaked, but no one minded, and Nanay and I laughed there on the sofa, wrapped around each other as we crooned.

I reflected that here, the birthday person wasn't feted like in my U.S. childhood; rather, he hosted the entire party and honored all those invited for contributing to his life. As the party ended, I almost laughed as each woman reached into her pocket to retrieve plastic baggies that she had brought to take home party food. I was in an alternate universe where traditions were the opposite of the culture I had left behind. The culture here was so other-oriented compared to my me-oriented upbringing.

❋ ❋ ❋ ❋ ❋ ❋ ❋ ❋

The days rolled by as our relationship strengthened and Nanay and I had deeper heart-to-hearts about our accomplishments and disappointments in life. Only two years apart in age, we had such different experiences and outlooks on life. Most of her life had been hard - really hard, with so much physical labor tending to children, and daily sacrifices to make ends meet. I had modern amenities like a car, clean water, electricity, clothes washers, dishwashers, toilet, sewer, and hot water whenever I wished to turn on that tap. She'd had none of these.

Sitting at the dining room table after dinner, she would get a faraway look and recount her life in a soft monotone. Maybe she was afraid to show emotions, or those times were so bad that there wasn't much happiness to remember.

"I was used to farming when I was a girl in Leyte, so I knew how to plant the land here. It was easy when I only had a couple of children. We had to fetch water from the river, there was no piped water at that time. And of course, we needed to boil the water to use it in cooking, to kill all the parasites. We bought *uling* (charcoal) for our cooking fires from vendors who walked through the street when it was just a narrow dirt road."

I wanted to hear it all. "How did you do everything? Where did you do laundry? How did you get food? What if someone got hurt?"

"It was hard, Deb. I had five children and each of them had chores, but the younger ones couldn't do much. We had so little food and went to bed hungry. I took our laundry to the river to wash and then hung it in the yard. We didn't have a house then, just the *kubo* (bamboo hut) with a thatched roof to keep out the rain. Me and the kids. My husband worked long hours and when he came home, he was tired. *Manang* Ester, next door, has lived here as long as I have, and she became my friend. Over the years we helped each other and we have a few secrets ha-ha. She is my longest friend."

Even with such a chasm between our experiences, some of our deepest hopes and dreams were the same. Mostly about our children and wishing for a closer relationship with them, as well as hoping that they could reach their hearts' desires.

"You know that Oliver applied to go to the U.S.?" Tess asked.

"No, why does he want to go there? Does he know someone?"

"He wants to be a teacher. He first applied about 10 years ago, but he was refused. He has applied two more times, and they told him maybe in another 10 years. I never understood why they wouldn't let him into the U.S. Do you know why your government won't let him come? Do you know anyone who could help him?"

"No, I had no idea they refused Filipinos. If you know people, especially if you have relatives in the U.S. I didn't think it was a problem. Maybe it was because he was young and didn't have a profession, or could show he had a way to earn a living?"

"Yes, maybe that was it, he was young at the time."

"A lot of people in California are Filipino, I read that one out of six people is Filipino in San Francisco! I thought their family members just came and went whenever they wanted. But it would be very difficult to live in the U.S. on a teacher's salary, especially with three children."

"Why is that? Don't teachers make good money?"

"Most teachers in the U.S. either have an *asawa* (spouse) who has a good job, or the teacher has a second job. Many people in the U.S. are leaving the teaching profession because it pays so poorly and is very stressful. Parents of students in the U.S. can be difficult."

"Oh, I don't think Oliver knows that. Teachers here aren't paid well either, but we thought the U.S. was different, that all people were paid well and that all the medical is paid for. Plus, your government takes care of all citizens for life and even gives you money when you are old."

"No, it's not quite like that. And there are lots of qualifications to get benefits like insurance. You can't just go there and get a job. He would have to get a green card and have a sponsor I think, and that would take time to work out. But I don't really know anything about the restrictions."

"And then, of course, he got married and has a family now. *Sayang* (how sad, what a lost opportunity) that he will never go to America."

Another son was doing well enough and lived a few hours away but worked two jobs and had a young family; I only met him once when he came home for All Souls Day. Her youngest son worked in Dubai and rarely returned. But both Tess and I shared our biggest regrets about our daughters.

"I didn't know how to be a parent to her. She was my firstborn. Her father was gone working overseas and the boys were younger and needed me. The worst was that I was so strict with her. I was hard-hearted. She had a curfew as a teenager but was *pasaway* (stubborn and disobedient). She wouldn't listen to me and stayed out beyond the curfew. So, I locked her out."

My eyes widened and my eyebrows arched, but I said nothing. I couldn't imagine locking one of my girls out all night. But I could envision Tess's furrowed brow and how tight her lips must have been.

"She slept on the front porch and the next morning apologized to me. But she was so angry inside. Then she got involved with an American serviceman and had a baby. They lived here for a while, but then they moved to the U.S. Oh, Deb, I have made many mistakes in my life."

"Hah, who hasn't? My relationship with both of my daughters is horrible and I can't seem to fix it. Mothers and daughters have so much to forgive each other."

"It seems both our hearts are broken," she said, as I agreed in silence.

Her daughter divorced and remarried another U.S. serviceman, whom Tess respected, and they lived in Texas. At some point, her daughter asked Tess to come to live with them to help raise her grandson, and she did, as grandmothers do. Her days in the U.S. sounded almost as long as the ones she'd already experienced raising her own children in Olongapo. The amenities were nicer, and she got medical treatment for her diabetes, but it didn't sound like proximity to her daughter improved their relations much. Tess sounded used, although she never spoke those words and loved her grandchildren. After ten years in Texas, the family moved to Germany, and Tess went with them for another three years. After they returned to the U.S., Tess decided to return to Olongapo to help raise Gelo since both Joie and Joseph worked outside the home.

Gelo and Nanay had a strong bond, and he came over every day after school; I was his curious new playmate. After his homework, we played Monopoly, and I introduced him to UNO and Jenga. He regularly beat me, to his great delight and belly laughs.

Our Peace Corps small group for language instruction was tight. We all lived on the same street, except for Bryce, who lived with his wife Krystal in another *purok* (a small, distinct neighborhood). Our language instructor, Kit, had a place on the street above us and called us her Peace Corps babies, even me. Peace Corps rules for our training group, or "cluster," were that the five of us ate breakfast with our respective host families at 7:00 AM, ran up 27 stairs to attend language lessons from 8:00 AM to noon, ran downstairs back home for lunch, and then, as a cluster, took a jeepney to our cultural lessons with another cluster of five a few miles away, from noon to 4:00 PM.

Bryce had a knack for word association, and I credit him for getting me to the intermediate level of speaking Tagalog. He mimed words like *gagamba* (spider) and *mabalahibo* (hairy) with hilarious gestures and guttural sounds. Sports-minded Chris who lived right next door with Tess' best friend Ester, loved playing card games and baseball or football (soccer) with the teenagers in the *purok*. Annie was a few houses down, with a delightful family and a toddler who occupied her spare time. Paj lived at the corner with her wealthier, but more stern hosts. We were not allowed to go anywhere without a chaperone and had to be accounted for at all times. A little odd for a 59-year-old independent woman, but I abided.

Fresh in our instructors' minds was the story of a 40-year-old volunteer who had been murdered only three years before in the Ifugao province in the north. Starting out on a simple hike near her home, she never returned. The Peace Corps was a bureaucracy with rigid rules, but our instructors had known the well-loved volunteer and promised themselves such an act would never happen again, the murder had brought pain and shame to the country. So, our group was on a short leash.

Host families had been recruited and vetted by the Peace Corps and were paid a monthly stipend to house us. It was only about $3 a day, but that went a long way in the provinces, and with both Joseph and Joie working, we ate well. Before Nanay's new refrigerator arrived in our house, our fish or pork meals were fried early in the morning, before the heat became oppressive. Then, covered with a plastic vent to keep off the flies, the plate was placed in a moat of water to dissuade the ants. I got sick the first week.

The Peace Corps had supplied us with a medical kit, along with a manual "Where there is no Doctor, A Village Health Care Handbook." While I reviewed the sections on parasites, snakebites, and ticks, I assumed my sickness was just what we call food poisoning, and I popped a Lomotil. It happened so routinely and embarrassingly that Lomotil became my best friend forever, or at least for my time in the Philippines. Much more palatable than the problem that Krystal, the young wife of Bryce, had. She hadn't noticed any symptoms until she excreted a live 12-inch worm into the toilet. There was a reason the Peace Corps distributed that handbook.

My medical kit alerted me to one of the cultural traits of the Philippines: everything belongs to the family, yours is ours, and there are no secrets. Joseph, the acting patriarch of the compound, worked long hours of manual labor in the hot sun and infrequently got migraines. My kit was put away at the bottom of my pile on the bedroom floor. I tried to keep neat piles, but it was difficult without a table or closet and was compounded with that huge, dilapidated box containing Tess's son's entire Olongapo life.

When I returned for lunch during our noon break, Tess said nonchalantly, "Deb? Joseph had a headache, so I gave him one of your Advil."

"Oh, where did I have Advil?"

"In that kit the Peace Corps gave you, that red one. I took two for him."

"Okay, I hope he feels better."

Tess had gone through all my things while I was at class and taken inventory, probably on the first day of instruction. She knew more about my stuff than I did. There is no such thing as American privacy in the Philippines, and the host family calls all the shots.

Carmen, another volunteer in my cluster, quickly found this out. She was told by her family that she had to be inside before 7:00 PM every night. Granted, it got dark by 6:30 PM, but her host father was almost abusive in his haranguing of her curfew, and we were horrified that he actually locked her door to keep her inside. Carmen was a vegetarian, and we laughed at her attempts to order food.

"I will have the vegetables, because I don't eat meat," she would say.

"Yes, yes, no problem, Miss."

"Can you make sure there is no meat in it?"

"No meat, yes Miss."

And she would be served a mound of vegetables...mixed with minced pork. We never saw thick hamburgers or steaks, but all vegetables were intermingled with ground pork or chicken, and the meats were bred to have high-fat content. Less than a year later, Carmen gave up and ate meat with the rest of us.

But I lucked out with my host family in Olongapo. Even with our inauspicious start, over the weeks we became close and remain so today. The day the refrigerator was delivered, I was in class, and when I arrived home, Joie (the initially nefarious daughter-in-law) squealed, "Not yet! You can't come in, *Tita* Deb!"

Wondering "What on earth?" I sat on the back porch with the dog, melting in the October sun. Getting the all-clear, I went to my bedroom to find the cardboard box from the refrigerator encased in Contact paper of pink and white roses and equipped with a dowel and hangers. Joie and Tess had painstakingly architected a closet for my clothes and had even spent precious money to decorate it. I wiped away a tear as I grinned thank you.

Tess took care of me, even offering to heat up bath water for me because we only had cold water. And chiding me whenever I returned hot and sweaty from hiking up and down the 27 steep stairs to my language class. I stood directly in front of the electric fan, trying to get some relief.

"Stop!" she would squawk, "You will get *Pasma*!"

Pasma apparently happens when there is a combination of the elements of "cold" and "water." Somehow, 'bad' cold is allowed to enter the body and causes clamminess and sore throat with flu-like symptoms, or "*pas-*

ma." I tried to explain my understanding of germs and illness to Tess, but she, and the entire family, refused to hear me.

Thus began my education of Filipino superstitions, which were only superstitions to us foreigners. To our host families, these were 'facts.'

"Don't smell the damp earth after a rain, you will get a stomach ache,"

"Don't use a red umbrella, it will attract lightning,"

"When someone sings off-key it will rain"

And these are only a few about the weather.

Our next-door neighbor, *Manang* Ester, who was the host for my friend Chris, had a profusion of them:

You should not sleep while you are hungry because your spirit will go to a place where there's food and it will become trapped there. Of course, no one personally knew anyone this had happened to, but there were plenty of stories.

Dropping utensils means that someone's coming. If a spoon falls, a woman will come. If a fork falls, a man will arrive. I dropped a fork at Ester's one night and said I hoped a man would arrive.

And once, after I bought *pan de sal,* my favorite yeast rolls for our meal, Ester yelled at me when I placed the change next to my plate on the table,

"Stop! Do you want me to lose all the little money I have left? Put that in the other room!" Neither did I leave my purse on the floor, it had a similar meaning.

If you choke during a meal, it means that someone far away is thinking of you. When I choked, it meant I encountered something unexpected in the food.

Don't cut your nails at night, or on Fridays. Apparently, spirits gain power with this action. I cut my nails whenever I wanted and never saw a ghost, but maybe they just avoided me.

If you sleep with wet hair, it will make you crazy, bald, or blind. I did not experience this, although some might agree with crazy. Wet hair cooled me off in our house with no ventilation and suffocating temperatures. We arrived at the end of August, the start of the rainy season, with unrelenting heat and torrential rains. On the corrugated tin roof of our home, rainfall was deafening, which could drive you mad; no conversation could exist during heavy rains. Sometimes we sat in the dark, or with candles because the electricity shorted out. With those conditions, wet hair felt like a blessing rather than heralding a curse.

My family and Ester all believed in ghosts and in the white ladies who lived under the weeping fig and acacia trees. They each had at least one encounter with a white lady and were terrified of ghosts, I never saw either one. The white ladies were purportedly a specific type of female ghost while *duwende* were the little people who lived under rocks or anthills.

One of my favorite television programs at the time was "Dwarfina," about a queen who gave birth to a beautiful princess but shamefully, a tiny person, so she was given up to be raised by the tiny *duwende* living under the rocks adjacent to the castle. I'm not sure if Dwarfina's origin was ever explained in the program since I spoke intermediate Tagalog and had only watched a handful of the 83 episodes. Did the Queen have an affair with a little man? Did the king have recessive genes? In any case, it was the start of a profitable career for the actress, Heart Evangelista. Heart met and married a real-life senator and had the most opulent televised wedding I had ever seen. Happily, ever after.

One of the first times Tess and I were alone, talking at the dining room table by candlelight during a brownout, something scurried just out of my sight. I thought it was a lizard, and animal-freak me ran after it, intrigued. Instead, I tracked a spider the size of my hand to an inside window ledge.

Tess laughed as I recoiled. "Oh Deb, it's just a house spider, they don't bite."

I still wonder how she knew that and suspect it was just another Filipino tale, just like, "if a gecko falls on you it sticks to you," which I knew wasn't true because a large gecko had in fact fallen on me. But I noticed that this big black spider carried a flattened ball of white underneath it, bigger than five cotton balls. As we watched in fascination, tiny babies began descending from that white cloud, like firemen called to duty. They rappelled down long silky strands to get to the base of the window and scurried off, not waiting for their brothers and sisters above them to land.

We watched 100 tiny spiders slide down and scuttle off into the nooks and crannies of the house. A scene I will long remember, and the forerunner to another scene with this mother spider.

The records show that 2010 was the least active Pacific typhoon season in history, which amazes me. I had been through two significant hurricanes in the Northern hemisphere, but never a typhoon, and its arrival felt darned momentous to me.

Each family in the compound shuttered themselves inside, and Joseph securely covered his pigeons so the driving rain and flying dirt wouldn't harm them. Tess and I barricaded all the windows, brought 'Tika in from her porch station, and toweled her dry. Of course, the electricity shut off almost at once, and we listened to the battery-powered radio first by candlelight and then in the dark until the heavy rain on the tin roof drowned out all sound. With no hope of conversation, I gave up and crawled under my mosquito net to enter a fitful sleep as outside debris bombarded the windows.

I awoke to a brilliant sunny day, my first experience of the transient life of a typhoon that passed quickly and intensely, and left sun and destruction as a reminder. I looked up and saw with a gasp the mother spider on top of my mosquito net; she looked dead. I kept my camera on the floor beside my bed, just in case something unexpected or curious happened. This defined that purpose, so I eased my hand out, slowly picked up the camera, and pointed it above me, never taking my eyes off the spider.

Then I yelled for Tess, who slept on her good ear, and was nearly deaf in the other, "Tess, can you come get this spider off my net?" I was, after all, still a pampered American. On the off chance it was still alive, I didn't want it to leap at me when I tried to get out. Tess was chuckling as she came in to help, but as she got closer, she said, "Deb it's not on the outside." Oh, yuck. I had been sleeping with the spider cocooned in my mosquito net all night. Maybe it's true that house spiders don't bite.

MY NEW ROOM

WITH MANANG ESTER IN OLONGAPO

TESS IN HER FLORAL DUSTER

GELO'S CONFIRMATION DAY

THE SPIDER

Chapter 4

Educational Excursions

Matibay ang walis, palibhasa'y magkabigkis
A broom is sturdy because its strands are tightly bound.
A Filipino proverb meaning, 'People and families gain strength by standing together.'

Our Fortress	
Ang mga puno ay aking ina, na sumasangga sa akin mula sa ulan,	The trees are my mother, shielding me from rain.
Ang aking ama ay bundok, kumukupkop sa aking ina	My father is the mountain, sheltering my mother
Ako ay isang batang lalaki, protektado ng aking pamilya.	I am but a boy, protected by my family.

DURING OUR THREE-MONTH TRAINING IN OLONGAPO, we had neighborhood assignments. Our cluster of five joined with another local cluster for projects and trips. The crew included six women, all in their twenties (except me), and four young men. As cultural neophytes, we learned many ways to define what "family" meant and experienced how interconnected Filipino society was with the ties that bind.

Our first assignment was to observe, as well as teach, English classes at Old Cabalan Integrated School. The school was a few blocks away, an easy walk. The high-school-aged boys and girls giggled, trying to squirm close to the young white Americans. Words like *kilig* don't translate well, but I could see the definition in the giddiness of the girls flirting with our volunteers, that sudden dizzy rush you get upon seeing your crush. Gaggles of girls and bevies of boys surrounded us until the bell rang for classes to begin.

We had heard that the Philippines had either a 'rainy' or a 'dry' season, and that day we were steeped in the meaning of 'the rainy season.' By afternoon, the door couldn't keep the rain from streaming flashflood-like into, through, and out, under the back wall of the classroom. The only ones alarmed were us foreigners; the students and teacher sat nonchalantly and continued their lesson.

Acceptance of "what is" was obvious in that the instructor had the only textbook. This class of 25 high school students had one teacher, 12 desks and chairs, one textbook, one chalkboard, two broken pieces of chalk, and a rag to wipe the board. Yet these youth were the most attentive and compliant that I had seen in my years of teaching; all conformed with their green and white checkered uniforms, and the routines of the school.

The teacher took a piece of white chalk and began to copy text from his book onto the green chalkboard, verbatim. There was no discussion, and no cue was given that we could see, but quiet descended and everyone took out their notebooks and began copying from the board, verbatim.

Each student wrote the same words in their notebook, most keeping up with the teacher, just one word behind the last text he printed on the board, the silence a grim demonstration of what textbook or rote learning was.

Line by line, there was no discussion, just the sound of 25 pencils scratching on paper and one piece of chalk scraping on the board. Class was dismissed as soon as students finished transcribing what amounted to half a page, 30 minutes of 'work.' Students closed their notebooks, put them into their backpacks, and left without a word.

Outside the rain poured and I stood, woebegone, at the back of the room.

57

In addition to our daily lectures and neighborhood tasks, we went on several field trips to expose us to issues in the Youth and Family sector. We quickly became familiar with the unofficial four-tiered government structure of the 81 provinces of the Philippines:

- The province itself, ruled by the Governor (our province was Zambales)

- The city or municipality, headed by the Mayor (Olongapo was one of 13)

- The village called a *barangay*, (Olongapo had 17 of these, and Old Cabalan was ours), headed by the *Kapitan*

- The smallest, although not formal, unit was a neighborhood of 20-50 houses, labeled a *purok* headed by a *purok* leader. My *purok* was Forestry.

Focus usually stayed within our *barangay* of Old Cabalan, but some trips took us further afield.

The most memorable, as in traumatic, trip for me was to a children's home, a 90-minute drive from our *barangay*, run by a group of nuns affiliated with Mother Teresa. This was the first time I would see children like the ones to whom I would be assigned, and I was anxious to better understand what my life would be like. In the U.S., we have Special Education classes for people with disabilities. In the Philippines, they call such children "Special," but there are few places where they are allowed in schools, let alone educated. This field trip would take us to an orphanage that served "Special" children and I could see their classroom setup and curriculum.

The van left early, taking Route 3 east from our meeting place at the barangay hall, and wandered through green fields of sprouting rice and bucolic scenes of farmers with carabao, or *kalabaw* (Philippine water buffalo). Some beasts plowed farmland, others lay deep in mud shielding themselves from the blazing sun, and all were roped with an iron ring through their nose. We passed into the Pampanga province and drove through small hamlets lining the twisting highway, most just scattered houses with no community buildings. Turning off the main thoroughfare, we headed north, through lush forests at the foot of Mt. Malasimbu, stopping at an orphanage for girls and another shelter for abandoned old women whose families either didn't want them or couldn't care for them, before continuing toward the facility that housed about 40 school children and 10 Special children.

We continued northeast, skirting the base of the Zambales-Pampanga Mountain range, and crossed the Pasig-Paseo River before finally jerking onto a dusty, rutted road. Nondescript buildings grouped in the distance, deliberately set at the farthest outpost from the rest of Angeles City, un-wanted, like a leper colony. The van slowly bumped us down the quarter mile of rutted road to a crowd of jumping children and smiling caretakers waiting outside.

"*Mabuhay!*" "*Magandang tanghali!*" (Welcome! Good Noon!) shout-ed the children and adults alike as we coasted to a dusty stop.

Having finally arrived, we were formally introduced to officials and staff as "representatives from the United States who were in training to serve the Philippines."

"Welcome to our home," said the directress. "Children! Gather round and greet our guests."

Most of the children at the home were not "Special," but were orphaned, or abandoned by parents who could not pay for their care. Dozens of children of all ages surrounded us, eyes large, spying the toys and games we had brought for them. Smiles, laughter, and chatter all around. The directress clapped her hands, but the children were too excited to settle down. We had been taught in our training a common and fun way to gain control of a crowd and in unison, we yelled "Hel-lo-o!" The children yelled back "H-i!" Then we chanted, "H-i!" and they responded "Hel-lo-o!" Now we had their attention.

"What shall we do with these balls?" our sports leader, Chris asked, taking the balls out of the vans.

"Can we play?" some of the smaller boys asked.

"Yes! Here, take a ball!" said Chris, keeping to simple English, and then saying, "*Halika, laro tayo!*" and ran into the field with 15 boys of varying size trailing him.

The men, with whom the children seemed enamored, kicked balls high in the air for the youth to run after. So much laughter. We reveled in the camaraderie as much as they did. While the boys played on the field, some of us women volunteers styled girls' hair in shiny black braids as they touched our whiteness, our blondness, our foreignness with their arms wrapped around ours.

Breaking for lunch was a chance to practice our Tagalog at the outdoor canteen. There were plenty of giggles from the children as we mispronounced words, but that was the way we would learn, from these accepting youngsters.

"*Ulit!* Say it again!"

"*Nga, nge, ngi, ngo ngu.*" "*Ngiti,*" I said, and the children collapsed in gales of laughter.

"What! I said it right that time," I said, pretending to be offended.

"It's okay *po*, you are a *Lola* (grandmother) and have a hard time saying *nga*. We will help you, *po*. Try it again, *po*. *Ulit na!*"

Everywhere in the Philippines, particularly in the provinces, respect was shown to one's elders, with 'seniors' afforded the highest esteem.

One of the most beloved demonstrations of respect was the *pagmamano,* where a younger person takes the elder's hand and places it on the younger's forehead. *Pagmamano* is a request for the elder's blessing. '*Po*' was the everyday term showing the societal value of respect and deference for age and authority. These children may not have parents and may have been abandoned, but they were reared with Filipino values, uber-polite, and well-loved by their housemates.

Following our after-lunch games, we left the main school for a tour of the complex. With uniformed staff in bright green in the front, we strolled dirt paths to the far back of the compound where they tended the children with special needs. This was my specialty area for which I had been hired, and I was eager to see their classrooms and teaching methods. As we walked farther from the eating pavilion, we spoke more softly, and quiet enveloped us. The last structure was merely a small concrete house with three rooms, and we quietly opened the front door. The staff who ran the facility smiled with pride as they stepped aside and motioned for us to enter.

No child talked or laughed or cried; the silence was heavy, with a soft murmuring of repeated phrases. There was a wrinkled poster of children surrounding a smiling Jesus in a field of sunflowers hanging on the wall, but not much else. I didn't see any blackboards, books, or toys. It wasn't what I would call clean, but not dirty either. There were three cribs in the center of what must have been the living room of the house, one window let in light, but not much. Two people sat in plastic chairs near one crib; the man looked through slat barriers at the sleeping child, while the woman held a wooden rosary and was the source of the quiet murmurs of prayers.

One of the staff smiled and said, "Hello, Jacob! It looks like you are having a good day today!" But there was no movement in the crib and the child just lay there; I had assumed he was sleeping.

"Jacob was wrapped in a blanket and left at our door when he was only two," she said.

"How old is he now?" one of our volunteers asked.

"He is six now and doesn't speak, but we are lucky that we have visitors from the church who come to talk and pray with him."

"Did you make the furniture?" one of our men asked.

"Yes, we built the tables and the rack in the kitchen, but the cribs were donated to us from a Christian mission in Laguna, and look, they even gave us three adult sleeping cots so that we can sleep here with the children. There is always at least one of us who sleeps in the house, and we all live on the property, so we are always available to help if a child needs us."

The smaller bedroom held two cribs and chairs for visitors. As usual, the heat was stifling. The boy I remember most was 15 years old and in a crib with only a diaper, in part due to the heat, but also because of his inability to regulate his body. He was as tiny as a five-year-old, with smooth skin, his body atrophied like a patient in the last stages of AIDS. As the loving attendants turned him over to show us his face, he didn't move or make a sound but drooled with unfocused eyes, his head lolling, and limbs flaccid.

The room smelled of urine and something else, decay and hopelessness. This was no school for Special children. There were no classrooms or educational tools in sight. These children were in a vegetative state and had no cognitive function. Flashback to a Robin Cook novel where body parts were kept in suspended animation, waiting to be utilized in an inhuman plot to serve a diabolical regime.

It was I, the one with the Master's degree in Special Education, who ran crying from the room gasping, "I can't do this!" over and over, inconsolable until one of our instructors came to me and calmed me down. I viscerally felt the hopelessness that I later saw in the haunted faces of the parents of such children, who had no escape from their prison. This was my first exposure to the lack of education on such disorders, the misunderstanding of Special Education, and the urgent need for basic medication and therapies that might help them. But these children were so severely disabled that nothing could help them. An epiphany about what I might have to face.

In the Christian Philippines, some parents viewed their disabled children as a burden from Jesus, their cross to bear. Other parents abandoned their children, as these children had been. In the U.S. with 300 million people, there were 800 developmental pediatricians; the Philippines, with one-third of that population, had only 40 such pediatricians who understood intellectual disabilities, or only 5% of the U.S.

For the first and last time, I felt like running away as fast as I could...because I knew if I had to serve only children like this, who had no hope of learning how to feed themselves and would never interact with another person, I would fail and be utterly miserable for two years.

Such a flagrant emotional outburst was reported to Manila and the head of the program. Arnel called me.

"Debra?"

"Yes, hello Sir."

"I wanted to call and talk with you about what to expect on your permanent assignment. What you saw last week at the orphanage is not the same as where you will be assigned."

"Oh?"

"Yes, your school is dedicated to returning Special children to regular school. Don't worry, it will be fine."

"Okay, thank you for letting me know. I'm sorry, but I don't know how to help those children and I panicked."

"It's okay, you will be able to use your skills to help children, I assure you."

Calming down, I was relieved, not yet realizing I was prey to another Filipino trait of manipulating people by telling them whatever they wanted to hear to get whatever it was that you wanted.

A month later he asked.

"How would you like to work for a small SPED NGO?"

"Oh my, that would probably be the last place I would want, Sir."

"Ah, but you will love the place. It is in a rural setting smaller than Olongapo. You will like it and they will like you. It is a very small NGO that needs to be taken to the next level. You can help them organize and get funding through grants.

"Well, I like the sound of a rural town, and I like helping organizations grow. If the children can learn, I will be okay. And as long as it is not extremely religious."

"It is probably the most difficult assignment I have, but you have the background and knowledge to succeed."

And so, I would discover the negative aspect of *pakikisama,* getting along with others. Inadvertently, I agreed to what Arnel had wanted all along. In this case, the manipulation was done to me by Arnel and the Peace Corps, but at another level, the school misled the Peace Corps with grandiose statements of what they did in order to have a harmonious and fruitful relationship.

After my outburst and recovery, we returned to Olongapo and, as a group, took on a project for our village's small center for abused girls. The Department of Social Welfare and Development (DSWD) handled all the Youth and Family issues in the country, from children in conflict with the law to orphans to incest victims, as well as Special children. We visited the facility where about 30 girls lived in a dull concrete, multi-storied building.

That first day, one of the officials approached me and wished me a very friendly, "Good Morning, *po!*" Following with, "Welcome to our center for girls. How long have you been in Old Cabalan, Ma'am? Are you married?" My eyebrows raised as I told him no. Then he asked, "How old are you, *po?*" My eyes widened and my brows arched way up; I tsked and ignored him in a very American fashion. The first thing the panel of officials did when they sat on stage and self-introduced themselves was to state their age, marital status, professional title and how long they had been with the agency. Thus, I sheepishly found out that age, marital status, and title are the most important identifiers one possesses and are readily publicized when introducing oneself. From that time on, I made my age public and flaunted it.

The girls' stories were heartbreaking; girls from six to sixteen years old, sexually abused, by uncles, brothers, and fathers. The girls were taken from their homes to keep them safe, then housed here pending family trial. These were some of the most beautiful children I had ever seen, and most broken, betrayed by parents who were supposed to protect them.

A tour of the facility showed us where the roof leaked onto their beds, flooding the lower floors, and shorting out light fixtures. The mayor had told them to cut service to their leaking water pipes which cost the city money. As a result, these young girls had to fill buckets from the lawn faucet and haul them to the second floor to pour them into a 50-gallon barrel situated in the middle of the bathroom. Only then could they bathe. They had to repeat the process to fill a similar barrel in the kitchen for cooking. We decided we would go to the mayor on their behalf but suspected it would be a lost cause since, before our involvement, the girls seemed primarily to do without.

As we discussed tactics, a lawyer arrived from arguing a case in court, saying that the judge had ruled again for the father and that the child was to be returned to the family. The lawyer nearly broke down in tears recounting her long hours fighting for the girl. She knew the abuse would continue, sanctioned by the courts. In the system's eyes, the child's well-being was not dependent upon her physical or emotional safety, but on her being with family, regardless of how that family treated her. The lawyer looked downtrodden, but she would be back in court the next day, fighting for another child.

Our group agreed that our priority would be to repair and repaint the large communal room that had flaking paint from the roof leak and to section off a corner to make a library. We were exuberant and so dedicated to making a difference. Most of us were young, twenty-seven was the average age of our Peace Corps batch, so manual labor and energy were abundant. The U.S. Navy supplied paint for us, which was a luxury in the Philippines, and they even helped us plaster one day. Exuberant, yes, tidy, no; what a mess we made, but what fun we had with the older girls helping move the bookshelves and steady the ladder. Colors are bright in the tropics, but paint is expensive with a limited choice of colors. So, our library walls were painted white with blue, green, red, and yellow highlights. We sanded and painted the bookshelves, stocking them with books donated by The Asia Foundation.

For the official dedication of the library, the girls dressed up in ruffles and bows and socks with sparkles. My favorite child was model-beautiful, only six years old. She had a round face with eyes like big brown pools and she could gaze at you like a sphinx. That is until she laughed when her face would break apart revealing brilliant white teeth in a beautiful smile. But only until she re-composed herself. Watching those angelic little girls, who had lost their innocence so early surfaced memories of my two daughters' upbringing: sheltered, loved, and safe, and I wondered how these girls dealt with their trauma. On the outside at least, they laughed, drank Coke, and thanked us for the books and the puppets we left them, giggling behind their tiny hands, like laughing was a secret.

Watching them surviving, 'in spite of,' reminded me of the movie *Life Is Beautiful*, where even in the worst conditions of a World War II concentration camp, there was something to laugh about, live for, and celebrate. I think that was the heart of the message I saw on the omnipresent posters plastered on provincial churches, storefronts, and vehicles: "God is Good All the Time." Those propaganda signs infuriated me and caused bizarre reactions: sometimes I wanted to laugh out loud in derision, and other times I flushed with anger. Watching these precious girls, I silently cursed God for allowing such widespread indecencies to go unpunished and unstopped. But I was trying to become Filipino, so I told no one.

Tess and I grew closer in the compound as the days wore on, and we learned each other's stories. Not only were we close in age and loved the color purple, but we were born on the same date in May and even shared the same blood type (another piece of personal information that everyone seemed to know). She told me her story of how she came to Olongapo as a young woman.

Tess was from the province of Leyte in the east and came to Olongapo as a teenager during the time of the Vietnam War (known as the Resistance War Against the United States in Vietnam). Subic Bay had been a huge U.S. naval base since its establishment in 1898 at the end of the Spanish American War when the U.S. acquired the Philippines as a U.S. territory. Tess related that her family life was unhappy, due largely to her step-father who mistreated her. A childhood friend of hers who was expecting a child in Subic asked her to come and help her with her home and new baby. Tess purposefully boarded a ferry in Tacloban and headed to Subic Bay, 24 hours away, where she worked for a couple of years as house-help. She left her friend and started waitressing at an eatery just outside the entrance to the military base, which is where she met her husband. She had stories of women who came to Subic as call girls for U.S. servicemen. The U.S. military convened at Subic Bay, from posts around the world, for their R&R (Rest and Recuperation). Girls were in high demand and jobs were plentiful, profitable, and full of promise.

Tess recounted her story in her quiet, understated way without emotion, and my mind filled in the blanks of what must have been a terrifying trip for a sheltered 17-year-old from Leyte. I didn't ask, but wondered who had suggested this route; could her parents have agreed to this, or was it the thinking of a trapped, romantic teenager?

"I lived in poverty with my family, and there was no use for girls there in Leyte, no employment which is what my family needed. I couldn't afford to go to college; it never entered my mind. In my family, there was no talk of school, just of working to put food on the table. And then there was my stepfather. I quit school before I was 15 and this was my way out.

"I also heard friends in town spread *chika chika* of the riches a girl could earn in Subic, where the American base was. This was 1966 and the American War in Vietnam was going on. For many it meant living as a prostitute, but many girls had no hope here, so what were they to do? I was lucky to have a house-helper job with my friend. I took a boat that left Tacloban at night and arrived in Subic Bay the following night, 24 hours on that boat in not-so-calm seas. There were times that I thought I was crazy, a few hours when I was terrified, and times I was excited to leave Leyte and go to a place with some opportunity. But I was mostly just scared of traveling alone with people I didn't know. I was only 17 and knew nothing about life.

"When I left my friend's house to work at an eatery at the entrance to Subic's U.S. Naval Base, I saw so many women, especially in the evening, gathered just outside the gates, waiting for the military men to exit."

A reciprocal arrangement had been reached between the U.S. Navy and the city of Olongapo: If the mayor of Olongapo promised unlimited access to women for soldiers on R&R, the Navy would foot the medical bills to keep the women clean and healthy. At one point there were 60,000 women employed as prostitutes for the U.S. military's pleasure.

I found out about this arrangement when we took a 'field trip' to the PREDA Foundation, founded by Father Shay Cullen. Father Cullen was a big man with a heavy Irish brogue; he dominated the pulpit, a room, and our group of volunteers. Cullen was an outgoing, charismatic, and confrontational Irish missionary priest, who fought against child trafficking since he first came to the Philippines in 1969. In 2021, PREDA and Father Cullen received their fourth nomination for the Nobel Peace Prize, the latest from the German Parliament. Father Cullen's disturbing book *Passion and Power* detailed the harsh realities beneath the surface that tourists never see, the dark underbelly of politics and money. The chapters were stark and raw, rather than romantic and uplifting, and he named names.

As part of our introduction to Olongapo, we made "courtesy calls" on government organizations, and unexpectedly met some of the characters mentioned in the book. Notably, we personally met Olongapo's Mayor Gordon, that is, James "Bong" Gordon, *aka* Bonggo, who had recently debuted an album as a singing cowboy titled *Deep Inside My Mind.* Slight of build, he was the epitome of the slick politician, with a ready smile and slicked-back black hair. But as we watched, the small politician doffed his baseball cap, donned a 10-gallon black felt cowboy hat, picked up his electric guitar, and performed two mournful songs for us. The most unique courtesy call we ever made.

Bong's brother, and former mayor, Richard, was the very person that Father Cullen claimed had started the sex trafficking ring of Olongapo, and he was then Senator, making a bid for the Presidency. Richard and Bong's father, James Sr., had been the first elected mayor of Olongapo City who succumbed to the fourth assassination attempt on his life. James' wife, Amelia, took over and her son, Richard, helped her run the city government. The only time a Gordon was not mayor was during President Ferdinand Marcos' Martial Law in the '70s. The Gordon political dominance, known as a 'dynasty' in the Philippines, continued with Bong's wife, Anne, who became Vice-Governor of the entire province. Only in 2013, after Bong, did a non-Gordon start serving as mayor (although the Gordon clan promised a comeback).

Easy to imagine how Cullen's daily life could be fraught with conflict with the Gordon government. Pushback also came from some of the religious communities who benefited from Gordon's rule, and, of course, the U.S., which relied on the local sex trade.

I bought Cullen's book, devoured it, and gave it to my Olongapo family to read, enlightening to them, and doubly fascinating since they had lived through those times. They liked reading the stories they knew firsthand, and others that confirmed rumors.

It was an outright sock-in-the-gut revelation for me and brought to life the love/hate relationship Filipinos had with America that I felt so frequently. The American bases had been ousted by the Philippine government in 1992, but vestiges of that time were obvious today. It made me recall the speech of my program director from that first introduction in Cavite. Hate the American but love the resources - the human conundrum.

Some nights, Joseph, Joie, Tess, and I would drive to Subic, get an ice cream at the Mini-Mart, and, with Gelo in tow, meander along the shore by the hotels. The lights were magical, and the darkness hid the shacks, trash, and poverty beyond. Remnants from military base R&R were still obvious, with brash, hopelessly young American servicemen buying drinks for ladies of the night, and we watched their blatant and crude foreplay as we strolled by with our cones. My patriotic views of America were severely under attack after only a couple of months in this country.

Tess' fate was not of prostitution; her future followed a chance encounter with a man that led to marriage and motherhood. She claimed that he saved her life, but it made me wonder if the life she was rescued into was a big improvement. She raised a brood of five on a pittance, almost entirely on her own, scraping together food while her husband worked. And, as is common for many Filipinos, as Tess waited for him to come home, he had liaisons with other women and would return home drunk, having spent their money. Certainly not a marriage I would have wanted, but what was her option? I tried to understand.

Life is hard in the provinces with little economic opportunity for the masses, a plight only heightened for uneducated women. Often their chance at a 'better life' is tied to marriage. In the Philippines, marriage is for life. It is the only country in the entire world where divorce is illegal; well, except for the Vatican where there are 450 celibate priests and their guards. Only rich Filipinos (celebrities and politicians) could afford to buy annulments from the Church, the cost starts at around $10,000 for no-contest and five to ten times that if contested. Annulment is thus a moot point in a country where the average annual salary is $3,300. Maybe it is precisely because of these costs that it is more commonplace and accepted that men have side wives and families, often residing mere meters from the original wife.

Those first three months in the Philippines had my head absorbing the culture and trying to make sense of it from my biased upbringing. I was lucky that my family spoke excellent English, and we talked about ideas; other volunteers didn't have that luxury. Discussions comparing and contrasting what was accepted in the U.S. versus the Philippines taught me so much, broadly:

- One accepts the mores of the culture into which she is born, programmed by the greater society in order to feel she belongs, with the ultimate goal of perpetuating societal systems and structure.

- There is no right/wrong or truth, "Truth" is what works in that culture.

- Most people in any given culture seem immune to examining their own culture objectively; we accept, and then promote, our societal norms as reality and truth.

It was fascinating to begin to scrutinize the assumptions I had accepted throughout my life in the U.S. These first three months were just the first stepping stone to analyzing my basic values, and finding them lacking. I began reviewing the mores of this new country with the hope of understanding. For such a religious nation, bigamy and illegitimacy were accepted, and people weren't even aware of the dichotomy. People I met blasted the U.S. for its high divorce rate and that effect on families, not considering their own acceptance of Overseas Foreign Workers (OFWs) who left spouses and families for years, nor unwanted illegitimate children, or fathers with multiple families. Nor did they see the impact of these on the fabric of society. Each of us seems bound by, and blind to, our own culture's social constructs.

One of the saddest things to me was the spousal acceptance of a woman's lot in life. Even with his spending, drinking, and perhaps unintended emotional abuse, Tess, then 62 years old, was anticipating death to be reunited with her husband.

"I've raised my family and now I am waiting to rejoin him," she said once.

"Good grief, Tess, you aren't dead! Let's go to Subic and get you out. Let's party a little!"

"Ha-ha. Oh, Deb, you are so funny," was her only reply.

Tess seemed to feel that her life was over; she had diabetes and other ailments that hindered her. She'd had a hard life and was just happy to have food on the table, two of her four sons and grandchildren in the compound, and that new refrigerator, of course.

Our relationships with our daughters, on the other hand, gave us plenty of material for regret and bonded us in our sadness and feeling of failure as mothers. In Asian countries, you often hear women friends call each other "Sis," and Tess and I became sisters of a sort. The three of us women, Tess, Joie, and I, talked long into the night about our womanly hopes, dreams, and regrets.

We emoted over board games at the kitchen table with Gelo, who was eight at the time. Gelo was a bright little boy and a spoiled only child who loved to eat. One night we had pork chops as a treat and Coke. Nanay was diabetic, and I was stunned when she had a glass of Coke.

"You can't have that!" I blurted with concern and a little vigor.

She chuckled and said, "Just a little."

The few people I knew in the U.S. diagnosed with diabetes had changed their diet immediately to exclude sugar, which I thought was standard procedure. Not so in the Philippines, where diabetes was common. People were too poor to afford medication, or equipment to check their insulin levels, but believed that they could have just a bit of anything proclaimed as a forbidden food, including sugar.

This night, the pork chops were large, we each got one. They were full-fat Filipino chops, not lean American-style. Fully one-half of the chop was pure fat, not marbled meat, but solid white fat an inch thick. And that was the prized portion here.

I asked Gelo, "I'll trade you this white piece for your meat half," feeling so guilty I couldn't even identify it correctly as fat.

"Really *Tita*? Yes! Yes!"

I ashamedly wondered if I contributed to his poor diet and weight gain. Joie just laughed her gay and contagious laugh.

Joie was full of vibrant positivity and was the wholehearted laughter of the household. She sang *karaoke* with an entertainer's voice and gestures and could have been the main event on a cruise ship, she was that good. She dutifully massaged Nanay's feet when they were swollen and gave her full-body massages at least once a week. Joie performed all of this after returning home from work, cooking dinner, and doing laundry.

I was shocked once when Joie punished Gelo by pouring hot wax from a taper candle onto the back of his hand. Contrary to Peace Corps training, I stopped her the third time she did this, I couldn't bear to watch him cry in pain. We talked a bit about it, and I think she ended this method of punishment, but maybe only just in front of me. Gelo turned out to be a wonderful young man, so I guess it didn't cause any lasting damage, and with my parenting failings, who was I to comment?

Cultural differences are hard to navigate; how does one know when to intervene and when to stay silent? Joie never took offense. She and Nanay taught me so much about the assumptions and expectations of the culture in which they grew up, many of which I rejected outright, and others I came to understand, although not embrace. But in subtle ways, I was acclimating to Filipino life.

The Philippines is 85% Catholic. Strangely, both my host families were not. My Olongapo family were Mormons and received frequent visits from missionaries, which I strove to avoid, at the same time they conspired to force an introduction. If I saw the very young, very blonde, and very white missionary coming down the street, I would run out the back door, hiding from the missionary by staying with Chris, the volunteer living next door. Once, memorably, I didn't make it.

"Hello, nice to meet you, Debra," said the young man with a bible and smooth face.

"Good afternoon, nice to meet you, too. I'm sorry, I missed your name?"

"You can call me Elder," said the 18-year-old with a beatific smile surrounded by peach fuzz.

"But, what's your name?" I persisted.

"You can call me Elder," he repeated.

My hackles rose. I have a thing about blindly following instructions, so I didn't call him anything. I skirted religion and asked about his excellent Tagalog. He gave me several great tips about inclusive and exclusive pronouns, explaining that LDS (Latter Day Saints) missionaries had intensive language instruction at the temple before they left the U.S. and that most arrived fluent in the language, ready to take up their mission. We conversed pleasantly, and I relaxed. Then he began the questions.

"Do you believe in Jesus Christ the Savior?"

"Umm, I like several of the prophets," I hedged.

"Well, that's all right."

I thought he, as a missionary, was quite progressive with this statement...until his follow-up:

"As long as you believe in God," said with a penetrating, questioning look.

"Umm... sometimes."

I can't remember what transpired after my uncomfortable statement, but after that encounter, Joie forewarned me when "Elder" was to visit so that I could be elsewhere.

For three months this family cared for me with love and kindness, acceptance and tolerance. I lost weight walking up and down those 27 stairs twice daily to language class and jostled with the locals in jeepneys with my little Peace Corps subgroup of five trainees. At the end of the three months, my language ability was officially assessed, and passed as "Intermediate Tagalog." The official Peace Corps tester, flown in from Manila, was surprised and commended me that I did well for someone so old.

My host family couldn't attend the formal Peace Corps induction ceremony in Manila, where Hilary Clinton was to speak (she canceled). Joie gave me a prized embroidered blouse of hers to wear for the event; my Hmong friend, Paj, did my make-up and hair, and I lost 10 years. The two of us, who had been initially rebuffed, had made it through training.

DEBRA PRITCHARD

Aged 59, I realized my childhood dream of becoming a full-fledged Peace Corps Volunteer. I was headed to my two-year assignment, on the island of Palawan, to reenact *Eat, Pray, Love*.

SCHOOL GARDEN

OLD CABALAN PARADE

MULTI CAB

THE OVERLOADED
TRICYCLE TO SCHOOL

GIRLS' LIBRARY DEDICATION

DOING LAUNDRY THE
FILIPINO WAY

Chapter 5

PALAWAN - THE LAST FRONTIER

Huwag kang magtiwala sa di mo kilala
Don't trust strangers.
A Filipino proverb meaning, 'You can never be sure that people you don't know truly have your well-being in mind. Don't put yourself in their hands.'

Foreigners

Sa kabila ng mga dingding na kawayan ay nagkatitigan kami	Across the bamboo walls we stare at each other
Ang una nating pagkikita, intimate sa iyong tahanan	Our first meeting, intimate in your home
Ang iyong pagtanggap ay walang tiwala sa akin.	Your welcome does not trust me.
Gusto kitang pagkatiwalaan	I want to trust you
Nagmula ka kay Moses, nagmula ako sa lupa	You come from Moses, I come from the earth
Kapag nag-uusap kami hindi ko pa rin maintindihan.	When we talk I still don't understand.
Baka magsinungaling ang mga salita mo.	Your words might lie.
Hindi dapat pagkatiwalaan ang mga estranghero dito.	Strangers should not be trusted here.

THE FLIGHT TO PALAWAN, the westernmost island of the Philippines, took 55 minutes from Manila, and each passenger was allotted 17 kg of luggage or 37 lbs. My possessions for two years made it with room to spare: my backpack, duffle bag, and, most importantly, my snorkel and prescription mask. My favorite thing in the whole world is to dive and snorkel, and I had high hopes for this island they called "The Last Frontier."

The flight was glorious; below us, enormous white clouds and turquoise waters speckled with hundreds of islands, mostly uninhabited. My nose was pressed against the window the entire time. Landing in Puerto was a geographic revelation. Approaching from the water, we sailed down the runway towards imposing craggy mountains. The rocky heights and lush primeval beauty were unexpected, a Jurassic Park that somehow unsettled me.

On November 10th, 2010, five of us PCVs arrived to live on Palawan; the others in our contingent were 25-27 years old; I was 59. Bryce, the young husband from my cluster, and his wife, Krystal would live just a couple miles from me and I felt lucky. Bryce was assigned to the DSWD (Department of Social Welfare) where he would work with children in conflict with the law, and she, along with Petra and Will, the other two education volunteers, would be teaching English in the local national High Schools. I was committed to a small school focused on Special children. PCVs were again entrusted to host families to keep us safe and ease us into the unique culture of the province. We would remain in these host family homes for at least three months and were expected to do all we could to acclimate to the community.

The Philippines is a tribal nation of over 7000 islands and 120 spoken languages. The indigenous peoples (the Aetas), geography, and wildlife of Olongapo were vastly different from Palawan, where the customs of the Batak and Palaw'an tribes were considered to be closer to Borneo traditions, and wildlife and geography also more Borneo than Philippine. Thus, we needed to learn new histories, manners, and even phrases of Tagalog, which could mean something totally different here. In Tagalog, the word for ant was *langgam*, but farther south in Cebu *langgam* meant bird. *Ilaga* in Cebuano meant to seethe, in Tagalog it was a rat. Linguistically, it reminded me of a trip to China decades before when I was five months pregnant. The Chinese sentence that a tourist might use was "I want to ask you" but if you got the tone wrong, you might say "I want to kiss you," which could really get you in trouble. I foresaw similar challenges here and bigger potential trouble. Host families were there to help us navigate tricky linguistic and social circumstances, at least in theory.

Arnel, the head of the Peace Corps Youth and Family sector, told me he had assigned me the toughest job in the country because I had experience and could handle it. Looking back, I think a high schooler with a smile would have done better. It turned out that a college degree, a knowledge of disabilities, and science in general, was suspicious in this expansive province with no professional support. In this land entrenched in superstition, patriarchal deference, and a willingness to say anything to deflect blame and save face, I would blunder. A submissive, agreeable teenager available to take the children for daily walks might have been a better fit for this assignment.

My host family, and the leaders at the school to which I was assigned, were devout evangelicals who referred to themselves as "Born Again." As Arnel had told me in Manila, "The school was begun by a husband and wife and is operated on a shoestring. I don't know how they make ends meet. They are doing God's work. You will like Pastor, he is charismatic, and his wife has worked many years for Puerto Princesa's Department of Social Welfare. They have been married about 10 years and have two boys."

Suitably impressed when he told me about this back in Manila, it was much later that friends on Palawan filled in some blanks for me over a lunch conversation.

"Before he was Pastor, he was a well-known dance instructor."

"Sure," I laughed.

"No, I'm serious. A friend and I took lessons from him years ago. He and his brother were the instructors. They rented a space and tutored ladies in ballroom dancing.

"Did you learn how to dance?"

"Yes, he was a very good instructor."

"Smooth, eh?"

"Very smooth. He was handsome and very smooth on the dance floor; the ladies loved him."

"How weird. How did he go from being a social dance instructor to a religious pastor? Did you know his wife?"

"No, not much. She is older than he is, maybe by 10 years, I don't recall how they met, but maybe she inspired him to study the bible. I don't really know. I remember he worked with a pastor at Life Church, the one across from Adventist Hospital. It's a Born-Again church, and somehow he became a pastor himself."

She rolled her eyes. "Only in the Philippines," she grinned.

"They formed a church group and used to meet somewhere in town, but then moved way out on the South highway. I think after they started the church, they decided that his wife could retire from her government position and start her own school for Special children. It's out in Tagburos. Oh, you know that. Did you know that there used to be mercury mining out there? I wonder if that's why there's so many illnesses and mental problems out there....."

We got off-topic, but she had told me a lot about this couple I lived and worked with. The church was composed of perhaps five to ten families, and five of those were relatives. Church members were recruited to be teachers at the school. They seemed truly devoted to their tiny church community and the fledgling school, but these teachers from the congregation had little, if any, teaching experience and no education credentials. Their instruction methods were self-taught and not found in any textbook I'd ever seen.

But their loyalty seemed significant, as evidenced by the fact that they were rarely routinely paid. At one point, the school received a grant from the Liliane Foundation in The Netherlands, but it was a small amount more focused on helping parents afford the tuition; it didn't pay the teachers' salaries. Pastor told me that they were provided for by the church, but once I saw a neighbor give one of the teachers an *upo,* one green winter squash, and the teacher was ecstatic that she had food to cook for dinner that night. I silently questioned a lot in those early days, and even more later.

Few PCVs had to work at the family business and also lodge with the same family. It was not an optimum situation. If there was any tension at either school or home, there was no escape. A novice to this new culture, I stuck my foot in my mouth innumerable times. Inquisitive about everything and expecting an exchange of ideas like my first host family, I asked a lot of questions, questions that were incomprehensible to some, and perhaps made them view me as suspicious or rude. Further adding to this tension, gossip spread so quickly that everyone knew each other's business, and less factual embellishments were always added for flavor, to make the *chika chika* (gossip) more enjoyable.

In our training in Manila, I was always worried about religion. "Can we ask to not be placed in a religious organization?" I asked with some trepidation.

"Oh, certainly. You won't have to participate in anything you don't want to," was the pat response.

"Yes, then I would like to request that for my placement, I be assigned to a non-religious NGO."

Yet, here I was, in an uber-religious enclave.

I recalled an exchange with other volunteers at our training in Olongapo.

"Isn't religion a little over the top here?" said one.

"Yeah, but it's all Christian, so that's okay with me," said another.

"For me, religion has committed some of the worst acts in human history." (me, of course).

"But, don't you think that religion has done a lot of good too?" said a young man who hailed from the San Francisco Bay Area. "Look at Catholic Charities and Mother Teresa's work."

"To me, it seems that they are cleaning up after the mess they made, starting with the Crusades." Yes, I did have problems with organized religion.

To each his own belief, but placing me, an outspoken, independent woman (not a good thing in the first place) with a profound distrust of religion, into an extremely religious organization seemed like trying to mix oil and water. Or worse, was a formula for implosion.

Religion wasn't the only cultural aspect that I grappled with. The culture of family economics also seemed foreign to me. I recall a communication with my host, *Kuya* John, a tall man with thick hair and a quiet manner, wherein we discussed the working situations of the members of the family. He, the oldest brother, or *Kuya*, as he was called, and Tina, the family's oldest sister, or *Ate*, were the only members with paid employment. He worked at the power company, and she was a social worker. As *Kuya*, he was responsible for taking care of everyone, from his parents down to his siblings and their families. Not only did he support his family of six, but he also supported his sister and the Pastor, along with their two children and another brother, and that family of five. And all of them worked at the school which didn't make any money. Kuya's father, the patriarch of the clan, had died years ago, so *Kuya* also supported their mother. The entire family was his responsibility. The only similar family structure and obligations I had seen was on a visit to Kenya years earlier and that 'oldest brother' had made no bones about feeling burdened and resentful. Not so *Kuya*.

This was fascinating to me, and I asked him (foot in the mouth) for clarification.

"So, you are the only one who gets a paycheck? How does the school pay the teachers?"

"Well, *Tita*, the church takes a collection from all of us and some parents of students can pay full tuition. And now we have the grant money once or twice a year."

"But how do your sister's and brother's families have enough money?"

"Well, I am the *kuya*, and I help them. My father died five years ago, so now I am the head of the family. Because I am the oldest brother, I take care of our family. My oldest sister is the *ate* of the family and helps a lot with making sure the children go to college."

"Is it okay with you that they don't have jobs and you have to pay for them?"

He stared at me blankly. Probably the same way I would have looked at him if he asked me (as many did) why children in the U.S. were "kicked out" of their parent's home after college and expected to be independent. It's just the way it is, the accepted norm of your society. Most children in the U.S. don't begrudge their parents for expecting them to move out of the family home, it is built into the social structure. The same as most firstborns in the Philippines accept their societal role. While those of us from other cultures seem to cast aspersions on anything unlike our own.

The *kuya* and *ate,* the eldest boy and girl in the family, are customarily responsible for shouldering monetary obligations for housing, livelihood, and education for family members needing it. That baffled me at first, but employment in the Philippines, especially on the distant island of Palawan, was difficult to come by. Locals made jokes that a cousin studied criminology at college and was now a security guard; or graduated in transportation management and became a multicab driver, or had a degree in petroleum engineering and pumped gas onto barges. It was a sad joke to me.

The swelling population of the country is so large, and industrial output so limited, that there aren't enough jobs to support the greater portion of society. So, many companies can get away with hiring employees for a six-month contract, without any benefits or even fair wages. This makes job security almost non-existent. The rare full-time employment opportunities are frequently saved for family members of people who already have their foot in the door, and nepotism is accepted as a way for uncles to help errant nephews and cousins. Often, the best chance for a family to prosper is to invest in the education of one child and send him abroad to make a decent living. He in turn sends a large portion of his wages home to support those left behind. Cultural norms ensure the whole family survives.

Many *kuyas* and *ates* I came to know supported siblings who never found a secure job, and they also supported their siblings' non-working husbands or wives and children. For an American this felt like free-loading and disrespectful; not so to a Filipino, it was family. As an American who had lived and breathed a culture that values fierce independence and self-sufficiency, many of the aspects of this collective culture seemed incomprehensible to me, but I was beginning to gain more understanding, as they said, little by little.

Kuya was proud of the remodel they had done to their house. Twenty years before, they had squatted on unused, non-titled government land. When they first arrived, I don't think they paid anything since the government could reclaim the land. Later, they did pay taxes and may even have gotten a formal title. As *Kuya's* salary increased at the local power company, their income was more secure. Thus, after years of saving, he was able to build an indoor kitchen and eating area and two small rooms for his older children, as well as make quality upgrades to beautifully tiled floors and walls.

The house was located on Maunlad Street, which translates to "Prosperous." I'm not sure if he had anything to do with its naming, but it suited the family's aspirations. The younger two girls (by ten years), slept in the same bed as their mom and dad, as was typical. I learned months later that the oldest boy gave up his new room for me.

This teenager's name was Genesis, and he slept in the kitchen on the hard tiled benches against the wall. I felt terribly guilty when I found out he had given up his room for me, but I knew not to say anything. My room was tiled and had a single cot in it. The room was about three feet longer than the cot and about two and a half cots wide. My first night there, it poured rain, as in buckets from the heavens. There was a big window in my room, with glass louvers that looked onto a grassy area between our house and the neighbor's. As the rain increased, it morphed into a marsh, and then a lake, and the frogs came out. Like nothing I had ever heard before; it was a chorus of frog happiness as loud as a chainsaw symphony. Some instinct had me grab my computer and record the amazing sound. Listening to it now brings me back to the wonder I felt and makes me smile with nostalgia. That was the first of many sounds that transfixed me and only the first of many nights that nature prevented a good night's sleep.

After a couple of hours, the rain and frogs subsided so that you heard only *Kuya*'s snores until sometime after midnight when another sharp sound woke me again. It echoed off the tiled walls and I froze in bed trying to identify it. At first, I thought perhaps a creature had gotten trapped in the wall, but it didn't sound like a bird or cat and a snake didn't squawk like that. I tensed every ten minutes or so to the harsh croak, an intense double-toned bark that repeated seven times in diminishing decibels. No one else got up, so I guessed it wasn't life-threatening.

Rigid in bed, I heard Genesis go to the bathroom, and called out in a loud whisper, "What is that?"

He smiled, and pointing to a crack in the wall, said, "*Tuko.*"

I pointed my phone flashlight at the wall and saw a big, blue lizard face with rust-colored splotches on it, and a bright red tongue, silent at that moment. Still confounded (could a lizard really make that loud bark?), I went back to bed and dozed off.

At 2:30 AM I awakened again to a loud mechanical alarm, ringing over and over at perfect intervals to not allow sleep. It seemed, though again, that I was the only one to hear it. Finally, after about five minutes, I heard someone turn it off, get up heavily and shuffle to the shower. The church held its first service at 3:00 AM, before work, before school was in session, and hours before the sun. *Kuya* lumbered out of bed in the dark, dressed in the bathroom, and rode his motorcycle in the black morning through the rutted roads to the 3:00 AM service. I only made that service twice, the first time nodding off as the sun rose, oh so slowly.

The Peace Corps had told us we didn't have to attend religious services, but evangelicals seemed to get points for bringing souls into the pack. So I was constantly invited to events, and I attended a few times in an attempt to build stronger relationships with my host family. Pastor seemed particularly interested in my conversion. When I first met him, he spoke about his faith, including how converting people was important. I joked a bit and politely asked him to please not try to convert me. His grin and hungry promise said it all, "I'll get you before you leave."

During my first week in Puerto, about ten evangelical leaders met at Life Church to discuss their new character program. This was a curriculum they had proposed to the Department of Education and hoped to implement in all grade schools the following school year. I've long been a proponent of character education for youth. Character education as I knew it taught children the basic values and ethics for getting along in society, like compassion, cooperation, integrity, and honesty, actions that contributed to the individual and to society. A true believer, I was ready to get involved, excited to attend, and to learn what they were doing.

The meeting began with a prayer beseeching "Lord God" several times to open everyone's mind to the learning, to rejoice in the opportunity to help educate children and to serve God. The prayer was peppered with erratic supportive utterances of "Yes, God!" and "Amen!" from the attendees. I probably squirmed a little. The meeting was in Tagalog, and although I had to pay close attention, I could understand everything being said. The pastor in charge was visibly excited as he presented a formal slide show highlighting statistics of the school population.

"Imagine," he said as he systematically locked eyes with each person at the table, "all the souls we could convert if we got them young. If we get into the schools with character education, before Catholics or others, we will bring so many souls to Jesus."

All eyes were fixed on his and were glowing with fervor. Bodies leaned forward, magnetized.

My eyes flashed and my heart fluttered. This was a plot to infiltrate public education and serve up their version of God. My stomach followed my heart and churned. I had unwittingly agreed to help them. Ugh. A newbie, I had no way of knowing the Life Church motto: "Win Souls and Make Disciples." The lead pastor continued his slide presentation which enumerated, instead of the character attributes to be taught, estimates of just how many students the program would reach: thousands upon thousands.

Abruptly, the projector blurred and the room went dark. Was this a sign? But no, it was just the first of what would be a near-daily occurrence for me, the famed "brownout." The electric company had a poorly designed and ancient distribution system, so that overloads and shorts occurred daily in the province. Brownouts were when only a portion of the city lost power; theoretically, blackouts happened to the whole city, but everyone magnanimously called those brownouts too. This first brownout plunged everything into quiet blackness...and stifling heat. Someone opened the doors for the light and ventilation to come in, but there was no wind and the pervasive heat followed.

The zealous group continued their discussion, and I made some excuse to take a jeepney home. But, "home" was the same evangelical family and offered no relief, or anyone to talk to about my misgivings. The only people I knew were the Born Again church members.

During this time, my day began around 6:00 AM, before dawn. On Palawan, the light lasts between 11½ and 12½ hours every day of the year, and there are but two seasons: rainy and dry. Electricity was expensive and families in my neighborhood had a grate for a charcoal fire for cooking, no aircon, and no oven. Life is organized around the sun's light and heat.

The coolest average temperature is 74F in January and the hottest 91F in April, but conditions often make it feel even hotter. To maximize both the light and lowest temperature, people wake up by 3:00 AM to kindle the morning charcoal fire that would cook breakfast, warm the water for a 'bucket shower,' and heat water for laundry. Those same people went to bed around 8:00 PM after dinner, when it had already been dark for two hours.

In our family, the father (*Kuya*) got up first to attend the 3:00 AM church service and the rest of us rose around 5:00 or 6:00 AM. By then, he would have returned with warm *pan de sal* white rolls for our breakfast, which we ate with steaming Milo, heated on the charcoal fire. Something I never quite got used to was the smoky flavor of bread and cookies cooked in the charcoal ovens of the neighborhood bakeries.

By 6:30 AM, the mother got the two young girls up and into their cold shower. She brushed out their wet hair while their older sister, the already showered *Ate*, ironed their school uniforms.

The father usually started the fire for our hot water for Milo, cleaned up, and waited for the two teens to finish readying for school, which started at 7:30 AM. The three of them hopped astride the motorcycle and the father transported them to their high school. Then he returned for the two younger girls, and with their wet hair trailing behind them on the motorcycle, he dropped them at kindergarten and only then continued to his office.

Filipinos pride themselves on their ability to wear many hats and take on different businesses to make ends meet. People work hard and long hours in this culture; I've never seen such industrious people. This family also owned a van called a multicab that was licensed for public transport. As with most commuter vehicles, theirs had a name, the same as their son, Genesis, painted in red just below the windshield wipers. Their driver arrived at our gates before breakfast and began his long monotonous day going back and forth the same four miles to and from the city; the fare was 10 pesos, about 20 cents, back and forth all day long. Salaries weren't openly discussed, but I suspect they paid the driver two to three dollars a day, the Palawan average. And they took the proceeds. The only time I had an interaction with the driver was receiving a text message stating he could not come in that day because he had 'LBM'. I had no idea what that was but quickly found out: 'loose bowel movement,' usually from parasites in the drinking water, a common occurrence. People spoke freely of such impediments to coming to work. Some bodily functions rolled off tongues nonchalantly in public like dysmenorrhea, diarrhea, and high blood, even though the prevention and treatment for these weren't understood. Discussion of other functions was *bawal* (forbidden), and it confused me to know the difference. Loud belches were fine, but audible flatulence not. It was like cramming 20 years of cultural assimilation into a month of learning; otherwise, you unintentionally offended people, something I was quite good at.

Brennie, the mom, spent at least two days a week doing the laundry by hand in huge 10-gallon plastic bins, one to soak the clothes, one with soap and infrequently charcoal-warmed water to wash, and two for rinsing. With four children and a husband, there were mounds of school uniforms, bed linens, towels, and *pambahay*, those casual 'around the house' clothes never worn out in public. Most days the yard was full of hanging attire that the teenagers were responsible for taking from the clothesline, folding, and ironing when they returned home, before they began their homework or started cooking dinner.

This was the first time in my life that I went hungry. There were seven of us to feed, and with all the other expenses, we didn't eat well, although we had plenty of rice. My Peace Corps funding was sent directly to the host family, so I ate whatever they served. A typical meal would be one large chicken breast boiled in a stock pot to suck every bit of juice, oil, or nutrition out of it. Leaves of *malungay* might be plucked from trees to add some greenery and nutrients, but we mostly ate the *sabaw* (broth) with an enormous plate of rice. I wondered how the teenage boy had the energy to work at school, do the laundry, and cook and clean up dinner on rice alone.

In contrast, the younger children had no chores, just perpetual play. Their antics were tolerated, even when they marked the newly remodeled walls with crayons. There was no punishment, harsh words, or even a reprimand, just smiles which confounded me. The youngest was a devil-child who delighted to annoy me. She loved to fondle my big derriere while she chanted "*Malaking puwet!*" (big butt), staring straight in my eyes. After asking her to stop and brushing her hand away, I started walking with one hand protecting my rear before her father finally reprimanded her.

"Stop, *Tita* doesn't like that," was all that he said, and she stopped, at least when he was in the room.

For Christmas, I bought each of the little girls a pair of fancy ruby glass earrings and wrapped them. They liked the flashy glass, but on Christmas night I discovered the younger with a hammer and knife, scraping the gems from their settings and smashing them to smithereens. The parents laughed out loud as they watched their darling, while I vowed that was her last present from me. Given my measly monthly stipend, those Christmas earrings cost me a lot that I didn't have, and I steamed for those kids to not even take care of the gift. Another cultural lesson: that things were different here. And a life lesson: enjoy giving the gift and let it go. I seemed to be evolving into Buddhist practices without even trying.

The Peace Corps taught me more indirectly, without any formal training session. The small stipend we received gave us a comparable income to those we served, something I appreciated immensely. In the Peace Corps, you are not the 'savior,' living in a luxury hotel and bestowing wisdom; you work alongside the community you serve and experience life as they do. This is the service I think every wealthy country should require, a humbling assessment of your privileged life.

My friends in the U.S. worried about me, especially my lack of good chocolate, and so sent me surprise Christmas packages. The problem was that there was no mail delivery on Palawan unless you were known. Early on, I walked into the Post Office in Puerto and asked to speak to the postman who delivered to Tiniguiban. He had me write down my name on a scrap of paper, but he either lost it or totally forgot. My friends asked if I got their gifts, so in late January I returned and helped postal employees search through a jumbled pile of unclaimed boxes in a back room. Behold! my packages, riddled with rodent holes and droppings. Rats had gnawed through and eaten the homemade cookies and candies long ago. They must have really been hungry rats since only shavings were left from the perfumed Estee Lauder gift soaps.

That first Christmas on Palawan, my host family held a party at home. We all had fun playing the typical games like Pinoy Henyo, where you write the name of something on a piece of paper and tape it to the guesser's forehead, so they can't see. They start by asking, "Is it a thing?" "An animal?" "A place?" "A person?" "A food?" And then go from there until they guess the word. It was made popular on the noontime TV show *Eat*

Bulaga!, which I thought was a vulgar title for "Eat S _ _ _ !", but it turns out it translates to "It's Lunchtime...Surprise!" and is entertainment while eating the midday meal. My contribution to our Pinoy Henyo game was Vice Ganda, one of the flamboyant regulars on *Eat Bulaga!* A youngster immediately guessed it, after I thought I had been so clever.

Other typical party games were 'Bring Me' where the game master calls out an item, like a yellow pencil, a coin purse, or a watch, and the first person to bring it to him wins. Another was something called "Trip to Jerusalem," equivalent to the U.S. musical chairs. There were other games for children, but the adults who played were slap-happy, loud, and laughed for hours. There was no question which of my two cultures enjoyed the simple life more as the slapstick family times clearly showed. From the *lola* (grandma) to the *apo* (grandchild), everyone was lively and in the party spirit. What a cleanup we had that night.

During the day, Brennie sold hotdogs from her freezer. She bought them in bulk for a discounted price and then stored them for purchase by her neighbors. Certainly, she was no Muhammad Yunus, the pioneer of small loans for poor entrepreneurs in Bangladesh, but she did supply bridge loans for the neighborhood, lending homemakers cash to get by until the next paycheck. We are talking about loaning perhaps two to five dollars at a time, but where two to five dollars is an average day's salary, it was a big help. Most people lived paycheck to paycheck, never needing a bank and many government agencies did not pay regularly. Nonetheless, utilities like water and electricity expected on-time payment and summarily cut off your supply if you were 14 days late. So, her business thrived.

They had a tiny television, a 12-inch square, on which I began my addiction to the series *Dwarfina*. The girls and I would watch it together, and they would explain the Tagalog words that I didn't understand. We watched the news, the national fiestas, and a lot of cartoons; Tom and Jerry was popular. I knew the cartoons, having grown up with them in the '50s; it was peculiar to see them broadcast here, 50 years later.

On Saturday morning January 9th, I was watching a religious celebration televised from Quiapo, Manila, the Feast of the Black Nazarene, when *Kuya* came out toweling off from his shower.

"See *Tita*?! Idols! They pray to idols!"

He was not happy and delivered a quiet rant to be sure I understood that Catholics were bad. *Kuya* also disliked Mormons because they had multiple wives, among many other complaints. I tried to be solemn and respectful but was figuratively scratching my head. Weren't all these guys Christians? They all believed in Jesus as the Christ. Good grief, even they couldn't get along. The criticisms and customs were strange to me, and my culture was just as foreign to my hosts. While they were welcoming, they culturally ascribed to the saying, "Don't Trust Strangers." Hospitality and trust were two different things entirely, so I decided to concentrate on the children at the school.

TUKO IN THE WALL

PAN DE SAL AND MILO
BREAKFAST

DOING MY LAUNDRY

CRISPY PATA

'PINOY HENYO'

THE LITTLE GIRLS AT
HOME

THE FAMILY MULTICAB

Chapter 6

SCHOOL DAZE

Wala kang masasabunot sa kalbo
You cannot pull hair from the bald
A Filipino proverb meaning, 'You cannot expect a person to give something he or she does not have - whether it be materially, mentally, or emotionally.'

Walang Pamagat
Untitled, *excerpt*
Diana Gamalinda

maraming beses ang malinaw na likidong many times the clear liquid truths
katotohanan

tumakbo sa aking mga daliri-magpakailanman run through my fingers—forever elusive.
mailap.

EVERY WEEKDAY AROUND 7:30 AM, the school's bird-egg blue multicab fetched me before transporting the better-behaved Special children to the school. We picked up ten students every morning at their homes. It was an hour-long rough ride over back roads of dirt and rocks and views of gated homes and squalid shacks where the children lived. A bruising drive that scraped my old body, but also fun, breezing along with the wind whipping my wet hair dry in the heat. We meandered through neighborhoods that I didn't know, and I could observe parents and *yayas* (nannies) interacting with their youngsters. The children we picked up were the more communicative, and their chatter and laughter were infectious; we always rolled into school smiling.

Someone had donated the bird-egg blue van to Pastor and the school when it was faded and already on its last legs. Holes had rusted through the metal floor so that you had to watch where you stepped. On rainy days, we arrived wet from the leaks in the roof, windows that didn't close, and splatter through those rusty holes from the road below.

As with most multicabs, the plank seats were covered in plastic tarps from old political elections or sales promotions. Metaphorically sitting on the faces of politicians promising better times or beauty contestants promising eternal glamour was cathartic. Paper posters didn't last long in the humid and rainy weather, and candidates were glad to have the additional free advertising. Even if they lost this election, there was always the next time, and most leaders were elected on name recognition. PT Barnum was right about there being no such thing as bad publicity.

The Marcos family knew this well. Ousted into exile in 1986, they caused the most significant public uprising in the history of the Philippines, The People Power Revolution. All the locals laughed when they told me at election time, "Filipinos have short memories!" It didn't seem all that funny to me. By the time I lived on Palawan, 25 years after the Revolution, Imelda, of shoe fame had returned and was elected Senator. Her son Bong Bong was Congressman and daughter Imee was Representative. Short memories, indeed. Bong Bong would eventually reclaim Malacanyang as the country's second President Marcos. Not that name recognition victories were unique to the Philippines. Wikipedia has a whole page for international stage and film actors who became politicians, think Ronald Reagan, Brigit Bardot, Arnold Schwarzenegger, and Volodymyr Zelensky. Some turned out better than others.

As happy as the politicians were to have the free advertising, the school was glad to have both the seat coverings and the van itself. With the van's frequent breakdowns, the driver was often forced to use his personal tricycle and had to make multiple trips to pick up the load since trikes usually fit only five people. But not our trike; that vision of eight children sitting in each other's laps, happily hanging on to the trike for dear life, is an indelible memory.

The school served about 12 students in the morning, returned them home at noon, and picked up a different group of 12 after lunch, a mish-mash of disabilities all day long. These children had issues far outside my specialty area, and they'd had no medical, behavioral, or psychological interventions in their lives, at least not treatments common in the Western world. All but a few of the students were profoundly disabled. Each had intellectual disabilities and some had physical problems as well. Most were non-verbal; some could communicate basic needs but were not interactive. Several were violent, inflicting harm to both themselves and others, and many had maladaptive behaviors.

In the Philippines, only a developmental pediatrician has the authority to diagnose a disorder, but those doctors are rare. Because we had no such doctor in the province of a million people, the labels applied by the social workers at the Department of Social Welfare and Development (DSWD) were usually wrong. There were only 40 developmental pediatricians in this country of 105 million people. Twice as many specialists lived in the state of Florida than in this entire nation, and there were none on our island. Therefore, the document keepers at the DSWD made a guess, typically a bad one since they had no training in Special Education. However, I had seen plenty of 'labels' in the U.S., both in college and in my certification for educational therapy, so I was familiar with diagnostics. When developmental pediatricians made an annual visit to Palawan, we conferred on official diagnoses.

Numerous students at the school had Down syndrome, identifiable from physical features, and they were usually friendly and compliant, the most interactive of the children. The correlation of a mother's age to the incidence of Down seemed unknown, even to credentialed teachers, and why bring it up now to these aging mothers at the end of their ropes? There was so much to do to educate everyone about 21st-century research, from city counselors to caretakers to teachers to pediatricians. Everyone needed to be able to deal with the SPED population, much of which stayed hidden from sight.

Many students had Autism, and all but one of those were non-verbal with violent behaviors I'd never seen in the U.S. Imagine a child unable to be understood from the time he was an infant and helpless to connect with another human. Over years, many retreated into their inner world while others acted out. Perhaps one of our boys could be functional in society; the rest had profound Autism and would never live alone since they had no access to early, significant, long-term, and trained intervention.

There was a set of twin 10-year-old boys with ADHD and autism in perpetual motion, whose mother could hardly cope. The mother reported that her husband hit them regularly out of frustration. It's easy for an adult who has never had a child with severe Autistic or ADHD behaviors to advise a father not to strike out in anger or frustration. Far more difficult to live with an oppositional or unreachable child 24/7, and maybe for life. The two boys were non-verbal and didn't interact with others. Like many twins, they had their unique communication that was incomprehensible to us. Plainly out of control, they ran around the open room throwing toys, turning fans and lights on and off, on and off, and finding stimulation however they could.

Several students had general retardation, as they called it on Palawan, where SPED standards were decades behind the U.S. But, their behavior was manageable and they didn't get much attention as long as they were compliant. All my years of training meant little in this place.

With no foundation of understanding and no trained therapists or interventions, the children ran wild. Because many of the well-intentioned, devoted church-member "teachers" lacked basic teacher education, they could accidentally trigger explosive behavior.

My workspace was a visual cacophony with bodies in constant motion and crescendos of sound, and it was overwhelming for me to think of any way to help.

School began in the common space that held church services on Sundays. Fitting that we began with prayers, and then we sang Christian songs with hand movements like *This is the Day* (the Lord Has Made). The adults held our hands over those of the students, moving their arms to the music like a pantomime; only a few children could start without assistance. My first month there, I learned the morning prayers and lyrics to the songs, all in Tagalog.

The second month, the school was set to perform the Christmas story at the Capitol building and rehearsed every day. With my high energy, it was hard to sit and be passive for hours, so I started writing a handbook about different disorders. Teachers had asked me to help them with behavior, and I thought a manual and some visual aids might be a step forward.

This was the first of my follies, and I repeated it so many times, thinking that I could improve their day when they didn't want to learn new ideas. They were exhausted and at the end of their ropes; they just wanted me to wave my wand and fix things. All of us were overwhelmed with the magnitude of the problem. Palawan had no educational courses in Special Education, no professionals for interventions, the school had no credentialled teacher, and I had never faced such severe behaviors. Where to even begin?

All those complications were there, even before the huge issue of trying to explain new theories with a language barrier. Most of the teachers spoke little English and understood far less, and I could manage only toddler-Tagalog.

In this biblical land, I questioned why God wouldn't want all of his tribe to communicate. When my children were young, I tried to read Bible stories to them and was horrified at how violent the scenes were and how nasty this God could be. The story of the 'Tower of Babel' fit that view of an angry god. At one time, after the great flood and Noah's heroism, all people spoke one language and understood each other. I would have appreciated that. But, then humans constructed The Tower in Babylonia to try to reach heaven. God was furious at humanity's hubris and blasphemy (according to the Bible). God's angry reaction was to scatter people far and wide, and confound them to speak 72 different languages. That may have worked for him but set human learning and kindness back a few eons.

In my career, I'd never had to convey concepts and explain them in a foreign language. So, even if the teachers believed I could help, my rudimentary skills limited any basic instruction on regular or SPED teaching theory.

The Christmas performance was a success, in part due to the narrator, a boy with Asperger syndrome, (known now in the U.S. as high functioning Autism). His name was Kobe Bryant. Names in the Philippines fascinated me. Some highlighted qualities like "Lovely," others were from the Bible, like "Genesis" and some added a random 'h' for uniqueness like "Jhun" or "Dharryl," but even more, like Kobe Bryant, praised celebrities. At the first rehearsal, Kobe read the narration from the script as the actors moved across the stage.

The action appeared to the audience as rather chaotic because the children did not respond to cues; an adult had to lead them through their role. Viewers experienced a double vision stage play of two people acting as one character; definitely not The Christmas Story most folks were used to.

During the second reading, I noticed that Kobe was watching the action on stage and no longer had any paper in his hand, yet he was narrating perfectly; he had memorized the script. The brain has always intrigued me, and Kobe's was incredible, memorizing an entire hour's performance verbatim, after one read-through. Kobe and I bonded, he was seven at the time, and after finding out I had a chemistry degree he came up to me one morning and said, "Debra, I would like to talk about the elements."

"Molybdenum," I said

He countered, "Plutonium."

Back and forth we went, through the noble gases and transition metals until he tired of that.

He thought for a moment and said, "Let's move on to compounds now."

"Water."

"Ammonia."

"Carbon dioxide."

And off we went. Such a remarkable mind, as genius in accumulating facts as it was lacking a social component. That boy was a bright spot of possibility in my day.

The Christmas season also brought more parties than I had ever imagined; I attended ten that first December.

"Oh Deb, you must come with us. It will be fun. All the officials will be there," said Pastor's wife.

"Um, okay, what should I wear?"

"Oh, nothing special, but maybe you could speak to the government heads about the school while we are there."

"Will you be with me, to introduce me?" I could do this in my sleep in the U.S., but it was terrifying here on a provincial island an hour's flight away from Manila. What if I screwed up?

"Yes, we will point the officials out to you and tell you who they are. Then, you can go talk with them. We will be close by." She looked at my face and chuckled, "Don't be afraid, we will be there to help you."

It was a lovely tropical night, clear and warm with that post-thunder-shower, still-damp earth scent, and the setting was an open area outside a nondescript public building. I didn't know the sponsors, the Goh family. I didn't know party protocol at all. I did know that there were several NGOs, government officials, private businesses, and religious organiza-tions in attendance, and understood that my job was to chat them up. The grounds looked festive, with white lights strung overhead and tables laden with all sorts of Christmas delicacies - *bibingka*, *embutido* and *buko pandan*, all under a copse of trees. The affair started at 5:00 PM, and we got there only minutes late. When food was involved, people tended to be punctual. Attire ranged from colorful work uniforms to hot-looking suits and flowery dinner dresses.

After the prayers and introduction of dignitaries, Pastor and his wife paraded me out to the government officials who might help them, but then they vanished. The Peace Corps had told us such fanfare was normal. Many in charge assumed that foreigners had money, and the perceived competence of the NGO improved with the appearance of a foreigner. There was an added status afforded any organization that had a dedicated foreign volunteer, but it seemed I was on my own.

Appearances and connections were important during the Christmas season, and I wanted to help. So, I began chatting and promoting the school programs with several officials who looked imposing. Little did I, and my culturally naive do-gooder mentality, know that 'helping' entailed layers of cultural nuances and was not straightforward at all.

"Good evening *po*. You are with the Health Department here in Puerto?" I said to a tall, dignified man.

"Good evening, Ma'am; yes, I am the head of the Department of Health for all of the Mimaropa region. Our offices are on the island of Romblon. Palawan falls under my jurisdiction."

"Ah, I am a Peace Corps volunteer, new to the island. I have been here only one month now. I will be working with Share A Life School. We serve children with intellectual disabilities who cannot attend regular school."

"Oh, interesting. The school is here in Puerto?"

"Yes, *po*, located in San Jose. May I ask a question, *po*?"

"Yes, certainly."

"Do children in public school get tested for things like vision and hearing?"

"Yes, of course. Schools assign nurses to do the testing. We try to do that every year."

"Do the Special children who cannot attend regular school also qualify for testing?"

"Certainly they do."

"Might our students be examined?"

"Surely; we can do that. Why don't you call my office next week, and we can set that up."

He handed me his calling card, in the Filipino way, with two hands holding the outer edges.

"Oh, that would be wonderful. Several of the children seem not to hear well. Thank you, *po*. Thank you so, so much."

I was ecstatic and ran to find Pastor. It seemed that this was exactly why they had brought me with them to the party. But, when I told him, he stiffened and refused (in the Filipino way of not-refusing but refusing) to speak to the man at all.

I pestered him for days, until Pastor finally told me that there would be *utang* involved and he had no intention of requesting services. Dejected, I tried to understand. *Utang na loob* is a cultural trait that means if someone does you a favor, you owe them. It is an unvoiced commitment, not with a contract or anything obvious but *na loob,* on the inside. And if you die before you pay back the obligation, your heirs assume the debt.

Once again, I was confused since I thought that my purpose in being at the party was to help them get what they needed, without involving them. Why was it such a big gift for the health department to do its job of screening students for hearing issues? But, that's how Pastor saw it, and the children suffered while he presumably saved face. My 'lessons learned' were piling up and every one seemed embarrassing and of the foot-in-mouth variety, yet I continued.

"Ma'am Debs, can you help us with the children, *po*? We cannot teach them anything. They won't sit down. They don't listen. We try so hard."

A frustrated group of teachers assailed me.

"Well, yes, I can help you, but you won't like what I say."

"Why not? We don't understand. What do you mean?" said the one with the best English, while the others hovered, watching her face for signs.

"It isn't the students who need to change their behavior," I said.

"What do you mean? Who then?"

They chattered about who they thought I might be talking about, and they ticked through each one:

"Pastor never knows what to do. He doesn't even get involved with them much."

"Ma'am doesn't know how to help the hard ones. She doesn't have to be in the classroom all the time."

"Oh, are you talking about the parents? They are crying for help too!"

"Umm, not really. I am talking about you. You, teachers need to be firm with them. Right now, if a student doesn't do what you ask them, then you do it for them."

"No. They are the problem, not us."

That societal trait of refusing to be the one at fault was obvious here. Perhaps we needed to do some perspective training and self-reflection. I tried again.

"When you do everything for them, they can't learn that there are natural consequences for their behavior. So, if they break the pencils or tear the paper, the natural consequence is that they cannot draw. But you pick up the pencils and give them new ones and new paper - so they don't learn. There is no reason for them to change their behavior because they know you will get them what they want - no matter what. They have learned that if they just wait, you will do it."

"We can't be mean to them!" they wailed.

Filipino society indulged children, and parents enabled them, sometimes into their teens. Toddlers were still given bottles at four years old, and their mothers hand-fed them from their plates until they were six or seven. It would be difficult to impossible for me to change their thinking, my training was based on Western behaviorists. In the U.S., even infants slept in another room after a few months; here, teenagers still shared the bed with their parents.

These schoolchildren were mostly non-verbal, with Autism, Down syndrome, ADHD, and the teachers assumed they were stupid. Every day during breaks and lunch, teachers sat next to students and teased them, taunting them in singsong and physically poking at them. They ridiculed behaviors the children had no control over. I was appalled.

"You do understand that they know you are making fun of them? And that they don't like it?"

"Ha-ha, Ma'am Debs, you are so funny, *po*. They don't feel anything, that's why we tease them. They don't understand."

The teachers couldn't believe that these children knew what was going on around them. Because students were non-verbal, and many had extremely odd behaviors, most people thought them closer to animals than humans. And treated them accordingly. In a superstitious society like this, disorders were not understood and were feared. How ironic that while the teachers said, "We can't be mean to them!" they were abusing them and sentencing them to an imprisoned life.

A month after I arrived, there was a fluster of *chika chika* as we walked up the path to the school. The adults whispered amongst themselves. I tried to keep up with the rapid Tagalog gossip and slang to understand what had everyone so upset. Some of their animated comments I could decipher:

"They killed him!"

"He was only a boy!!"

"I heard it was the father. He is American you know."

"The poor mother!"

"And the poor boy!"

"How horrible!"

The sister of Pastor's wife was a social worker and told me that a 13-year-old boy with autism had been murdered the night before. All during lunch, the teachers fomented gossip: that the foreign father, an American heathen, had killed him and on and on. It was uncomfortable for me, feeling they questioned my morality as an American foreigner and somehow blamed me by extension. The next day, we got the truth.

Thought to be inhabited by the devil for his incomprehensible autistic behaviors, the boy had been taken to the mother's church for exorcism. The priest and devout Christian congregation encircled the boy, determined to drive out Satan, and they beat the child repeatedly with heavy sticks, to death.

As the days progressed, I saw how a lack of knowledge and education, coupled with fear and no professionals, resulted in unintended cruelty to these youngsters. One of the teenagers at the school had undiagnosed autism and his family kept him in a covered cage for years, outdoors next to the pig enclosure. Without understanding or intervention, already socially-odd children acted out. They became unruly and unmanageable for their caretakers, causing parents to respond with equally extreme behaviors to manage the situation.

Again, I felt my values shifting. What could be expected when no one had access to medical or therapeutic intervention? The local social welfare workers weren't educated for this, and teachers had no credentials or training. Again, I was out of my depth, dealing with behaviors I'd never seen, and had no competent professional to support me even as a sounding block.

One of the girls named SheilaMae was a big teenager, weighing perhaps 300 pounds, who would casually spread her legs and pee whenever she needed to. She was non-verbal and did not interact at all or show any interest in the external world. Her father brought her to school. The tiny, older man with unruly white hair had a gentle smile and a humble spirit. Recounting how he chained his daughter to her bed at night because he said she would harm both herself and his wife, he was near tears. She more than doubled him in size and physicality. I understood their fear one day after I had called out to a neighborhood puppy just outside the entrance to the school. Loving animals, and thinking I could pet him, I gradually coaxed him inside. SheilaMae had been watching, standing placidly about 15 feet from me. Suddenly, something visibly switched in her head, and she silently propelled herself at the puppy with a taut, fierce face, kicking the tiny pup 20 feet through the air and sickening me.

While I couldn't condone the extreme measures parents took to control these children, I understood. Their methods began to seem almost reasonable with the lack of any professional support and the severity of the behaviors they had to deal with.

Sean was one of my favorites, a beautiful boy, as many youths with autism are, taller than me, severely autistic, and non-verbal, although he often seemed to interact with me. I thought we had a connection and tried to show the teachers how to calm him once when he was hitting others. Wrapping my arms around him, I hugged him gently but securely, just as taught in textbooks for a calming effect. Everything was going well until his mouth chomped down hard onto my forearm which had black, blue and red teeth imprints for a month from broken blood vessels. Sigh, so much for my teaching people anything.

A few mornings later, during song time, I sat behind Jake on the mat and moved his arms with mine to the movements of the song, until he forcefully threw himself backward and laid all his 250 pounds on top of me, flattening me. By this time, I had learned to laugh at myself much the way the teachers laughed at the children. Jake, who seemed to plan out and take pleasure in his fiendish pranks, pinned me one day into a corner of the concrete kitchen. I simply had to wait him out; at least he didn't bite me.

In the afternoon session, a seven-year-old boy named Gian arrived with his reticent mother. For three solid hours, he screamed a high-pitched keen almost of pain and threw himself on the floor. His behavior worsened with his mother around, so we asked her to just drop him off with us. Since the school was far from town and down a long dirt road, she had nowhere to go, and I wondered how she coped, hearing his continuing screams. Every day for three hours, Gian would cover his ears and scream, writhing on the floor with his backpack strapped on.

The school was a crazy place, and although Arnel had assured me that they returned children to regular classrooms, that was obviously impossible. I'm not sure who pulled the wool over whose eyes, the owners over Arnel's, or Arnel over mine.

The day I bought a bicycle changed my life. Finally, I could escape, and I pedaled away from the house on rock-pitted Maunlad Street. Biking miles, all the way to the bay, screaming in the wind, and propelling myself faster and faster. Freedom! It was exhilarating in the 90-degree heat just to feel free and not worry about what I was doing wrong or how not to offend someone with what I said. Walking on eggshells debilitated me.

In January, the Pastor's wife showed me a flyer. "This is another school in Puerto that has a few SPED students, and they bring doctors here once a year. These are doctors called," she looked at the paper, "Occupational Therapy," she said. "One of our students might go to see them, would you like to take her?"

"Really? I can go? I used Occupational Therapy with my SPED classes in California!"

"We don't have it here - what is it?"

"Our class therapist worked their bodies with a lot of movement and balance exercises and sensory activities – it made a huge difference. Lots of kids who couldn't even walk a straight line learned how with practice. It kind of re-trains the brain. It's amazing what OT can do!"

"Haha, you sound like YOU are an OT yourself!" she said.

"It's a wonderful and well-tested therapy. Let's go together, you will love it!"

"Oh, it's at Salve Regina. You can just go and tell me what they say."

"All right," although I couldn't understand why she wouldn't come with me.

I ended up going alone and meeting people who changed my trajectory. Salve Regina School had purchased a small property in Tiniguiban, close to where I lived with my host family. Salve built K-6 classrooms and a covered court for Physical Education. The woman who owned the school was a teacher continuing her teaching credential to get a Master's in Special Education. She had a grandson with autism whom she visited in Australia. So, Special Education was top of mind for her, and she dedicated one large room for Special children. Knowing the importance of SPED training, she hired the only credentialed SPED teacher on the island at that time, Teacher Hercel.

Salve Regina became the only school that I would recommend to parents with a Special child. Teacher Hercel was miraculous, and I admired her immensely for her progress with the students and her incredible patience. I could teach older children, but the younger, or more severe ones were a challenge for me. While I hated the repetitiveness and consistency needed to make behavioral changes, Hercel made it look easy. She and I were the only credentialed SPED teachers on the island, and I wasn't teaching; both of us felt a burden of responsibility. Salve had a lot going for it: the head of the school had a prime interest in Autism, Hercel was a professional educator trained in SPED, and one of the families enrolled at Salve had a strong SPED network in Manila. The family was the sponsor of the OT visits. Serendipitous for all and specifically for me.

This first meeting introduced me to the dynamo of a woman who brought the two stellar OTs to Palawan. Angelie Espina Mendoza, known as Angie, was truly an angel for the SPED community. After that first introduction, I recalled mainly her merriment and energy, and that she came up to my shoulders.

Angie coordinated all the paperwork and logistics, with rapid instructions lilting with tinkling laughter, efficiently moving parents, children, and therapists about. She spoke as easily with the parents as with the doctors and teachers, and everyone loved her. Her filing system recorded patient history and discussions the pediatricians had with the parents on their last visit. Doctors prescribed medication or behavioral exercises for the family to do until the doctor returned in nine to twelve months. Compared to what I had seen so far on Palawan, that day was organized, efficient and impressive. Angie and I bonded immediately. We were as mismatched in appearance as the tall, skinny Mutt and short, squat Jeff cartoon characters, but our hearts were aligned for the children.

At 27, Angie had a daughter with Down Syndrome and channeled her energy into researching how to optimize her child's outcomes. Angie was a chemical engineer from the University of the Philippines and undertook the most devout research project of her life, accumulating a wealth of information on the genetic disorder. In Manila, she united parents of children with Down syndrome who coordinated a network of therapists to serve Special children. The Manila group even funded professional visits to different provinces like the one at Salve Regina. When I met Angie, she was 36, with 10-year-old Bea, whom she called her "Million Dollar Baby," due to multiple heart surgeries and ongoing therapy and medications.

The year before, Special Olympics Asia Pacific approached Angie to start a chapter on Palawan. Although the formal documents had been signed to officially establish a chapter, not much had happened over the last year. I had been involved with Special Olympics in San Francisco and was so impressed with the OTs, the school, the teacher, and Angie that first day, that I jumped right in, and said I could get the NGO set up and organized. Our energies and intent were similar and we fueled each other. Unfortunately, my enthusiasm unintentionally drove a wedge between me and my own school, and my encouragement for us to join forces made matters worse.

Sadly, the owners of Share A Life School wished to believe and promote themselves as the Puerto Princesa experts and refused to collaborate meaningfully with Salve Regina. This was my introduction to another Filipino trait that sociologists called "Pinoy Pride," the deadly pride of hubris, or thinking you can do things better than anyone else and promoting yourself to be bigger and more successful than you are. Termed *Amor Propio* in Tagalog, there is a meme of a kitten looking into a mirror and seeing a lion that perfectly captures the attitude. Additionally, Filipino culture was based on the concept of *hiya,* or shame. For Pastor or his wife to appear at another school and accept their instruction could be shameful. Appearance, not substance, was the key to success, and hierarchy was crucial for reputation.

Accordingly, I worked with Angie after hours as we organized the Special Olympics Philippines Palawan Chapter - or SOPPC in terms of inescapable Filipino acronyms. Together, we made it a functioning organization. I wrote articles of incorporation and bylaws, registered them with the SEC, and assumed the role of Secretary. Our official inaugural induction of officers was held under the shade of a huge mangrove tree on the beach as we were barefoot in the wet sand. Quickly, though solemnly, we said our pledge to serve, were inducted, and headed for the macaroni salad and sweet spaghett snacks to celebrate. Every function I attended on Palawan required food, which was atypical at U.S. business meetings. I learned that it was the first requirement for any successful endeavor and was the first item budgeted.

Back at Share A Life School, I gave the teachers training about how to change behavior in Special children. We made visual aids for the non-verbal students with Autism and charts for them to follow. Youth from the church drew pictures for us and we paired the drawing of the action with English words. Then we placed the laminated signs in appropriate spots around the school, with illustrations like "Turn off the fan" "Brush your teeth" and "Wash your hands." The funniest language mishap showed the back of a boy in the bathroom facing the toilet zipping up his pants - the caption said, "Flash the toilet." No one understood my hilarity.

To effect change, you need a systemized curriculum and intensive timely interventions that both the school and parents work on together, especially when working with seriously impaired students. With these children attending only three hours a day, and no commitment from parents, it was clear that change wasn't going to happen. The teachers and owners didn't have the understanding or tools necessary and were exhausted shepherding the two groups for six hours. Any additional effort just wasn't going to cut it.

The teachers tried hard to follow instructions from the owners who were not trained schoolteachers themselves. One teacher came to me in confidence, since she questioned the directions she'd been given.

"Ma'am Debs, none of the children can speak, but I am supposed to teach math by rhyming. How do I do that, *po?*"

Teachers in the U.S. had access to manipulables for teaching math and assistive technology for learning spoken and written language. Here, they didn't have even one SPED manual or textbook telling them how to start. We discussed how to demonstrate math by using physical objects, like rocks, but the teacher still was directed to rhyme. She later completed her teaching credential and left the school.

Pastor's wife attempted to write up individual education plans for each student, but they were lofty, mostly unattainable educational goals and progress was so slow that it seemed more like a babysitting service. I understood the need for parents to get a break, I just wished the school could be more truthful about what they truly did.

As I found and Filipino sociologists noted, as a rule, appearance is more important than substance in the culture. Having a good story, told with a pleasant face is best. This was the antithesis of my entire life, where success was measured by task completion and competence. It took me years to unlearn much of my Western values and appreciate interrelatedness and harmony. These people were a service to the community because, without them, there was nothing. They were pleased with their work, and it was my issue, coming from another universe, looking for what was missing. I felt the need to help improve what they were doing, yet ultimately felt overwhelmed, worthless, and hopeless.

After I had been there for perhaps a month, Pastor proudly, and righteously, told me that the Peace Corps had sent a specialist for a six-month stint the year before.

"She was a Filipina American and had her family roots in the Philippines, she understood our values. She was a professional and well-known in her field. She watched how we dealt with things and gave us high marks. The Peace Corps appreciated us because of her. Now she sends us presents every Christmas, for us and the children in big *balikbayan* boxes."

I Googled the woman. Like me, she also was an educational therapist, and in fact, we lived only five miles apart in California. It boggled my mind that she had praised the work being done at the school. She told them that they were doing a wonderful job and that nothing needed to change. Now I understood their confusion and anger with me and their reluctance to put in any extra effort. Maybe her going with the flow was better than mine fighting against the current for all the good it did.

These folks had big hearts, but their methods were tough to handle. The only teacher who could control Jake held a thick rubber band stretched between his thumb and index finger. Most of the time, he would just threaten Jake with it, but often he snapped it on Jake's skin. And always, the adult laughter following, which I came to realize was part of the culture. But the meaning of those laughs depended on the situation, and with the teachers, I got the sense that their nervous giggles showed their embarrassment of not knowing what to do.

There is an iconic attitude in the Philippines called *bahala na*, 'come what may,' or, 'it's up to God.'

"Oh, I heard a big storm is coming, what shall we do to prepare?" "*Bahala na, po*, God will protect us."

Or, "How will we feed everyone at the event?" "*Bahala na, po*, God will provide."

Or, "Who do you think will win the election?" "*Bahala na, po*, God will decide and grant the Philippines peace."

Bahala na designated that we mortals will do the best we can do, but it isn't up to us, *bahala na*. For me, it was overwhelming how much the teachers should be doing but weren't even aware.

Watching them make fun of the children made my stomach twist and hurt my heart, but the cultural divide was deep. Sharing no common theoretical understanding or mutual language was an immense hurdle. I disagreed with their last Peace Corps adviser and wondered if she had really felt more like me but just took the easy way out. She was only here for six months, and what could be done in that time?

As I was to find out, just about as much as I could accomplish in 10 years, very little. There is a saying in the Philippines that I came to despise: 'little by little.' For someone nearly 60 years old, I often said that I would be long underground by the time progress was made. I needed to find a way to cope with all this, or I would go mad.

PAPER BEAD NECKLACE

COMPUTER FUN

MUSIC TIME AT THE SCHOOL

STAND INFRONT OF THE URINAL

FLASH THE TOILET

FLASH THE TOILET

MATH CLASS

BRUSHING TEETH

Chapter 7

BREAKING FREE AND DEATH

Huwag magbilang ng sisiw hanggang di pa napipisa ang itlog.
Don't count chicks until the eggs are hatched.
Originally an English proverb from the 1500s, also a Filipino proverb
meaning, 'Eggs are extremely delicate, and not all of them go on to become
chickens. Don't act on the assumption that you have something before you
do.

Solace

Natagpuan ko ang aking tahanan sa tabi ng karagatan	I found my home along the ocean
At lumangoy sa humahampas na alon	And swam in the breaking waves
Hanggang sa naging magaspang sila, ginugulo ang buhay ko	Until they became rough, tossing my life about
Umaaliw ako ng mga kaibigan at magkahawak-kamay kaming naglakad patungo sa malayong dalampasigan	Friends comforted me and we walked hand in hand toward the distant shore

AT THE MINIMUM THREE-MONTH MARK, I moved out of my host
family's house against their wishes.

"But *Tita* Deb, we will worry about you!"

"You shouldn't live alone; you won't be safe!"

"But what if something happens, you are old already, *po*."

"You can just stay here; we will take care of you."

It felt more that they would miss the money the Peace Corps supplied rather than real affection, but that could have been my own projection. As a culture, very few live alone in the Philippines, especially older women. Big families often reside in compounds, sometimes partitioned in the same structure, sometimes in small homes situated around the parents' home.

Although I said I was leaving, I first had to find a place that was approved by the Peace Corps as "safe." There were no realtors on Palawan, no CraigsList, or MLS, you found an apartment by taking an eight-peso multicab ride to a neighborhood, getting off and walking through dirt streets looking for a 'room for let' sign in the window, or knocking on doors and talking to see what was available. It was hot, I was the only white person for miles around, was old, and spoke Tagalog with a three-year-old's competency - a high anxiety situation for sure.

I worked up my courage, practiced my pre-school Taglish, and flagged down an already packed multicab. Holding the steel bar, I crouched down, hunchbacked, and stepped over eight pairs of feet. "*Pasensya po*" (I'm sorry). For having such a national reputation for being hospitable and respecting elders, I never understood why passengers didn't just move down and make room for the newcomer, especially if they were old. But, this was the norm, so I crouch-waddled up to the front to sit near the driver and gave him my fare, "*Bayad po.*" A bumpy 10 minutes later I called out "*Para, po!*" for the driver to stop, and had to again step over 80 toes to get out. The multicabs weren't like taxis or trikes; they stayed only on the major roads. So I began walking down the long street looking for anything that looked like a room for rent. And I spied a sign.

"*Excuse po. Paki mayroon ka bang ang room for rent po?*" I spoke my practiced query.

The apartment owner blushed as she responded in Taglish, "*Sorry po, nawala na,* my son needs it now."

I had no idea how to compose a follow-up sentence asking if she knew of any other rooms for rent close by, so I smiled, "*Ah, okay-lang, Salamat po.*"

I saw several friendly faces and wished them good morning with a wave but saw nothing more for rent.

So, with sore feet, I trudged back to the highway to wait in the hot sun for another multicab to pick me up and take me 'home.'

Luckily, the school owners took pity on me and asked around...that word of mouth, which I simply could not manage. They surfaced a few possibilities and kindly drove me to inspect them in the school's tricycle. Some of the rooms we saw were abysmal, with daytime rats and cockroaches. One had a smashed, but still alive, foot-long gecko in the door jamb, its bright red tongue lolling, while another shared the toilet with the male landlord; no thanks. We finally found an acceptable place at the back of the Almonte family compound in *barangay* Santa Monica, only five minutes from the school. After seven months in the Philippines, an abode I could call my own!

It was a native construction of nipa palm, called a *bahay kubo,* also an iconic childhood song. At night, with the lights out, the moonlight shone through the woven leaves that composed my walls. The prismed moonlight looked to me like stars from a primeval time as I lay in bed. My stateside friends were horrified when I told them about the critters that wriggled through those starry walls.

There was a small, heavy wood dining room table and I bought a wooden settee and chair for the living room from a furniture stall in the *palengke* (market). Humidity, mold, and venomous insects prevented any softness of upholstery or carpeting and the floors were plain gray concrete.

The kitchen and bathroom were both outside the back door, along with a refrigerator. There was counter space to put my few dishes in a dish rack with a cover preventing larger vermin from licking the remains of my meals. There was no hot water, so dishes weren't quite as sparkling as in the Dawn commercials back home.

The bathroom was rather despicable, even with my low expectations. There was a seatless *inidoro* (toilet bowl), black with mildew, that you 'flushed' by pouring buckets of water into it. It sat at the edge of a tiled room that tripled as the shower and laundry room. There was no showerhead, just a rusted pipe, and a pint-sized *tabo,* a water dipper to pour water over your body for an imitation shower. I got quite good over the years at washing my clothes concurrently with my body. Certainly, it was efficient and during most months, I took two or three showers a day due to the high heat and lack of air conditioning. The Philippines calls the bathroom a CR or Comfort Room, although few recall what CR stands for, and the term was ironic for any CR I ever visited.

I bonded with my landlord, Ma'am Helen, who allowed me to paint and spiff up the place, all at my expense. She did agree to be responsible for taking down the bedroom ceilings of nipa palms which were deteriorating and smelly. The day they tore down the ceiling, they discovered a huge dead rat which relieved the nauseating smell in the second bedroom. My only overnight visitors were other volunteers who lived in similar situations, so we accepted my little home for what it was.

In the large outside kitchen/bathroom area, I laid plastic flooring as the dirt floor creeped me out. During heavy rains, roof leaks turned it into a river of mud. One weekend, my fellow PCV, Petra, jeepneyed over from Aborlan, two hours away, and helped me lay the vinyl floor and paint the walls, which was an enormous task. We volunteers stuck together, sharing camaraderie and productivity, and Petra was a great companion without whom, it just wouldn't have gotten done. So, at least my space became habitable, by my revised definition of the word.

On one of the first days in my new home, Helen showed me something that Santa Monica was famous for. She took me by the hand and walked up to her concrete house. She motioned me closer.

"See this Deb?"

"The brown decoration?" It looked like terra cotta pottery squiggles all over the white stucco walls, a haphazard modern design.

Her eyes crinkled and she laughed heartily. "No! Look here. Grab that big rock."

I handed her the rock and she proceeded to knock several of the thick tubes off the wall. I didn't see anything and wondered what she was doing.

"*Ang bahay ni anay.* These are the tunnels where the termites live," she said, as brown powder and fragments clung to her clothes. They were mud tubes built of soil and wood and probably termite poop, and as big around as my little finger. It took a lot of effort to scrape off even a square foot of the squiggles, which covered the house, but we cleared a big space. Although we had termite inspections in California, where both builders and homebuyers feared termite damage, I had never even seen one, so I was engrossed, pun intended. I learned later that California termites are different, only termites in moist conditions like the tropics make mud tunnels. I thanked her for the demonstration and resumed my laundry. Two hours passed and Helen called me back over. I was mindblown to discover that the mud tubes had already been rebuilt where we had knocked them off and were just as thick as before.

I had watched my host families do the laundry and helped as they would allow, so I learned laundry Filipino style. The Filipinos I knew were fastidious, whites were bright white and clothes were ironed before wearing, even if they later wrinkled in the humidity. Shoes were scrubbed weekly and even white tennies were spotless. And all this was done without a washing machine or dryer or Tide spot remover. My synthetic blouses stretched into odd shapes from the intense scrubbings. I loved doing the laundry for some reason but discovered that during the rainy season, laundering was difficult, not the washing, but the drying. Often it took three to four days for dresses hanging in my little dark rooms to dry. I frequently wore damp, slightly mildewed slacks, having few to choose from. And the wet weather attracted more than just mildew.

Neither the nipa fronds nor my plastic flooring kept out critters very well, notably during the rainy season. One stormy night I had a variety of 20 amphibians chirping in the living room with me, big Busuanga toads, dime-sized juveniles and tree frogs that had suction cup feet spotted the walls and ceiling to my delight, as well as a few bullfrogs. That night I took my bucket shower with another dozen, just the frogs and me enjoying the water together. I was glad that people wore *tsinelas* (flip flops) in the shower, some things still grossed me out, like slipping on a frog.

The sunny days penetrated the dark room to make it feel cozier, although I did find three different scorpions, the first when I was sweeping. Fast, long, gray, and thin, it got tangled in the *wallis tambo*, a broom made of soft reeds, and as I swept, it did a double flip in the air before landing on the top of the dining room table. Quite pissed off judging from the stance it took with front pinchers open and back tail coiled and ready, a nano Scorpion King. I ran to the main house and got Helen's husband, who returned with a hammer and lightly tapped the thing to kill it. I've always been fascinated by creepy things (and learned that a scorpion is not an insect, but an arachnid), so I kept him on the windowsill until he disintegrated in the strong sun. Another fellow was quite the opposite in stature, short, brown, fat, and slow, prompting another run to Helen's husband, and another return with the hammer, but no scorpion. Her husband told me this one was poisonous and to be careful as he had no anti-venom, and to be sure to wear shoes. That night I didn't get up to pee. The third variety was rust-colored and tiny. I had my own hammer by then, a quick tap dispatched him.

Unfortunately, many of the critters that came through the walls were small as a pinprick and could get through my mosquito net. I love to read, and since I had no television and it got dark year-round at 6:00 PM, I tried to read under my netting. The consequence of reading by flashlight was a nightly bug-disco, resulting in lots of bites and some difficulty breathing which, in addition to the mold and dampness, turned into asthma. I visited a Peace Corps-approved doctor who said that although I had only lived there three months, if I wanted to make it out of the Peace Corps alive, I needed to find a new place with concrete construction. Very bummed, I took a trike to Divine Sweets and sat at the last empty table, ordering a leche flan and an iced tea to drown my sorrows. Forlorn, I nearly missed the proverbial window opening as the door closed.

"Hello Ma'am, may I join you at your table? There seem to be no seats available."

"Yes, please join me," I responded with a smile. Maybe some conversation would take my mind off things.

"My name is Mark Antony," he said. My thoughts strayed to Caesar and handsome Roman centurions. "How long have you lived in Puerto?" he asked.

"About six months now, but I just learned that I have to move, and I don't know what to do," I replied morosely, poking at my comfort food.

"I'm only here to visit my family in Brooke's Point, I live in Malaysia. But, my brother and I own a house about ten minutes from here and it is vacant. Would you like to look at it?"

Feeling skeptical of this stranger, but also desperate (he did seem heaven-sent), I hopped in a tricycle with him as he told the driver, "Go to the end of Libis Road, to Bountiful Village." That sounded like a good omen to me.

The road was decent for the first mile, but then turned to potholes that were numerous and deep, and tricycles are unstable enough on newly asphalted roads. I clung to the sides of the trike as we bumped along the now dirt path. As soon as I saw it, at the end of an unnamed street, I wanted it. The bright white house with turquoise windows was lovely, even though the property needed some repair and upkeep. But, it was spacious and light, and I grasped at this opportunity. I told Mark Antony if I could get out of my lease that I would take it.

I returned to Helen's and told her my sad story, but she wouldn't let me out of my six-month lease, even though I had painted the place and installed flooring. Due to the medical issue, the Peace Corps agreed to pay the rest of the rent (it only totaled another $100), and I committed, a little too quickly. The Peace Corps wasn't happy with the pictures of the house that I sent them; they wanted the windows to have iron bars and insisted on new locks. I didn't have many options, and with the Peace Corps authorities far away in Manila, I decided to move forward even though the requirements hadn't all been met. Mark Antony had his lawyer draw up the lease and we met to sign. The lawyer was surprised that I expressed any security concerns.

"You aren't afraid, are you?" he asked me.

"Well, I'm new here, I don't know what to think," was my reply.

He laughed, then looked me in the eye. "Are you in politics?" he asked somberly.

"Ha! Hardly," I said.

"And you aren't campaigning for anyone?"

"No."

"Not marching in protest for a cause?"

"No!"

He grinned, "Then you have nothing to worry about. Here in the Philippines, politicians kill off their competition, people in politics are the only targets on Palawan."

He and Mark Antony laughed uproariously at their joke, which turns out wasn't much of a joke and didn't do much to ease my mind. No need to tell the Peace Corps and worry them.

Not only politicians died though. Over my time in the Peace Corps, I saw several deaths and how different the attitudes and customs of life and death were from my home country. I returned from a trip to Manila to find that the mother of Pastor's wife had died.

"What!" I said, tears springing to my eyes. I had liked the woman who was close to my own decade and would miss her. I had met her at her home in Bahile and had spent time with her on several occasions, including my second Christmas in the Philippines. I had been given, and readily accepted, an invitation to her son's farm in Bahile, a little over an hour's drive from the school. It was a great family holiday with toddlers, puppies, and *carabao*. I had also seen her own home in Bahile that her sons had built for her. She, like I, lived alone and identified as an elder, she was perhaps 15 years older. We had some good conversations about life and children. "I loved your mom, what happened?" I asked rather stricken.

The Pastor's wife waved her hand. "Oh, she had high blood." High blood means high blood pressure, which, along with diabetes and high cholesterol is accepted in the Philippines and it is God's will if anyone lives. Going to the doctor in town is a rarity because of the distance, but more because a visit to a doctor cost around $6, and no one had that kind of money. Nor did they have money for any prescribed medication, so they skipped both the doctor and medication. People just died.

"We knew she had high blood, so it didn't surprise us," she said as she stared quizzically at me with tears flowing down my face.

"We buried her on the farm in Bahile and have been in mourning for 30 days now. We say prayers for her daily. The 40 days is over soon."

I am not religious but have always been intrigued by different religions and customs. In the Catholic church, there is no ecumenical rule stating anything about 40 days. But in the Philippines, everyone I knew honored

40 days of mourning, no matter the religion. On that day, prayers were said and the spirit departed earth into heaven. Muslims also have the custom of 40 days of mourning. All my friends called the day someone died the 'death date' and each year they honored their loved one, likely a parent, on his or her death date.

Parties at cemeteries were common with the requisite platters of food. There wasn't a specific 'funeral' buffet, but people made the favorite dishes of the departed to honor them, showing they were not forgotten, and friends and relatives gathered at the gravesite to have a meal with them and remember the person.

Another friend of mine died suddenly, without warning at only 43. Simon worked an organic farm with his wife in Sicsican about a half-hour from town. His diminutive wife, Jinky (the name Manny Pacquiao's wife made famous), sold their produce to restaurants. Jinky invited Bryce, Krystal, and me out to the farm and cooked delicious meals for us; Simon was a Brit, so Jinky had expanded her Filipino culinary repertoire to European tastes. They were organic farmers and tried to educate local farmers on organizing a farm for profit. They painstakingly taught farmers how to optimize a crop, what nutrients to add to improve pricing, how to budget to make a profit, and how to have a better yield the following year. Simon and Jinky had plenty of *sayangs* (wasted opportunities) with their work, but they never stopped. Simon was an expert on soils and how different kinds of soils affected both crops and their pests. He was working on theories of how different soil compositions repel the pests when one night, he sat in his chair and went to sleep, permanently. Jinky frantically called the ambulance, and some friends, who came immediately, but with the state of medical care on Palawan, it was futile. Simon had an enlarged heart and congenital problems of which no one, not even Simon, was aware.

His family was in the UK, and it took some time for his sister to be able to get to Palawan. Jinky arranged everything and opened their home to grieving friends and neighbors. There were photos spread around showing Simon's life, a lot of flowers, a delicious buffet, and Simon, in his glass-topped coffin in the middle of the living room. This was a first for me but was a common practice, and the deceased often stayed in the house for days. In my mind, this was at odds with the Filipino preoccupation with, and utter fear of, ghosts. I didn't understand why they would sleep with their departed relative in the room if they had such a dread. This was another of several dichotomies in cultural traditions I tried to reconcile. Later in the day, after people eulogized Simon and said their goodbyes, the funeral procession slowly wound its way to the nearby cemetery where he was laid to rest.

Angie's mother also died during my first year on Palawan, and she, too, entertained visitors in her closed coffin, lying in state in the foyer of Angie's sister's house. As was the custom, the casket was prominently displayed, and huge floral arrangements, sent as condolences from friends, surrounded it. Her mother had baked a secret recipe for empanadas, a favorite of mine, and that was one of the many foods served. There were chairs set up near the coffin and family and friends told stories of yesteryear, recounting mutual escapades of their youth before she was stricken with Alzheimer's.

This was where I first heard about the Filipino custom of gambling over the body, routine in the old days, and still a tradition in many parts of the country. Friends would keep watch over the body, playing mahjong, bingo, and card games, with the winner's pot going to the family to pay off funeral bills. The reason for the vigil was not for prayers alone, but distinctly Filipino in nature: to deter Aswangs. Aswangs are widely feared shape-shifting spirits believed to steal corpses. Folklore has it that the ghoul-Aswang would cunningly open the coffin, replace the body with the trunk of a banana tree, and slink away to devour the body. So, the family stayed awake together to fend off the evil creatures.

In Angie's case, they had a place for her mother at the big cemetery in San Jose, and the funeral was a several-hour affair. Her family is Catholic, and a priest said Mass. Several people paid tribute under a big tent, appreciated since it was a hot and rainy afternoon. The family constructed a covered mausoleum for her, but it wasn't finished that day. I'm not sure where she rested in the interim.

I do remember the completed mausoleum on All Souls' Day that year. I knew many families in Puerto by this time and All Souls' Day had come to feel like a big community party held at the cemetery. I took my flashlight and started with Angie and her folks, whom I knew well by now. I met a few relatives I knew and a couple I didn't, one who would become my landlord several years down the road. We reminisced about times together and they told stories of their childhood as well as of Mamita and Angie's father. I then went to the Mitra plot, then to those of a few of the Chamber members – a progressive dinner party of sorts.

As I recount this, I realize I saw a lot of death in my brief time on Palawan and a general acceptance of death as a life passage. Strikingly different from my birth culture which hangs onto life as long as possible, even bankrupting families in an attempt to thwart death.

The Philippine holidays surprised me with the mix of religious seriousness and happy celebration. Just as Magellan happily converted 800 Cebuanos in 1521 to this new religion, yet only thirteen days later died at the converts' hands. Symbolism and dichotomy are rife in Philippine Catholicism.

Holy days are a big deal in the Philippines, and, as noted, one of the holiest is All Souls' Day on November 1st. It begins the morning after the U.S. Halloween and is nothing like that frivolous holiday. Family members try to come home for Christmas, but it is imperative that they come home for All Souls' Day to honor their ancestors. It was a day of loyalty and tradition, and people planned their travel far in advance. Millions finished their work in Manila, and even overseas, and returned to their home provinces. It felt like Chinese New Year, known as the world's largest annual mass migration. For me, the word 'migration' brought to mind earth's seasonal migrations. Sometimes the significance and enormity felt like the Serengeti migration, with humans instead of wildebeest or zebra. It was primal.

It was marvelous but intimidating. On my first All Souls' Day in Olongapo, Nanay, and Joie cooked all day. Nanay got up early and walked to the cemetery about 10 minutes away and cleaned the gravesite, and I assume she chatted with her departed husband for a bit. She came back to finish cooking and we packed up something similar to a picnic into *Pula* since Joseph was at work with *Itim*. Nanay's two children who lived out of the country were not there, but the other three came and met at the gravesite. They were not wealthy and didn't have a grandiose tomb or mausoleum like I later saw on Palawan, but there was room for us to sit around the grave.

We had a late lunch with their patriarch, and the boys told stories about their dad. I liked him better hearing some of their memories. All Souls' Day is a family affair, recounting days gone by and catching up with each other's lives. Just by being together, they expressed their love for being a family. As usual, it got dark at 6:00 PM, and that's when the candles were lit all over the cemetery.

My friend Chris, from next door, met me and we walked through the graveyard, getting creepily lost a few times. It was also disconcerting to figure out where to step in the dark. I didn't want to step on someone's grave and there were no lights to show the way, only sporadic candles. We had only been there a couple of months at the time, and didn't know many of the neighbors, so we walked, feeling like two tall white interlopers in a sea of familial brown.

The thing I noticed most as we walked about was that this day brought the community together. The Catholic holy day originated in the 10th century as a day to pray for the dead, but here it seemed less religious and more like a societal equalizer. Everyone seemed of the same family, not the normal Philippine hierarchy. This was Philippine interdependence, and the mayor was in the same position as the pauper, grieving and honoring his ancestors. The other emotion was gaiety. I expected quiet and solemnity but on the contrary, families were laughing, some so hard they had tears, and laughter was the predominant mood, not mourning.

Strangely, as a child, I had always loved cemeteries, especially Forest Lawn in Glendale. My mother said I used to run through the grass, maybe because I felt free. When I got older, I read the inscriptions, the more historic ones had some very clever quotes written on the gravestones, like "I told you I was sick," or, "Go Away...I'm Asleep." I also loved seeing the dates of death and how long they'd lived; some revealed what they died from. I discovered that makes me the definition of a 'taphophile' which I didn't know existed. Most Americans I knew thought graveyards were morbid, but they reminded me of Egyptian tombs, Zoroastrians, and Indiana Jones. This was the first time I could be 'out' with my interest in death rituals.

People partied quite a bit; men used All Souls' Day as an excuse to get drunk. So, the cemetery got rowdy and loud, a consternation to the police.

Chris and I left probably around 9:00 PM, just when the party was getting started. We found our way home; Joie and Gelo had already returned since both had early mornings. Nanay's boys stayed until after midnight, and Nanay spent the night. She slept at the cemetery to honor her husband. I didn't understand her loyalty, but it made an impression on me.

I experienced All Souls' Day differently on Palawan mostly because I lived there longer. There were two cemeteries on Palawan. The older one was adjacent to the bay. I went to three funerals there; it was on a hill with only one entrance and exit, and you had to wait a long time to get in or out if the person being buried was of any civic importance. Sometimes I parked outside the grounds and walked in, wondering how the homeowners just outside the walls liked living so close to this space.

My favorite cemetery was the one closer to me in San Jose just off the highway, where Angie's mother was. That was where the 'newer' families had plots and there was space to build mausoleums for your loved ones. Some were quite opulent, looking like small homes. For some who had grown up in poverty, the grandeur felt inappropriate. The woman I lived with was as irreverent as I was when we visited the beautiful cemetery one sunny day.

"Ooh, I like the shutters on that one."

"No, this one is all marble, it would be easier to keep clean."

"But look at the architecture of this one, it has two stories, plenty of room for everyone!"

My very Catholic friend could never aspire to a home as nice as these crypts. Yet, at the end of our frivolous chatter, we stopped and became somber again. Death was the Great Equalizer and the circle of life ended here. So many generations, lives, and losses. Our human condition.

Death had rituals, but suicides were different. One day there was a commotion on Bennet Road in Old Cabalan about a block farther down from our house toward Santa Rita. I asked Nanay what had happened since medical personnel were there. She was sad but delivered the brief story in a monotone.

"The man who lived there had a hard life, Deb. He was always depressed. He lived with his mother, but she died last year. I think he hung himself."

"What will happen?" I asked.

"Nothing," she said. "It is shameful to commit suicide. No one will go there now."

It was unspeakable, and the only suicide I heard of; the taboos against suicide were strong.

There were other ways to shame oneself in death. The President of Palawan's Chamber of Commerce was an introverted young man when I first met him. He was elected President following an elder he esteemed, and as is typical, he wouldn't do anything to disrespect the elder, or even have a difference of opinion, so it was as though the former president still held that office. But, I liked the young man when he was by himself, outside of influence. He managed his family's hotel and acted as a web developer for several websites. He sought me out to give me an invitation to his wedding, and I felt honored. The reception was formal so I had a beautiful dress made for the occasion. I made sure to get to the cathedral on time at noon since it was hot and I wanted a seat. Not one person was there.

I passed a mother walking arm-in-arm with her daughter through the church.

"Please *po*, might you tell me if there is a wedding here today?"

"Oh, yes *po*. It will be a big wedding for the Chamber of Commerce President!"

"Yes, it will. But I wondered where everyone is?" I pointed to my printed invitation. "See, the wedding is to start at 12 o'clock. Where is everyone?"

Giggling behind polite hands against her lips, the woman said, "You forget this is Filipino time *po*. The priest will be here soon."

The priest arrived 'soon,' nearly an hour later, at 1:00 PM. The cathedral filled up a half-hour after that, and the ceremony began. It was opulent and lovely, with the parents of each accompanying the groom first and then the bride down the long aisle. The reception was held that evening in their hotel ballroom. I went home and lay about in the interim, figuring I had plenty of time with Filipino time.

I arrived as the reception was in full swing and my friends from the Chamber laughed at me, "Are you kidding, you think we'd be late when free food is involved?" Another lesson in protocol.

The marriage was short, and his fault entirely. As was his choice to allegedly embezzle money from someone not to be trifled with. Whoever it was, shot him four times sometime after midnight as he was leaving the hotel. He succumbed to sepsis when I wasn't on the island. I don't know if the Filipino superstition was followed to put chicks in the coffin with grains of rice. It was told that when the chicks pecked at the rice, the murderer's conscience would also be eaten away and the murderer brought to justice. It didn't work in this case and as far as I know, the killers were never charged.

There were other superstitions that I didn't know about at the time, but am certain that funeral homes made sure to get them right, such as these:

- Position the deceased's hands open – if they are clenched the family will have money problems.

- Place the deceased with his feet toward the door to help him enter the next world.

- Carry the coffin out head first so that his spirit doesn't come back into the house.

- While he is in the house in his casket, take his shoes off so that relatives don't hear him walking about in the night.

- Keep the altar candles lit at all times so he can find his way to the next life.

- Don't shower or comb your hair at the funeral – otherwise, you will bring bad luck to the family.

- Cover all mirrors with cloth so that you don't see the dead who might try to show himself.

- Pregnant women should not look at the coffin, or they can have a difficult delivery.

- Don't go straight home after a wake, go to the mall so that the deceased doesn't follow you.

- Pinch anyone who sneezes at the wake, sneezing invites the deceased to visit you, pinching voids that invitation.

Families grieved privately for their loss but also had support from others, recounting shared experiences, remembering good times as well as regretting times that would never be. There was a lot of laughter as well as tears at funerals. Neighbors and friends contributed money so that the family could afford to have a funeral. And, life went on quickly after the 40 days of mourning. But they remembered the day their relatives died and honored them annually on their death date with gravesite visits and picnics with favorite treats of the departed.

It seemed we were all together on a long journey, and through the coming-together and breaking-apart, those ups and downs in the ocean of life, we were all just reaching out to each other and trying to reach that next shore.

MY OWN KITCHEN

MY OWN BATHROOM

MY OWN BEDROOM

SHOWER MATE

THE SCORPION

Chapter 8

PRIDE, PREJUDICE AND CONFLICT

Aanhin pa ang damo kung patay na ang kabayo
Of what use is the grass when the horse is already dead.
A Filipino proverb meaning, 'Something came too little, too late.'

Too Late?	
Tulong!	Help!
Nauubos ang oras.	Time is running out.
Kailangan nating sugpuin ang dugo.	We have to stanch the blood.
huli na ba?	Is it too late?
May chance pa ba tayo?	Do we have another chance?
Hindi tayo tulad ng kahapon; hindi tayo maganda magkasama ngayon	We are not like yesterday; we are not good together now
Araw-araw naghahabi ang landas.	Every day the path weaves.
Hindi natin alam kung ano ang tatama sa atin.	Friends comforted me and we walked hand in hand toward the distant shore
Huli na ba?	We don't know what will hit us.

MOST PEOPLE THINK OF THE PEACE CORPS as hiring high-school graduates. Movies like the horrible *Volunteers* and sitcoms like my childhood favorite, *Mr. Ed,* have portrayed young impetuous teens (or horses) as irresponsible as they "run off to join the Peace Corps." In fact, all PCVs must have graduated from college, and more and more are enlisting after several years of work experience. Peace Corps service also helps alleviate student loans, and the average age of my cohort composed of 200 people, was 27. There were several newly married couples and a few 50+ volunteers like myself, but the bulk were singles on the younger side. Normal service is a total of 27 months, including three months in training, where you are housed with a host family to learn the basic culture and language. At the end of this period, your language skills are tested, you are inducted as a full-fledged PCV, and only then are assigned to a location to serve for two years. You again board with a new family at the permanent site for another three months minimum.

In 2007, the Peace Corps added a program for folks over 50 who wanted the experience, usually after retirement, although I got no different treatment as a 50+ volunteer and wondered if the program was more of a marketing tool to encourage seniors to join. That same year, they renamed the Crisis Corps to Peace Corps Response. Peace Corps Response was for professionals who had served earlier in their lives and were willing again to serve in a professional capacity for an intense, short-term assignment, six months or less.

In passing, I'd heard in mid-December of my first year that there was a new Peace Corps Response volunteer living just outside of Manila. He was a SPED behavioral specialist in the U.S. and had set up a computerized behavior modification program for students. I was ecstatic, seeing possibilities, or perhaps just feeling desperate, and sought him out by phone.

"Hi, my name is Debra Pritchard. I am a PCV on Palawan, and I could sure use your help. Could I convince you to come to Palawan for a week for Christmas?"

Palawan had been ranked the #1 island in the world by both *Conde Nast Traveler* and *Travel + Leisure* magazines that year; it was a volunteer's dream to come to Palawan.

After I explained what the week might entail, he said, "I would love to help you out. But I'll need to clear it with the director of Peace Corps Response. I have two weeks' vacation since my school shuts down for the holiday. Man, to spend it on Palawan, thanks!"

The problem was that the entire Philippines woke up every September 1st singing Christmas songs and starting the longest Christmas season in the world. On my first September 1st I was awakened with a jolt at 6:00 AM to Alvin and the Chipmunks blaring throughout the compound, "Me, I want a hula hoop!"

Christmas extends from SeptemBER 1st to the end of the year, known as the BER months, and all of DecemBER is spent on parties. Parties at your office, with your clients, with your family, with the family of your brother's cousin's wife, with your classmates who graduated 20 years before, etc. It seemed the whole country shut down and partied. I was determined to enlist this man's help but couldn't reach anyone in the Peace Corps offices for approval because they had already departed on vacation.

That Monday, I went into the school office.

"Excuse me, Pastor and Ma'am. You know the man I talked about?

"Yes, yes. When does he arrive?"

"Well, no one at the Peace Corps seems to be at headquarters right now, they left for Christmas vacation. The PCRV (Peace Corps Response Volunteer) is only available for the next two weeks. Would you be willing to share the cost of his flight here?"

"Oh no! How much will it be?"

"It's about 3,000 Php ($60) and then the hostel here. What do you think?"

"We just got a grant from The Netherlands," said the Pastor's wife. "When would you need the money? Later we will have enough, but we don't have it now."

"I can charge the ticket and hotel on my credit card. You can pay me back when the check comes in."

They were so excited to get another Peace Corps volunteer to help that they blithely agreed, and we called the PCRV together to let him know. We chatted a bit and then asked,

"Can you be on the afternoon flight Friday?"

"Heck yeah! I'll be on it!"

We held trainings for the teachers, and although he was taken aback at their lack of knowledge and the school's rudimentary operation, he said that his program could improve behaviors. Another one of my follies, first, thinking that it would be easy; second, thinking that they would be interested and could understand how it might help them; third, forgetting

I was a PR symbol and not meant to really improve things; and fourth, reckoning with the newly discovered cultural trait that would be my bane: *ningas kugan*. *Ningas kugan* translates to 'flaming cogon grass,' which is what a farmer has to clear from his field before planting. He ignites the tall grass that bursts into a conflagration of bright flames that just as quickly dies. Similarly, bright ideas flamed and extinguished without any follow-through, vanishing like smoke into thin air. Add to this the trait of *pakikisama;* broadly, getting along with others, and specifically, always trying to please the person you are engaged with, and I should have seen red flags.

You can easily see where this was headed.... over a cliff. The PCRV had a lovely vacation on Palawan on my dime, and I doubt that Pastor even remembers the occasion. He never paid one centavo toward the cost.

Before he left, the PCRV bemoaned the fact that every year there was a "sore eye" season in the Philippines with prevention as simple as just washing your hands. Sore eye is 'pink eye' or 'conjunctivitis.' But the Philippine version is extreme, with blood streaks in the eye that impair vision, and freak out those who look at you. It races through families several times during a season.

"I just don't understand it," he said.

"I've put up simple signs in English and Tagalog. And we have practiced over and over. But the teachers and kids forget to wash their hands. All they have to do is wash their hands."

But, they couldn't break old habits, and he failed miserably. The Filipino word we both identified with was *sayang,* meaning, "Oh how sad, what a wasted opportunity." It was a feeling of being so close to the finish line, but somehow falling flat on our faces and losing the race. Both of us had our arrogant do-gooder mentality dashed. All our projects, like sore eye preventions, were, but weren't, that simple.

My heart was more aligned with Angie and the Special Olympics than at my assigned school, but even so, I remained and worked long hours there.

My school did attend Special Olympics events but didn't collaborate or share methods or curriculum that would benefit everyone and provide a united front for Special children. Throughout this time, I helped the Share A Life school register as an NGO with the City Social Welfare Department (with reams of requisite documentation), trying to improve their reputation and professionalism.

They started an outreach program, going to distant *barangays* to educate small villages. I made PowerPoints, in English and Tagalog (obviously with grammatical help), for each major disability, adding photos of the children we served. On the weekends, we borrowed the projector from CSWD (the city social welfare office) and drove in the dilapidated bird-egg blue multicab for hours to meet with parents, local government officials, and children. Sometimes the CSWD needed the projector, and we went without it. Sometimes we had the projector, but the electricity failed and there was no slide show. Sometimes we had car problems. Sometimes the weather was inclement, as in 'pre-typhoon.' But the *barangay* would always serve us lunch and people seemed thankful for the little we could provide, with me being the circus curio for the townspeople.

"*Siya sobrang malaki!*" they would whisper (She's so big!). "*Oo, isang giante, pero maganda at sexy, di ba?*" (Yes, a giant, but beautiful and sexy, right?). "Sexy" in Tagalog translates more to "she's looking trim and fit!" than the salacious American definition.

While I loved these visits and meeting different people as my photographs remind me, they also reinforced my sense of hopelessness. People walked for miles to get to the barangay halls to meet with us, but we did little. There were no facilities or professionals on Palawan to help these children, there was only one credentialed SPED teacher on the entire island of a million people and only 15 pediatricians who dealt with normal childhood illnesses. None of the doctors had a clue about intellectual disabilities, and there were no therapists for speech, motor, vision, or language. The owners of Share A Life School truly cared and wanted to help, but their lack of education in SPED, along with the lack of any SPED infrastructure on Palawan hindered everything.

Often, I felt we were charlatans offering false hope. I, in particular, felt guilty, since I knew the interventions we promoted could never be delivered as the hunger in the parents' eyes so desperately wished. Pastor was an expert in salesmanship. Suave, handsome, and charismatic, he was a charmer; the Peace Corps was enamored - and clueless.

One of my life's purposes is to help people if they want it, not to lie to them or sell them snake oil just to make them feel better (as my American enculturated mind viewed it). This continual culture conflict between my direct, truthful, science-based, results-oriented mindset, and the Filipino way of harmony and avoiding conflict by saying whatever people wanted to hear took a toll on all of us.

Three teachers hesitantly approached me one day when the owners were gone to say, "Ma'am Debs, we don't agree with what Ma'am is telling us to do with the students. What shall we do, we cannot disagree with her." Yikes. They viewed me as their ally against their employers. I might know what to do in the U.S., but not here, especially with my volatile status with Pastor.

Pastor and I had a significant disconnect at the outset. The last Peace Corps volunteer, the professional via Peace Corps Response who was supposedly an expert in educational therapy like me, had told him that the school was doing a bang-up job. Pastor had been pleased with the school's progress and wanted to rest, not invest more time and energy. Thus, there was a conflict brewing at the outset. Me and my infernal altruism and focus on competency and organizational improvement (which, in my defense, Arnel had directed), clashed with the others' wish just to be gainfully employed and viewed as successful and godly. Add to that the Filipino trait of fatalism, *bahala na*, and perhaps my fate was already sealed. The emphasis seemed to be on smiling, being kind and compassionate, and praying for a miracle.

Pastor told me that the school was based on a miracle in the Bible, the book of John, chapter 9:1 where Jesus sees a blind man in the crowd, and his disciples ask him who had sinned, the man or his parents so that the boy was born blind. Jesus answered, "Neither hath this man sinned, nor his parents; but that the works of God shall be manifest in him." Then Jesus spat in his hand, picked up dirt, and rubbed the mud on the blind man's eyes, and told him to go wash in the lake. As soon as the man washed the mud from his eyes, he could see. So, in essence, they viewed the children as born this way on purpose so that Jesus could perform a miracle to show how great God is. Quite counter to my philosophy and profession.

In the spring, Pastor and I flew to Manila and met with other volunteers with their counterparts for a scheduled Peace Corps training. One of my PCV friends was a young woman named Aja who was a devout Christian. Her rationale about trying to gather her friends to her religion made sense to me, and I use it even now when explaining faith to non-religious friends. Aja said, "Debra, if I love you as my friend and believe to be saved for all eternity that you must believe in Christ the Savior, then how can I NOT try to bring you with me?" Because of her devout belief and the country in which we were serving, Aja was chosen to open the conference attended by 500 with a prayer.

She told me later that Pastor sought her out afterward and said, "I can tell you are a true Christian. How I wish you were my volunteer. Is there any chance you could come to Palawan and work with us?" It was obvious he didn't want me or my expertise, and I felt degraded and scorned.

The school claimed success based on 'little by little.' When, after three years, they successfully taught Jake to brush his teeth, using butter as toothpaste; when Gian screamed for only two and one-half of the three hours; when SheilaMae walked toward the toilet before peeing. These perceived successes were the manifestations of my misgivings and foreboding during our training excursion to the orphanage. Those feelings returned with a vengeance watching the hopelessness of these children.

Arnel had either lied to me or didn't know that this school was a haven for those who could never live on their own, let alone be integrated into a regular classroom. It was tough for me to feel I was of any use to anyone, and hard not to consider this education a farce.

Although my relationship with my host family was somewhat tainted by being the same family I worked for, many of the Peace Corps volunteers felt as I did, overbearing scrutiny and monitoring of every detail of our lives by the host family. But others loved the constant company and camaraderie.

There seemed to be two kinds of Peace Corps host families. The first was like Carmen's host father who locked her in at 7:00 PM, who monitored everything, and kept records of how much she ate. Those families seemed to value the PCV most as a profit center for the family. In fairness, provincial life was so different even from Manila, let alone the U.S., that families might just not know what to do with us, we were so foreign.

But the second type of host became a surrogate family to the volunteer, with relationships lasting far after our service. In my case with my first family, they weren't defensive, and we traded cultural stories and respected each other. When they found I wasn't interested in being converted and didn't want a conversation with a missionary, they graciously left me alone. Many volunteers had families like this.

To Americans, a Filipino family can be overwhelming with its close and invasive (to Americans) bonds and rules. But several of my PCV friends loved being included as family members and spent all their time with their families. Many learned to cook iconic Filipino dishes like Bicol Express and pinakbet as a result of the host mother's culinary skills and collected recipes to prepare back in the U.S. In other cases, a couple of volunteers didn't leave at all.

Perhaps four of the men married Filipinas and had children. One of the women PCVs on Palawan wedded a man from her worksite who returned with her to the U.S. He is now a well-known chef in Washington D.C. with reviews in the Washington Post.

An older volunteer married a woman he met at his site and lives there today, farming on her ancestral land in northern Luzon.

Another young man had a child with a woman, and, although they didn't marry, he supports and visits his child every year.

In contrast, a few immature men got women pregnant with no intention of having a relationship with them, which is probably not an uncommon occurrence during Peace Corps service.

One man married his wife and brought her and their child to the U.S. and now has three daughters living in the Midwest.

One of my PCV friends fell in love, but his girlfriend was in nursing school. He returned to the U.S., but kept in touch; two years later, she came to the U.S. and they married. Beloved by his family, she just had their first child in Texas.

Our volunteer experiences and long-term ties varied in large part due to our relationship with our host families.

I missed my first host family as I tried to acclimate from a give-and-take of ideas and philosophy to a life of family parties, parlor games, *chika chika*, and intense religion. I felt misunderstood and rejected when I asked questions about their culture. Maybe I wasn't as involved as I should have been; maybe my approach was too 'intellectual' and non-appreciative of the way they did things; maybe I was just too foreign. I remember an instance, early on, when I said to Pastor while planning an upcoming event, "You and I think alike." Hoping I was laying some common ground, I recoiled at his response. He nearly spat in my face, "I'm nothing like you."

I tried hard to roll with the punches, but that should have given me a clue; hindsight is great. Who knows what I could have done differently? I wanted to change the world and empower people. The irony was that I thought everyone on earth wanted to be empowered and was held back by a lack of confidence, knowledge, or opportunity. I was stunned to find, over and over again, that most people I met didn't want power. They wanted to follow, not lead, especially if *utang* might be involved. Young people were groomed to work for someone else for gainful employment rather than to start their own businesses.

And, the Catholic Church promoted it as well. Opus Dei once said in a presentation to the community, "We need to keep procreating and sending out our youthful workers. Most industrialized countries are aging and their birth rates have slowed. The Philippines needs to improve its birth rate to supply workers throughout the world and become the dominant nation of the future." Their thinking eluded me, who hoped to decrease the population and preserve the earth. Our mindsets were diametrically opposed.

At least two people approached me within that first year and asked me to start an NGO for Special children, promising to come work for me. I responded that I would do all the work to set them up and train them to run their own NGO for Special children. One looked at me in horror; the other laughed nervously, and both declined. They didn't think of improving the system for themselves or their community, they just wanted a paying job working for a foreigner who, as the myth goes, is rich. It was a good, but depressing lesson for someone trying to bend Martin Luther King's moral arc toward justice.

At school, after the first batch of children left at noon, Pastor would stretch out on a bench and nap. I was at odds, bustling about and expecting him and the teachers to want to learn new things, or at least try new things. They wanted to coast now after expending so much energy. What a thorn in their side I must have been, appearing to not appreciate them. During training in Olongapo, Arnel had told me that I was to help them network and improve their organization's infrastructure, to take them to the next level. So, I thought I was sent to help them improve, not to tell them how wonderful they were. Pastor once said to Arnel, "She isn't respectful and said that our teachers aren't credentialed." Well, they weren't. My idea was to get them and other schools working together and exchanging ideas. He thought that I was assigned to them and should be promoting them as experts. I just couldn't do it.

Between their prideful competition with Salve Regina, my professional objections to how they dealt with children, and my feelings of spinning my wheels, I sensed a growing undercurrent of conflict and emailed Arnel for help. He didn't respond for over a month until it was far too late.

I can't even remember what the breaking point was, but I left that day in tears on a public multicab, cried all the way into the city, and walked with my computer to Neva's, my favorite pizza place that had wifi. Pastor had angrily phoned Arnel after I left to say he wanted me removed, and Arnel, in turn, called me at Neva's just before closing time. Between sobs, I said that the break was irreparable; he said he would fly over the next week, and just lay low. I reminded him that I lived with the family, but he said to keep calm and all would be fine. I thought of those silly red memes with the royal insignia on the internet, "Keep Calm and Carry On." It may have worked for the British in WWII, but I couldn't even laugh.

Multicabs stopped running at 9:00 PM and I caught the last one. But when I arrived, only the teenage son, Genesis, was there to let me in, without a word and his eyes cast down. Everyone in the church had been summoned for an emergency prayer meeting - about me. I went to my room and shut myself in. The family returned late and went straight to bed. For three long weekend days, we avoided each other around the house, which was difficult because I didn't have a key to the front gate and had to ring to be let in. I had nowhere to go since my life revolved only around these people. I decided that shunning was quite an effective group punishment.

Eventually, the Peace Corps sector director, Arnel, came and somehow patched things up a bit, getting me and the owners back together. I was never told what he said to them, perhaps an appeal for them to remain in good standing with the Peace Corps, or maybe that it was all the stupid American's fault and to rise above it; I'll never know.

I arrived at the orchestrated reunion with a bright red nose and swollen eyes. Not only had I shamed myself and my country but I had failed. I apologized and Pastor's wife felt so bad looking at my messy face that she hugged me. We agreed to try again and the following day, Pastor told the teachers, gathered in front of me, "Debra doesn't believe, but she did say something I agree with: God helps those who help themselves. So let's continue to pray for a miracle, but also work."

Pastor and I were 'friends' on Facebook and after their late-night church meeting, I saw his post: "I met the devil today and overcame him. Heathens will never do good because they are heathens."

I needed Scotty to get me out of this dystopia and beam me back up to the Enterprise, hopefully in one piece. I refused to give up on this parallel universe and wasn't listening to the negative vibes all around. The tom toms were beating a foreboding bass and I was treading water without knowing how angry the music was.

COMMUNITY OUTREACH

PARENT AND TEACHER TRAINING

GRAND OPENING OF A SMALL SPED CENTER

DOCTORS VISIT

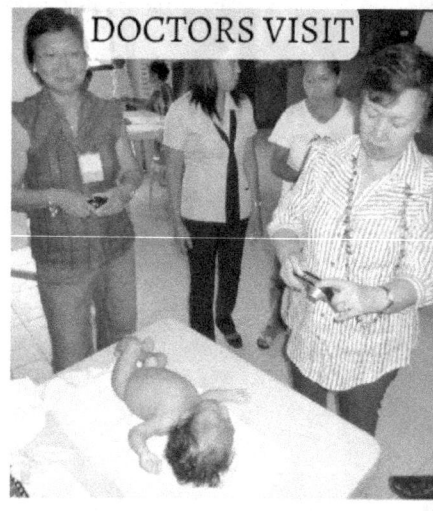

MEDICAL OUTREACH

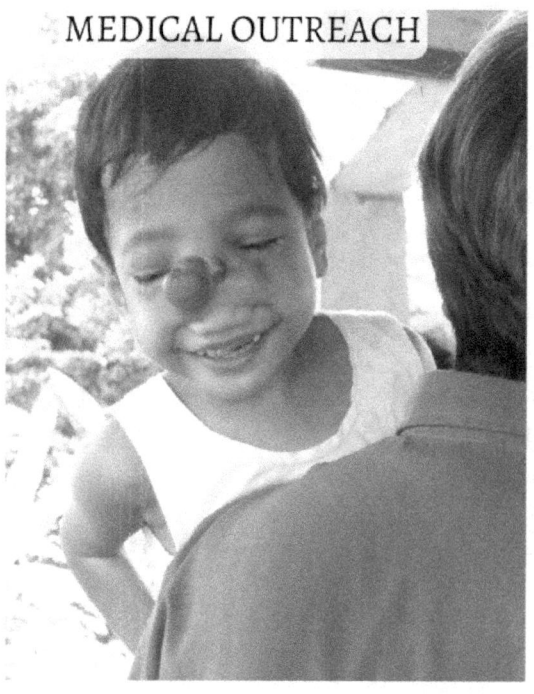

AND ALWAYS FOOD

Chapter 9

SAVIORS AND MENTORS

Ang pagkakataon sa buhay ay madalang dumating. Kapag narito na, ating samantalahin
Opportunity only knocks once: Grab it or you'll lose it.
A Filipino proverb meaning, 'If you see a way to make your life better, grab it!'

Saved	
Dahil sa pagkalunod, napaharap ako sa dulo nang ang isung linya ng buhay ay naglayag sa itaas.	Drowning, I faced the end, when a life line sailed overhead.
Hinawakan ko ang lubid, inilapit ko ito.	I caught the rope, drawing it close.
Kumapit ako.	I clung.
Ang barko ay aking minamahal.	The ship was my beloved.

THE PEACE CORPS ENCOURAGED PCVs TO ADOPT secondary projects at different organizations than their primary assignment. This policy saved me.

March 1, 2011, was the 50th Anniversary of the Peace Corps. All current Peace Corps volunteers on Palawan were invited to the home of a PCV who had served in the Peace Corps in the 1960s, Bart Duff. We arrived at his home, the bayside ancestral home of his wife, Paz, whom for some reason they called Baby. As a couple, they appeared a dichotomy. He, over six feet tall, eyes crinkled in a warm smile on his bespectacled, lily-white, freckled face, sporting a bald pink pate. She, the classically inscrutable Asian, delicately petite, with quiet, measured, slightly condescending tones and somber glances.

Their large, plantation-like home on Circumferential Road overlooked Puerto Bay and featured a huge wrap-around veranda, protection from that evening's tropical shower that cooled things off. Bart had invited two others who had served in the early years, so there were three 70-year-old PCVs, representing Nigeria, Pakistan, and the Philippines. Each of them had married Filipino nationals and were longtime friends, having retired to Palawan. There were nine of us volunteers, and this welcome was grounding for us. We all felt the camaraderie and connection between us and these elders, folks only a decade older than me.

"Let's show you a bit of our time in the Peace Corps, back in the 60s," said Bart. He ushered us into the large open living room where he had displayed photos of their Peace Corps service on the dining room table.

"Just look at this photo we took in the jungle," said Jack of Nigeria. "You know who this is?" he asked with obvious pride.

I gasped and gaped at the picture of Jack with the legend.... but none of the others knew who it was.

"He looks kind of like those pictures of Einstein," said one of the youngsters.

"Look at that crazy white hair," said another.

"It's Albert Schweitzer," I said, and blank looks stared back at me. "Who?"

Sigh, I was showing my age. Schweitzer was an icon in my childhood for his selfless acts as the doctor who established a 500-bed hospital in what is now Gabon in Africa, as well as for his hatred of colonialism. He was a polymath, a genius hailed as "the greatest man on earth," for whom Walt Disney named Schweitzer Falls on Disneyland's Jungle Cruise. The next generation had never even heard of him.

Bart hailed from Pendleton, Oregon, and had a Ph.D. from Stanford. He was an Agricultural Economist who met his wife at the International Rice Research Institute (IRRI) in Los Banos, Laguna, about 90 minutes south of Manila. He was a brilliant man and so humble, involved in many aspects of life on Palawan, and served as the Vice President of the Chamber of Commerce. I told him of my issues at the school, showed him my business resume, and asked if I could help the Chamber in some way.

Thank heaven for Bart Duff.

His wife claimed that we became partners in crime. Two idealists who worked for some unidentified intrinsic reward, definitely not monetary. Our idealistic "reward" was making general progress for the community, whatever it might be. We met, usually over food that he shouldn't be eating, and planned the strategy for the Chamber. Bart as Vice President of business development and me as the secretary, organizing, taking minutes and sending out notices. Bart was a foreigner and couldn't be President according to their bylaws, but he WAS the Chamber for the years I was there.

In addition to the Chamber, Bart hosted students from Michigan State University each summer and secured internships for them at various organizations on Palawan. I got to know the five who came during my first year on Palawan, both through work and play. Bart asked me if I would take them to El Nido and I jumped at the opportunity since I had not yet been to Palawan's #1 tourist destination. Puerto was abuzz and gloating to be featured in international tourism magazines. Was all the hype real?

The six of us piled into the van and paid $4 each to travel the six hours to El Nido on winding roads. In some parts, a *barangay* had run out of money, so only half of the road was paved, it was a wild ride, luckily in daylight. The driver wanted to return home to sleep in his bed that night and drove at breakneck speeds. It was the definition of cheap thrills, a terrifying experience without seatbelts. The cheery driver whipped down the twisty streets of the sleepy town, disgorging each group at the door of their hotel and off again in seconds. It was only noon and I headed for the beach; the five youths headed for the restaurant. It had been a long, tiring ride.

It's hard to describe the beauty of El Nido with its ragged karst cliffs looming beneficently over the town. A plethora of *bangkas* (native boats) floated in the picturesque harbor, waiting for tourists to board the daily tours. The days were glorious in the sun that made the turquoise and teal ocean sparkle. We witnessed a bounty of marine life like dolphins, turtles, sharks, and flying fish, and that was before we dived under the waves to snorkel. Over months, this became my spiritual haven, snorkeling and swimming with marine life in the fabled triangle of biodiversity. These were the early days when I could marvel at the plentitude of sea life. Before climate change killed the reefs and made it clear that marine life as well as humans were in dire trouble. What a marvelous few oblivious days those were in Paradise.

Bart had identified six major areas for the Chamber to focus on, and one dear to the hearts of several members was agriculture, the mainstay of provincial life. On this westernmost island of the Philippines, known as The Last Frontier, wild nature was its allure. Its capital, Puerto Princesa City, was known as The City in the Forest, with trees blanketing manmade structures. If you hiked into the hillsides and looked down to the bay, you only saw a magnificent canopy of trees.

Many of those were mango trees - a huge industry before mango pulp weevils invaded from Indonesia. For over 20 years exports were banned from Palawan, ruining industry and livelihood. The nasty bug lays its eggs under the skin of the young fruit where the winged insect develops. Once, I cut open a mango and screeched as a two-inch weevil flew out - FLEW out - of the fruit! Not so appetizing. Even finding a dead weevil inside is revolting, one of the ugliest bugs you'll ever see. Talking to a farmer in El Nido once, I found out that some farmers in the north illegally sent their fruit to Manila.

"Twice a month in the summer months, I pay a captain to take my mangoes to Manila. They leave El Nido late at night and must make good time to bypass customs. My mangoes are perfect, why should I be penalized?"

For the most part, no mangoes left the island and a previously thriving economy died. Thousands of mature trees were neglected for years, strangled by weeds, and starved by drought. Our small group of five including the City Agriculturist and her husband, and Governor Mitra's brother, MonMon took on the task of reclaiming Palawan. We met at the Mitra family ancestral home, Mitra Ranch, on their terrace overlooking Honda Bay. The patriarch, MonMon's father, Ramon, had been born in the penal colony on Palawan where his father was the superintendent. Ramon became a journalist, then a politician opposing Marcos. He nearly became President of the country, narrowly losing to Ramos after Cory Aquino left office. Ramon passed on his interests and physical attractiveness to his six handsome sons. The sons also shared his mischievous temperament, MonMon always had a gleam in his eye. They were actively involved in Palawan political life and the community, with MonMon's youngest brother, Baham, elected governor that year.

At our first meeting, we brought fruit and *merienda* (snacks) and met at the expansive ancient native *ipil* wood table outside the front doors and overlooking Honda Bay. In just 20 years, Palawan had lost 14% of its tree cover due to deforestation, mainly illegal logging. The prized *Ipil* (aka 'Borneo teak' or 'Moluccan ironwood') was still being felled, even with legal restrictions. I felt a bit of the weighty history that massive table must have held, looking far down onto the islands in Honda Bay as though from Mount Olympus, easy to feel superior from that high perch. It was seated at this table I saw my first waterspout, watching as the funnel descended from the enormous gray-blue storm cloud, and merged with the ocean, forming a solid wall of water sucked hundreds of feet into the air. Magical and awesome to witness.

MonMon was proud of his family heritage and showed us the family oil paintings inside the home, hung high on the walls of the great room. It struck me as odd that the paintings were so close to the front door and wind and rain, but they looked in perfect condition and framed two giants, his father and mother in traditional attire smiling down upon guests. After completing our meeting at that momentous table, MonMon showed us the zipline he was installing for tourists.

"You want to try it? We will formally open the zipline next week. I'll let you go free tonight," he joked.

I knew MonMon was essentially Palawan royalty so I didn't know the appropriate decorum for my response. I was so excited that I couldn't sit still and MonMon was delighted to show us the zipline. Bart declined, but the other three of us accepted. I went first. OSHA would not have approved. As I gained speed sliding down the line toward an enormous acacia tree, I realized the only thing avoiding a body splat was a Filipino teenager who looked half my size. There were no mechanics to slow or stop me, just that one Filipino, wide-eyed in a fighting stance as I sailed toward him. He grabbed my legs, hung on, and swung me around, avoiding impact by a couple of feet. I barely avoided peeing in my pants and that was the last time I went ziplining in the Philippines.

The five of us organized individual farmers, set up an NGO, and met with the governor to forward the issue to the federal level. We met with the elusive head of the Department of Agriculture's Mango Weevil Research Team, who spent a lot of the government's budget on mango research, supposedly to help the growers. However, the spending was most visible with several shiny new trucks, laptops with touchscreens, and little progress over 20 years. It was insulting that later her team won a national award for "saving the supermangoes of the Philippines from the dreadful mango pulp weevil (MPW)." Palawan was anything but saved. She used Palawan farmers for her research, but they still cannot sell their mangoes.

Our efforts showed how slow government progress would be for our farmers, so instead, we shifted focus to establishing a mango processing plant to dry and export the fruit. The contract for the plant was signed at that amazing *ipil* table, under the Mitra family portraits. Business was my strong suit; political deal-making, my nemesis. I'm very thankful that I didn't pursue a career in politics.

Bart and I brainstormed over leche flan at either Heavenly Desserts or Divine Sweets. Our sugar highs spawned ideas to vitalize Palawan and its economy. We outlined tourism opportunities from luxury medical stays to organized farm tours and heritage tourism. We were ahead of our time. The first all-inclusive farm stay, a glamping experience, happened ten years later. But, boy, did we have fun thinking of possibilities.

By this time, I appreciated the Filipino trait called *pakikiramay*, or compassion. One of our schemes was to showcase the cultural and historical hospitality of the country to refugees of war. The warmth of the people towards American prisoners captured by the Japanese in World War II risked villagers' lives. The prisoners were starved, yet forced to work hard labor constructing the Japanese airfield. Compassionate Filipinos would come to the fence at night and hand the captives scraps of food through the barbed wire. Even with such compassion, the war ended badly for those prisoners. When the Japanese on Palawan got word that the war was ending, they forced the prisoners into bunkers and threw aviation fuel on them, burning them alive. Anyone trying to escape was shot. Out of 150 men, somehow 11 escaped to tell the tale of the Palawan Massacre. The books recounting their story, Glenn McDole's *Last Man Out*, and Stephen Moore's more recent *As Good As Dead*, make for harrowing late-night reads.

Similarly, Filipinos embodied compassion during the American-Vietnam war (called The American War by Vietnamese as Americans call it the Vietnam War). After the fall of Saigon in 1975, about 400,000 Vietnamese fled by boat (coining the term "boat people") and escaped to the Philippines. Four years later, the UN helped set up the Philippine First Asylum Center at the mouth of Puerto Princesa Bay. Soon after, the Catholic Church donated land to establish an area now known as "Vietville" in Santa Lourdes about an hour north of Puerto. Over 2000 refugees built homes there and constructed a Buddhist temple, in addition to the stipulated Catholic church. The river was diverted into beautiful wide waterways overhung with lush vegetation. Today, the only remnants are renegade dragon fruit plants and concrete stairs leading to what had been a bedroom, now, just air. Another legacy of the compassionate Filipino people.

We never realized our dream of setting up a historical tour, but Bart championed a monument to the Palawan Massacre and recognition to the liberators from Oregon, his home state.

Because I volunteered for any Chamber project, my understanding of the culture deepened and developed, just as they said, 'little by little.'

Soon after I met him, Bart asked me to help his wife launch her dream of several years, a community kitchen empowering women in far-flung villages. I loved her idea to organize a communal kitchen with shared space to afford anyone the opportunity to start a business. But this was Baby's baby, and she didn't want Bart or his associates involved. So, after some initial help, I bowed out and she worked with the local government to establish the site.

The kitchen was eventually built in a remote community on the west coast, about three hours away. A painful road, three solid hours over pot-holes and ruts, often losing track of just where the road was. I traveled there by public jeepney once during the rainy season, and the ruts were so bad that the axle snapped in two. All passengers had to offload and stand in the rain until they affixed the spare axle. Who carries a spare axle?

The inauguration of that community kitchen was a triumph. The kitchen itself was small and basic. It was a concrete structure, painted white, with wire screens for ventilation. The generator had been donated and was the only source of electricity for miles around. Bart's wife spent weeks, and her own money, transporting women over the mountain to train them in sanitary procedures and hygiene. She also developed recipes for them to use local fruits from their forests, like mangoes and coconuts. The idea was to farm, harvest, process and package the bounty of the forest and ship it to Puerto for sale.

On the day of the launch, these properly trained women demonstrated their process of making and filling local coconut jam into labeled bottles. They looked uncomfortable and awkward with their white smocks, plastic gloves, hairnets, and sterilized implements to stir the food. The scene threw my memory back to how imperialists made their indigenous servants dress conqueror-style: Indians in Mumbai serving British generals their tea; the black butler in Atlanta with his white gloves shining his master's boots. Not quite the same, but I wondered how the women felt. Many had hands so tiny that the misfitting gloves flapped about. These were women who probably didn't wash their hands before making their own family dinner. They looked like actors in a movie who had not rehearsed and were embarrassed at their performance.

It was hot. There was no piped water, they had to transport it by buckets from one of the several waterfalls throughout the lush *barangay*. In the end, it was a short demonstration since they hadn't received a key ingredient needed for production. Everyone was relieved.

I recently heard that the kitchen didn't quite achieve what Baby had intended and that the government took it over, but it still serves the women in Simpoken. It was such a great idea, I hope it thrives.

Another sector that the Chamber, (well, Bart), targeted was Education. We wanted to upgrade the two universities to international standards and had high hopes of establishing a world-class environmental program with a marine life facility on the shores of Palawan's biodiverse seas. I now laugh at our idealistic optimism. But, for us, it was possible.

We set up a conference to teach university professors how to write a grant, something I knew. The head of the Commission on Higher Education (CHED) came from Manila, along with the presidents of both universities who selected professors for the two-day training. CHED had money left in their grant accounts and wanted proposals written so that they could fund projects. They targeted Palawan as the beneficiary, all we had to do was submit proposals. Everyone was excited.

Bart and I had prepared well, people were engaged, and it seemed wonderful...until I received draft proposals a couple of weeks later. The top two were in agriculture and aquaculture, a seed storage system for endemic plants, and an abalone fishery. I was dismayed to see the quality, not just the English, but organization and thought, even the research protocol was flawed. I had seen better from high school students in the U.S. I pushed my now-familiar feelings of misgiving and hopelessness aside and tried to salvage something that might receive funding. I didn't know their fields of study and had to ask questions, questions to which the professors had no answer. A case of dysentery stopped me from shepherding things forward. A personal *sayang.*

So, another sad, wasted opportunity that was attributed to God's will, *bahala na.* It seemed to be up to God a lot of the time here, but I didn't see God doing much to see things through. My private word for much of my work in the province, *sayang,* matched many of the results. We came so close on so many things, but we missed the bullseye and didn't pursue our ideas to fruition, wasting rare opportunities. I also felt a healthy dose of frustration as I put so much effort into these projects just to have them unravel into nothingness. People wrote what I considered a draft, but it was a huge effort for them and they considered it final. It was frustrating and demotivating.

As I got more involved with outside do-gooders, like World Bank, Rotary Club, and the IMF bank, I wondered how they kept going with so little progress forward and even less return on their investment. At least I wasn't investing millions of dollars as they were, just my time and effort, well, okay, my life. I felt fortunate that my career had been in the business world and not development.

The Chamber housed not only a wide range of businesses but also degrees of ethical standards. Most of the Chamber accepted Bart and me, viewing us not as outsiders, but as one of them, and liked the work we were doing, especially because Bart and I were doing the work. Many of them showed up to meetings to listen to what we'd done but few offered their help.

Bart was best at getting titled people from international concerns interested to come to Palawan. The Chamber members benefited, so they showed up to those events. In the Philippines, nearly every event someone attends results in a printed certificate of recognition. People collect them as documentation that they attended, and theoretically, learned something. Senior employees, government and private sector alike, had thick files of these. Bart's and my toils heightened a Chamber member's reputation and recognition with absolutely no effort on their part; we didn't care as long as we moved forward.

The first several meetings I attended at the Chamber were fraternal meetings, most held at restaurants owned by Chamber members. The Chamber picked up the tab for these delicious meals of seafood and wine, a windfall for the owner. That is until one normally quiet member spoke up at the end of one dinner.

"You know, I think each of us can pay for our own meal."

The members looked at him both aghast, and expecting the punchline to his joke.

He explained, "The Chamber budget should not just be used for our entertainment and serving us dinner. We should be doing something other than eating our membership dues."

I loved the man immediately, he had my kind of ethics. Not to say that the others didn't have ethics, but their ethics were primarily concerned with benefiting themselves. The Chamber was set up to promote business and businessmen, but they were unused to thinking that they should benefit anyone outside the Chamber members.

Many were also sexist, although the men would probably disagree. The few female members were relegated to organizing decorations and food for the events. It reminded me of my start at Shell in my 20s when crude sexist jokes and inappropriate touching were commonplace, when I was frequently asked to fetch coffee for my male peers at business meetings. Some of the women members of the Chamber had advanced degrees and owned their own businesses, but such was the society and the nature of 'women's work.'

The entertainment was also sexist. The worst instance I observed was when I was asked to attend a meeting at a restaurant in Santa Monica to discuss trade contracts with Borneo. The state university, Chamber, and local trades were trying to set a path forward now that there was a cargo ship between Palawan and Borneo to the south. The meeting was held on Mitra Road at the Commodore's Mansion. The Commodore was a retired navy commander who had built his home high above the bay with incredible views. At the white wrought iron gate was a big entry plaque reading, "Commodore N. Hernandez (Ret)" in yellow-gold letters a foot tall and beneath it in bright red, "Mansion." It was ostentatious, befitting its owner, who didn't greet or acknowledge me. He was a large, pompous man, rather like South American dictators are portrayed in Hollywood movies, leaning back in their seats as people fawn over them, currying favor.

The university president had brought his 30-year-old daughter who sat to my left reading a paperback novel while he and the Commodore laughed together, oblivious to her presence. The five men in attendance were segregated to my right, about five feet away, and were loud in their comradeship. I was uncomfortable in this good old boys' meeting where the men spoke rapid Tagalog with references to social events I knew nothing about.

There was only one other woman in attendance. She was from the university, I assumed a professor, although she didn't speak, and seemed to function as the note-taker. The men socialized, ignoring us three women on their left, all while their eyes slid to watch the servers and smile at them. Their smiles were not fatherly. I assumed the girls might have also come from the university because they were so young and didn't seem to have any catering experience.

They were half-clothed, the reason which I better understood after the meal. The men relaxed with their cigars while tinny music played on the radio. The girls began to sway up on stage, not with any dance expertise or routine, but provocatively in short shorts. It chafed me to be excluded from the before-meal business conversation, but this display rather turned my stomach. Sixteen-year-old girls giggling and flirting with 50-year-old men. To watch the university president relishing this, with his daughter seated at the table, was disturbing. I had seen enough of this in my life at Shell back in the day, although nothing as blatant as this. A nauseating throwback in time for me to have to go through it again. Their giggles still ring in my ears. One of my least favorite meetings that ruined any future positive perception of the participants.

That was not the norm for me and Bart. We fed on each other's idealism and had so many irons in the fire that we simply never stopped, or even slowed, for the negatives. Like how baseball players can have a losing streak but don't have the time to get down, there's always another game to attend to. That's how it felt to me.

Together we founded the Palawan ICT (Information and Communication Technology) organization. We intended to provide jobs for graduates of Palawan University's tech programs and evolve business opportunities. Our conferences focused on students and professionals interested in IT startups and call centers.

We worked with a delegation from the national ICT group in Manila who agreed to come help us set up an organization and to lay out the basic structure. I warned them that our members were beginners and provincial, asking them to keep things simple. We met at AA Plaza Hotel which had the only elevator on the island, in the fourth-floor conference room. The woman in charge took me aside on the last day of their initial visit and said, wide-eyed, "I had no idea people knew so little about the IT business or business in general, thank you for the heads-up."

So, we started 'little by little' but our enthusiasm was contagious. The 15 of us at that inaugural meeting signed our names in bright blue ink on an eight by twelve foot tarp as our commitment to see things through. Within a year, we hired our first executive director, a man with experience from Tacloban. We had several false starts and a lot of internal drama, but the organization remains today. It is still known as the Palaweño ICT Association (PICTA), the name we gave it at that first meeting.

Our 'little by little' positive outcomes resulted from working with men and women who wanted the betterment of the community, not just themselves. They exuded personal confidence and compassion rather than self-serving defensiveness. Maybe it was also that we were business-minded and had a common understanding of the actions needed. Whatever it was, it certainly rescued me and propelled me in a positive direction. I was weaving myself into the broader fabric of Puerto Princesa and loosening ties with the insular school.

FORMING PICTA IN 2012

MANGO GROUP WITH GOVERNOR MITRA

ORGANIZING MANGO FARMERS

TOUGH DUTY IN EL NIDO

Chapter 10

MAKING A DIFFERENCE

Ang palay ay parisan, habang nagkakalaman ay lalong nagpug-pugay
Imitate the rice stalk: The more grains it bears, the lower it bows.
A Filipino proverb, meaning, 'The more you acquire, the more humble and respectful you should become.'

Blessings

Pukyutan, Bulaklak, Bundok, Tao	Bee, Flower, Mountain, Man
Bawat isa ay may layunin	Each has a purpose
isang hiling	a wish
isang regalo	a gift
Mga pagpapala na ipinagkaloob	Blessings bestowed without
nang walang pag-iisip, nang walang bayad	thought, without charge
Bawat isa ay may pasasalamat	Each has a gratitude
isang utang	a debt
isang bono	a bond
Tayo ay iisa	We are one

OVER DECADENT *SYLVANNAS* OR MANGO TARTS, we conspired. Bart knew I wouldn't tell his wife what he was eating.

"Two years ago, we held our first Annual Economic Breakfast. How do you feel about getting the second one done, a year late?" he asked me one afternoon.

"Sure, what's it about?"

"One of the Chamber's objectives is to educate its members on business. This is a breakfast meeting, we'd have to figure out where to have it. Then the invitations and food and all. I was thinking of inviting the Secretary of the Economy to speak."

"Isn't that like a Cabinet position? Would someone like that come to Palawan?"

Bart chuckled. "It's a quick flight over, and if we do it on a Friday, we can entice him with tickets to the Underground River and a city tour. Palawan is exotic, The Last Frontier, you know. I don't think many government people get an invitation for an expense-paid business trip to Palawan. So there's a good possibility. At the worst, he might send his deputy. We'd take him and his entourage to Ka Lui before they left for their tour. I would expect a few of the Chamber to attend a dinner at Lui's."

"Sure, maybe a couple of the Chamber guys can meet with us to start the ball rolling. I'll set something up."

Two days later, four of us met at a member's restaurant, *Ka Inato*, for an early breakfast to hash out details and share logistical tasks. Breakfast was *lamayo* (dried fish) and rice, and yet another failed attempt at *durian* (the smelliest and least palatable fruit I've ever eaten... well, tried to eat), all washed down with an avocado shake.

"What will be our slogan for the meeting?" asked the restaurateur.

I started to laugh, but Bart glanced at me sharply and replied, "I've had some thoughts, what do you think about 'Building Palawan's Future'?"

I gaped.

"Or, 'Making Palawan #1 in Opportunity,'" said the other.

They agreed to: '*Gearing up to be Globally Competitive.*' Heavens, what high aspirations we promoted with that slogan.

But, as Bart taught me, in the provinces, such business slogans are important. As are different color-coded employee uniforms for each day of the week, monthly office themes, and nicknames. These provided unity, structure, and a sense of belonging and loyalty to the organization.

Even tricycles had names like 'Princess Cherry Pie,' 'Jhun's Family,' 'Cookie,' or 'Pam and Roy.' Trikes were the canvas upon which drivers painted their pride, stenciling the christened name of the trike just below the windshield. Each trike was so unique that it shouted to commuters, "Hi! It's Me! Choose me to ride with!"

Even politics was color-coded with the party in power painting everything 'their' color. For 20 years, Puerto's mayor had ruled with red. Red buildings, red gates, and even CRs with red signs thanking the mayor for blessing the *barangay* with the toilet.

By the time I arrived, many in the Philippines knew the showy Mayor of Puerto Princesa as Palawan's best promoter. He started a clean-up program with trash collection and a focus on the environment that highlighted Palawan's natural beauty. He also started Puerto's celebration called "Love Affair With Nature."

Strategically coinciding with red-themed Valentine's Day, the morning began before the sun rose. People gathered at the sea in San Jose to plant mangroves to prevent erosion and enhance the habitat. I woke up at 3:30 AM to walk three miles in the dark because public transportation hadn't begun. Environmental volunteers handed us a donated mangrove seedling and we walked into the sea to plant them in the muck. It was a gooey event with the mud sucking off my flip-flops.

Afterward, at Valentine's dawn, there was an outdoor Catholic wedding spectacle marrying 200 couples. The betrothed, all 400 of them, stood on a high stage, the women lovely in white gowns. Two priests in full vestments and biretta officiated. In the middle of the priest's pronouncement to the almost-newlyweds, the Mayor drove up with his driver and bodyguards. The crowd cheered. The Mayor was a celebrity and trumped the religious ceremony. He waved to the crowd, smiled beneficently at the brides- and grooms-to-be, got back in the SUV and drove away. Only then did the priests pronounce all married in the sight of God.

The Philippine constitution sets a term limit of three consecutive three-year terms for mayor, but there are always loopholes in the Philippines. Since he could not run after his third term, Mayor organized and accomplished a recall against his newly-elected successor. Mayor was permitted to finish out that term. Because his term had been theoretically interrupted by his opponent (and was therefore not 'consecutive'), he could run again.

By 2007, he had served 15 years, again reaching a limit. No problem for the politically astute. He went to great lengths to establish Puerto as a "highly urbanized city" (HUC) so that he could begin a new term as mayor of a HUC. One can only guess how he accomplished this since Puerto did not meet the qualifications of a HUC then, defined in terms of population (minimum 200,000) and revenue ($250 million annually).

Mayor's fame came from his coup to put Palawan on the map with the now-famous Underground River, a pretty inlet where boatmen navigate a cavernous network of stalactites and stalagmites. No scientists or tourism agencies were involved in the determination; the "New 7 Wonders of Nature" were elected by popular vote. The Mayor persuaded government leaders to install computer terminals, not only on Palawan but throughout the Philippines. He coordinated an international ad campaign for all Filipinos, including the 12 million overseas workers, calling them to action to vote for the Philippine landmark. A testament to "Pinoy Pride" in this country of 110 million, the Underground River won (how could the Galapagos think to contend with a population of only 17 million? Or the Great Barrier Reef with 25 million Australians, let alone Angel Falls or Kilimanjaro?). As the results showed, the Filipino diaspora is a force to reckon with.

An unexpected consequence was that the advertising worked, and tourists flooded Palawan to view the New Wonder. Tourists found themselves turned away due to a lack of infrastructure and overbooking, and vacations were thwarted. Many who did see the River were disgruntled that this was a Wonder at all, and posted disparagements on TripAdvisor. The publicity was a major embarrassment for the city that took years to remedy.

Nonetheless, Mayor promoted his success and again took a revived term as HUC mayor to the limits. In the Philippines, when a politician reaches the ultimate, when voters start to whisper 'corruption,' he usually turns to a family member to retain control and fealty. These political dynasties are common, such as the Gordons in Olongapo and the Marcoses in Ilocos, keeping power in the family. Dynasties held such power that even a family as disgraced as the Marcos family could be reinstated, and over the next decade, inch their way back to the presidential palace at Malacañang.

So even though the year before, the Mayor had pledged allegiance to his Vice Mayor for the upcoming mayoral race, his aspirations to transition out of power seemed to change when he finally had to yield his seat. He instead promoted his wife as his favored candidate for the race, essentially securing himself the right to rule for another term with her as his proxy. Awkward, since the mayor and vice mayor had married sisters, hence, the two men were brothers-in-law. Yet, most people expected his wife to win.

This was my first election, and I lived on the street of Mayor's campaign headquarters. I commuted by multicab and walked past the bustling activity in the dark on my way home, a bit scary. During the election, huge livestock transport trucks filled with standing farmers lined the street. Perhaps 30 men per truck had been brought in for the Mayor to buy their votes, it was a common practice. Many voters were illiterate, but a thumbprint was sufficient to receive a payout of 1,000 pesos (about $20) and a 50-pound sack of rice. By the time I left the country, the going purchase price had doubled to 2,000 pesos per thumbprint.

The political nasties began with confrontational divisiveness. The families of the two candidates no longer spoke, and neighbors argued with friends. You either adored or despised each candidate. Luckily, the only violence during that election was verbal. The surprising outcome was that the former Vice Mayor was elected, even after a recount demanded by the angry opposition.

This changed the hue of the city from red to a rather garish combination of bright yellow and blue. The new mayor modernized the city and made urban and commercial improvements. But now there are yellow and blue streetlamp poles, bleachers in the sports complex, street signs, and yes, yellow and blue comfort rooms. The new Mayor's slogan was "*Hindi Bukas, Kundi Ngayon*" – Not Tomorrow, But Today.

So, *Gearing up to be Globally Competitive* was an optimistic slogan for that first forum, and some might have believed that we fulfilled our aspirations. It was easy to get caught up in the passion of making Puerto Princesa ready for the global stage.

As Bart predicted, the Cabinet Secretary flew in from Manila for the breakfast and his staff stayed for the weekend. And, at Ka Lui's, I ordered the special dessert for them; one I could hardly eat. The coconut showcased an erect banana with skin partially peeled, dribbling pineapple syrup, with soft, round, reddish-brown guavas at the base. Lui had a wicked sense of humor.

For that first forum, we hosted about 150 attendees. Handsome men in formal *pinya barongs* (long-sleeved shirts of woven pineapple fabric) accompanied women in Filipiniana gowns and high heels. They sat and appeared to listen to the very dry National Economic forecast.

The next year our speaker was the well-respected Dr. Lilia de Lima of the Philippine Economic Zone (PEZA), who should not be confused with Senator Leila de Lima, imprisoned for years without trial for being an outspoken challenger of authority. Confronting a President, even over extrajudicial killings, had consequences in the Philippines.

Our speaker, Dr. de Lima, was all smiles as she encouraged the Puerto Chamber to develop the technology sector. Her department set up incentives for IT start-ups and call centers, Puerto had no such businesses. I'm pretty sure very few of the guests understood the details, but with 300 people attending, this was deemed another success. I still think that the main draw was the food and the chance to look sophisticated.

The following year was my favorite forum because it focused on the environment and was a multi-day event. Over 500 attendees came to hear prominent speakers like the head of the World Wildlife Fund, the Presidential Adviser for Environmental Protection, and Yeb Sano. Yeb then sat on the Climate Change Commission and went on to head the Asia Pacific region of Greenpeace. Yeb was famous for his passion at both the COP 20 in Doha and testifying at the UN's Climate Summit 24 in Poland. With tears rolling down his face, Yeb made an impassioned speech to the Summit as he received news in the middle of the conference that his family had survived the Philippines' first 'super typhoon.' Typhoon Haiyan (known as Yolanda in the Philippines) was the most powerful typhoon recorded and made a direct hit on Tacloban. Yolanda killed over seven thousand people, destroyed over a million houses, and displaced 4 million people. The world media broadcast Yeb's words:

"What my country is going through as a result of this extreme climate event is madness, the climate crisis is madness. We can stop this madness right here in Warsaw."

Of course, the madness did not stop, but handsome, soft-spoken, and engaging Yeb began speaking to youth. He led marches, protests, and fasts all over the world. Yeb was the Philippines' 30-something equivalent to Sweden's Greta Thunberg who inspired millions of global youth with her activism in schools. I had met Yeb the year before and we liked each other. Convincing him to return to Palawan for the forum was easy. We incentivized his attendance by sponsoring a romantic birthday weekend with his wife. At the last minute, she couldn't come, but Yeb had a fawning fan base who showered him with birthday cheer.

We held the workshop at the Capitol and Yeb got a traditional Palawan welcome for his presentation, an electrical blackout. Filipinos are renowned for their flexibility and resilience because so much is thrown at them every single day, and Yeb calmly modified his presentation as we opened doors and windows for air and light. The positive consequence of blackouts was their ability to bring people together and take upsets in stride.

Attendees stayed at the newly opened Princesa Gardens, the only 5-star hotel on Palawan at the time. I oversaw everything from registration to schedules to entertainment and the requisite *merienda*. Bart and I met to sample the menus we would serve and scope out how to accommodate the large crowd. Event planning can be heady, but it can also try friendships and that convention frayed several of mine. But it was spectacular and the local and national appreciation for our pristine environment was obvious.

Bart decided after that momentous and labor-intensive affair that we could only sponsor the forum every two years, but sadly, this was his last before his demise. And, like many efforts, without Bart, it evaporated.

Bart started so many different ventures that a few survived even without him. He organized the "Power Family," a group of energy producers. Palawan's electrical distribution system was antiquated and broke down regularly with consistent overloads to the system that caused daily blackouts. Restoration surges ruined expensive personal and commercial appliances which stalled commerce and communication. To this date, there can be daily electrical outages on Palawan often caused by a gecko, a snake, or a small bird shorting out the lines.

Who knows if or when they will renovate that system? Most tourists are oblivious of how the populace lives since most hotels have backup generators. As tourism and hotels grew, so did electrical outages for us residents. With the environmental lawyer, Attorney Gerthie, Bart formed a group to promote renewable energy. They named it Palawan Alliance for Clean Energy (PACE) and invited me to their first group meeting.

"I've invited Debra since she has a marketing background and I thought could help us get media attention," Bart introduced me to the few people there.

"Umm...I'm willing to help you, but it will need to be behind the scenes, I don't want to jeopardize deportation," I said, only half-joking, since foreigners were warned to not get involved with politics.

"We won't endanger you!" said Gerthie in her cheerful, lilting cadence of Filipino-English.

For being deeply involved in such dangerous and heavy legal protests, Attorney Gerthie was always cheerful. She was positive that the fight against lumber and mining ventures would be successful. I knew her as Gerthie, married to Dempto, a newspaper journalist trained in classical guitar. Drinking San Miguels and listening to his Thursday night gigs at The Gypsy's Lair was a favorite pastime of mine. His brilliant guitar reminded me of 'culture' on this island so far removed from anything cosmopolitan.

Dempto was an investigative journalist for the largest paper in the Philippines. His adroit inquiries uncovered many illegal schemes on Palawan, usually perpetrated by rich oligarchs or foreign concerns. Dempto wrote stories about the illegals: fishing, mining, logging, and wildlife capture. Or of Chinese nationals who sailed barges at night to our shore, dredging boatloads of sand to build military bases on the Spratly Islands. We called the contested islands Kalayaan and considered them ours.

I often wondered if Gerthie and Dempto discussed work at home and what their two teenagers thought. What a contrast their dinner discussion was from mine growing up; my dad was a grocery clerk. I learned from

Dempto that serious topics were not discussed in public. He came to my table to chat during his gig breaks, but only with superficial chit-chat.

Gerthie headed the Environmental Legal Assistance Center (ELAC) which filed lawsuits against illegal mining and lumber giants. She had an inherent conflict with the new governor, whose career began on Palawan with illegal foresting, culminating with his then-rank as the richest elected government official in the Philippines. His fortune grew proportional to the destruction of 30-60% of the forests over a 20-year period. The governor ironically also headed the Palawan Council for Sustainable Development (PCSD), of which Gerthie was an elected member. Like many things on Palawan, the Council started with best intentions and morphed into strongman leadership. I often heard about the Gerthie-Governor confrontations second- or third hand. Perhaps they were exaggerated, but it was obvious that Gerthie was a warrior. She had an understated demeanor and a lethal smile.

Her primary focus had been the huge nickel mining industry on Palawan that stripped resources and soil structure for a tremendous profit. The Philippines exported around $600 million in nickel exports and Palawan provided one-fourth of that. But mining destabilized the land and its processing wastes polluted the island, and provided for the island's main conflict. Environmentalists tried to protect the natural habitat while politicians and corporations protected their profit.

Bart and Gerthie started the renewables group to prevent coal's use as fuel for the electric plant. One of the new governor's *pares* (a male buddy) owned a coal mining company that supplied over 90% of the entire country's coal. The powerful governor had assured his friend that there was a market for that coal on Palawan, well known for power outages. Our electric system was so dysfunctional that the business community was in favor of anything that would supply semi-consistent electricity. Daily outages seemed at times contrived to encourage voters to approve the plant.

I became part of the opposition which continues fighting a decade later. Palawan was so beautiful, my paradise, and to think of the damage to the ecosystem of 250 endemic species was painful. Let alone the cost of human health. Much of my work was quiet since foreigners were forbidden to take part in such activities. Even working behind the scenes imperiled my visa. But, by this time, I had become environmentally 'woke.' The island and wildlife were being destroyed by human greed, and I wanted to help. I networked PACE with environmental groups like 350.org and Fossil Free. Together we composed an online petition that took the message off-island and into the international arena. Others in Gerthie's group organized local protests and bused-in farmers from affected municipalities to protest at the Capitol.

The governor and his friend tried first to establish the plant in Narra, near the nesting place of the endangered Philippine cockatoo called the *Katala*. The *Katala* Foundation responded by organizing several successful protests. So, the proposed site moved a bit north, right next to Western Philippines University (WPU) in Aborlan. The University campaigned against the coal plant with our slogan,

"Keep the Philippines' Last Frontier - Don't let Palawan become the 'Lost Frontier'." But, the governor retaliated. He announced he was withdrawing 2000 scholarships from students at WPU.

Journalists (including Dempto) and politicians sparred over this unscrupulous action, and PACE answered with community organizing so that the Aborlan site also was foiled. At one point, the governor (yes, the same governor who headed the Sustainable Development Council) planned to purchase land and set up the coal facility on his own private land. The purchase of that land was also prevented. Enlisting national and international civil society, PACE motivated crowds to come out at both Palawan and Manila government buildings.

The Philippines ranks consistently as the first or second deadliest place in the world to be an environmental activist, vying with Colombia for the top spot. Forest rangers and everyday citizens are regularly killed execution-style, often with their spouses and children. Most simply wanted to protect trees from logging, parrots from Manila cages, oceans from overfishing, and prevent mining filings from polluting land and water. The governor had been stymied by the people he had profiteered and abused through his illegal logging career. It must have infuriated him. But he was a hard-liner and continued to persevere. I read in the Palawan Daily News that the coal plant is proceeding, to be opened in 2023...in Arborlan, next to the university. Bart is rolling in his grave, or maybe just smiling *bahala na*.

Bart and I were of like idealistic minds, and few Filipinos understood us. At one Chamber meeting, I was exasperated with several of the businessmen. They couldn't agree to a blanket resolution because each of them didn't receive a specific benefit.

I finally blurted, "Good grief, what's in it for Bart and me!?"

To which the President looked at me with a questioning expression and said, "We always wonder that. Why do you work so hard and get nothing out of it?"

But we did get something out of it, just not monetary.

- I wrote a business plan to start the Palawan Ecological Adventure Trail from Puerto. It traverses the mountains to the west coast; that tourist trail is still pleasing backpackers today.

- The Palawan ICT group has changed the university's teaching focus from theoretical to practical. The first call center set up business in 2017, only four years after we first organized, and several more followed.

- Bart realized his dream of building a memorial for the 41st infantry division that liberated Palawan from Japanese rule in WWII. He lived to inaugurate the first Palawan Liberation ceremony, now celebrated annually in April.

- The abalone fisheries proposal spawned a new Aquatic Research facility at Western Philippines University in Aborlan.

- The mango processing plant in Irawan dries and ships mangoes internationally.

- The women's kitchen remains in Simpokan.

We made a difference in a few lives.

As for me, I got to work with Bart and become his friend. He saved my Peace Corps life by offering me an escape from a miserable situation. He was the only person I ever met who closed his letters as I did: "Blessings."

Bart was my blessing and my partner in crime...some of the best escapades of my life. I officiated at his funeral, attended by the community and his family. I made it through the program and my own speech, signing off with, "Blessings to you, Bart."

LISTENING TO BART

THE ENVIRONMENTAL CREW

WITH MAYOR

THE UNDERGROUND RIVER IN SABANG

YEB SANO WITH OUR PACE FLAG IN EUROPE

COMMUNITY KITCHEN

Chapter 11

LIVING MY BEST LIFE

Kung walang tiyaga walang gantimpala
Without perseverance there is no Reward
A Philippine proverb meaning, 'Keep on Truckin'!'

Keep On	
Tanging mga nakakulong na ibon ang nananatili	Only caged birds stay
Ang mga bata ay naggalugad sa kanilang sariling mga bakuran	Children explore past their own yards
Ang mga monghe ng Tibet ay nananatiling tahimik ngunit gumagala sa mga uniberso sa kanilang isipan	Tibetan monks stay still but roam universes in their minds
Bumahaba ang oras	Time stretches
Ipagpatuloy	Keep on

MY LIFE WAS FULL. I HAD THE CHAMBER WORK, my original Peace Corps assignment, and the Special Olympics. As a side gig, I tutored five college girls every Tuesday evening at the Mr. Donut in town.

The Philippine academic curriculum requires English to be taught beginning in grammar school. Provincial tradition focuses on rote learning rather than critical thinking or the Socratic method. Teachers who were trained in the rote system continued it, and Tagalog, not English, was the predominant language.

Questioning what a teacher said was counter to the culture of respect for one's elders and the cultural lynchpin of *hiya*, translated loosely as shame. *Hiya* demands personal restraint so as not to shame oneself or others, and children learn the principle early. On Palawan, many teachers don't speak, write or understand English well, and perpetuate a lack of skill in their students, who respectfully never question them.

The five college girls were social workers that I worked with at Share A Life School. One day the Pastor's wife begged me, "Deb, can you help them with English?" Then she handed me a client report.

The summary stated that the father had gotten pregnant when he was three months old and that his baby had been born to his grandmother.

"Oh my, this makes no sense."

"I know! I can't keep trying to fix their mistakes when I can't understand what they mean!"

"Why force them?" I asked, "Can't you just let them write in Tagalog?"

"No, Social Work licensing requires English competency. Can you teach them?"

When I was married, and my Broadway-loving husband overheard me on the phone, he would often cheerfully begin whistling a tune from *Oklahoma!* "I'm Just a Girl Who Can't Say No."

With the whistle in my head, the five girls and I agreed to meet where the wifi was free and there were snacks. Multicabs dropped us right in front of Mr. Donut. Every Tuesday at 4:00 PM, I bought them donuts and hot cocoa. We laughed a lot, but teaching adults English is tough and without a good foundation, it felt hopeless. Our attempts ranged from 1st-grade grammar to clinical terminology, and we failed at both. Ultimately, I gave up and made them a template of proper English, using blanks for them to fill in. They could enter birth dates, length of pregnancy, disability diagnosis, and other pertinent facts. Perhaps boring and redundant, but at least the report was understandable.

How invigorating to meet with young people who valued an older person's input. This was so different from my country of origin which discarded elders long before 65, deeming them of no future worth.

While the work was stimulating, I was also stymied at times. My U.S. experience didn't necessarily translate to this unfamiliar culture. As much as they couldn't imagine disregarding an elder's advice, I was ambivalent about advising them on specifics. My responses were always prefaced with, "This is what we would do in America, but that might not work here. Let's think it through." And, with that give and take in figuring out a solution, I learned as much as they did.

In those days, the Philippines did not have a three-year middle school education system. Children went from 6th grade straight to high school. So, they entered college between 14 and 16 years old. By the time I left, the curriculum changed to align with international standards, but these girls were young and dealt with some heavy issues. The university's Social Work curriculum required them to do fieldwork in their third year. They were full of idealistic questions, wanting to help everyone they could. Unusual to see such passion in the workers I knew; I loved that they were altruistic and devoted to their work.

One Tuesday evening, we ended our session, and I gathered my things into my backpack. But they sat there without talking, looking from one to the other like they had a secret, furtive yet hesitant.

"Is there something else?" I asked.

"We were wondering, *po*," said the one who often took charge, "if you might help us with one of our clients."

"Well, if I can, of course. What do you need?"

"He is a nice man but had polio as a child and cannot use his legs. He wants a wheelchair so he can get out of his house. Do you think you can help get him one?"

My thoughts flashed to such programs with Rotary International and other local NGOs like Bahatala that worked with the physically disabled. So, hearing that Broadway tune whistling in my head, I said that of course, I could.

"Where does this client of yours live?"

"Sicsican *po*, about 45 minutes away. We take the multicab."

"I would love to go with you. Do you think we could make a day of it and you could take me to several of your clients out there?"

I had only seen the 'Special' children at the school, didn't know what things were like 'in the field,' and wondered how families lived. I was naturally curious and thought since this was my calling, that I should know these things.

"Oh, Ma'am Debs, we would love that! You could help us so much, and we can help with the conversations," the five girls clapped their hands with delight.

"We will pack a lunch for us," said another.

"Be sure to bring water and wear good walking shoes," advised a third.

"And a *payong*, I mean umbrella, because it will likely rain," added the fourth, while the quietest girl just smiled.

"Okay. Is it far to walk?"

"We will walk back quite a way into Golden Valley and might walk even 10 km," the leader was back in charge.

"What time should I meet you?"

"We will start early, so we won't get too hot. Take the multicab north on the North Highway. Tell the driver to let you off at Golden Valley, he will know it. We will be there and greet you. We will have our breakfast there. Is 7:00 AM okay, *po*?"

Wow, these girls started early.

I arrived before 7:00 AM, but the five girls were already assembled at the side of the road and waiting for me. I didn't know Sicsican then and it felt far removed from Puerto Princesa. The girls had waited to get breakfast, so we strolled to the vendors' stalls along the highway. There were a lot of morning people at the *sari-sari* stores, buying groceries for their day, sipping coffee or Milo, and eating breakfast. Many ate *ulam* (an entree), which looked just like dinner, and always surprised me. Americans ate distinct foods for breakfast, lunch, and dinner, whilst Filipinos only had one rule: Rice must accompany every meal. In practice, *ulam* accompanied the rice.

We all got *ulam* and rice, bought some packaged cookies and snacks for later, and walked back to the unmarked entrance to Golden Valley. We were the only people walking on the path that morning; most people had left home long before and were on the highway headed to work in Puerto. The day was dry, although it had rained the night before and threatened to rain again. The road was very wide, and not paved, but nice and flat. You could have put 20 Filipinos or maybe 12 Americans across it, and we walked down the middle, the girls with their umbrellas opened, arm in arm, chattering.

Our first stop was on the main road, at a concrete and wood house on a lot with shade trees, the home of a teenage boy who was partially deaf. He had attended the deaf school in Aborlan about two hours away until they discovered he had partial hearing in his left ear. He no longer qualified for that residential facility, but regular schools would not take him either; he neither spoke nor heard well enough. As a youngster, he had been bullied for his hearing problems and was now of high school age. A bright boy, who had been taught to sign, he was returned to his family, who accepted their fate, but had nothing for him to do, only chores around the house.

The house was a good size and there were four younger children in the family. It had some yard space where they grew vegetables for the family's consumption. His mother was busy with his siblings and housework, and he often just sat around. There were no books in sight. When we arrived, the girls introduced me to his pleasant mother who chatted with them for a few minutes, with me just looking around. The mother took us to the back of the house, where the boy leaned against the concrete wall. The room reeked of urine, but no one seemed to notice. We spent quite a while first with the mother, and then when she left to do chores, with the boy.

Not only could he sign, but he could read lips in both Tagalog and English. My heart broke as he told his story with gestures through our question and answer.

"How long were you at the deaf school?"

"Three years."

"Can you understand what I am saying by reading my lips?"

"Yes." and he mimed that he could also hear a little out of his good ear.

"Do you miss classes?"

"Yes, so much," and he put his hand over his heart.

"Do you have friends here to talk with?"

"No, no friends."

"What do you do now?"

"I do chores and am the *kuya* for my brothers and sisters. But they are in school all day, so I don't do much."

My mother used to tell me to "count to ten" when I got angry, which I never did since it only made me madder. I had met so many people here who had no ambition or had nearly insurmountable life issues. Seeing this bright boy cast out of an institution that was helping him and depositing him in what amounted to an intellectual wasteland made me angry.

The girls brought the mother back into the room.

"Does he have people here that he is friends with?" I asked.

"No, he just helps me around the house."

"Is there anyone around who he can sign with?"

"Ha-ha, no one here knows that."

Uh oh, I felt my blood begin to boil.

"I'm trying to set up a group with mentors for deaf people. Some sort of a café for them all to meet and talk or sign. And for a teacher to work with them on their signing. If I can do this, could he come into town?"

"It's up to him," said the mother.

I banged my hand down on their table, hard, surprising all of us, and we all jumped.

"NO! It's up to YOU to encourage him. You are his mother, and he needs your support. He is wasting his life here, he is intelligent and has been taught a good education, but now he can't even communicate with anyone!"

Oh boy, crossing that line again big time, plus losing my temper. The boy watched us intently and his mother revised her statement and said that yes, he could come.

This was a hard day for me, and it had only begun.

We left the house and the girls looked at me as I sniffed away my tears of frustration while walking up the lane. After my outburst, we continued, stopping for a snack under the shade of two tall *ipil* trees. There was a cloudburst, and we waited under the umbrella trees until it subsided.

"Ma'am Debs, we will next take you to an easy one. Biboy, the boy is quite nice, although he cannot communicate. Biboy looks happy though." It was always the leader who told me technical information, the other four girls followed her mood and tone but said little.

"What is his diagnosis?" I asked.

"He had problems in the birth canal they say. He cannot walk or speak, and he can't control his muscles. His mother isn't there, but his *tita* cares for him. She also cooks for other families who pay her for food. But, she is home all day, usually in the kitchen. She is nice and will talk with us."

We walked up the path to the home and saw the boy in a stroller on the porch. He looked old, maybe seven, and his body leaned sideways in the stroller, his arms and legs spasming as drool slid down his face. Severe cerebral palsy had him and the stroller chained to the front door.

As we stepped closer, he became excited so that his head, arms, legs, and entire body contracted repeatedly and uncontrollably. He had a wide smile on his face.

"*Magandang umaga, Biboy,*" the girls greeted the boy. He smiled and his body jerked.

"*Tao po,*" we called. *Tita? Tao po!*"

Calling, "*Tao, po!*" pre-dates the Spanish conquerors, and is a loud announcement when visiting someone's home. The original phrase was "*Tao po ako, hindi aswang!*" which translates to "I am a human, not an *aswang!*" Old superstitions were common, ingrained, and accepted in the culture. Even accomplished professionals I met in the Philippines admitted to believing in *aswangs*, ghosts, and white ladies. Nowadays, the phrase just alerts someone that you are at the front of their house.

"Ah! Welcome, welcome! I don't have room for you all to come in, but maybe we can talk through the window as I stir this soup."

"*Siyempre* (of course) *po.*"

She explained that Biboy could not crawl or do anything for himself, so she chained him to the front door in the stroller so that he did not hurt himself. He seemed to like being out in the air, and he was out of her way so that she could cook to earn money for them.

This was a hard day for me.

Walking on through puddles of rain, our next stop was to visit Raymond, the polio survivor.

Raymond was about 40 years old and lived alone in a covered lean-to type of room made from bamboo. Open, and only about 18 inches above the dirt, heavy rains would have flooded it. There were no walls, the only privacy that he had came from something looking like curtains, strips of plastic, and burlap feed bags strung together. The front was exposed, and it felt like Raymond was on stage holding court, with us as his audience. He sat on some woven mats and was quite the talker while I was quite the listener, but it was so difficult because I lacked the language. My ears would hear the words and then try to translate them individually so that my understanding was always a few seconds behind my hearing. Since I could never keep up, I tried listening to the whole speech with contextual translation by the girls.

Swimming with his five siblings in the lake by his house when he was only six years old, Raymond was one of the three who contracted polio. One brother had died, and his sister lived nearby but had "brain problems." Raymond felt lucky. He was smart and loved to read books. Several popular titles sat on a table, English novels from who knows where. The problem was that his disease had progressed now, and he was going blind, he couldn't see to read anymore. He had muscular arms and got about by first sitting, then picking his legs up to cross and lock them. Large hands supported his body as he 'walked' with his arms since his legs were useless.

His late parents had been his caretakers, but for the last many years, his brother's wife assumed that role. Until she had five children to care for. They built the room on stilts for Raymond, but their house was a couple of blocks away, and she had to go back and forth to tend to him and bring him food. Exhausted and panicky when looking at her future, she took action.

One day the previous year, she asked a neighbor to stay with her children and Raymond. Spending money they didn't have, she took a multicab into the city to plead with the city government. Neighbors had told her the Department of Social Welfare could help.

She entered the building near the sports complex and asked the receptionist, "Please, may I see Ma'am Angara?" She was instructed to take a seat. After 20 minutes, she went back to the desk and asked again.

"Ma'am Angara is not available *po*. The Deputy Director, Ma'am Lopez has an assistant who will talk with you. Go down the hall and you will see the sign CSWD. Go in that office and ask for Maria."

So, she did. But Maria had no answer for her when she explained the situation. "Wait *lang po*. I will ask Roddy to speak with you."

So, she went to Roddy, having no idea who he was. But Roddy did not have an answer and sent her back to Ma'am Angara's secretary, where she again sat and waited.

She had now been several hours at the DSWD, and as it neared 5:00 PM, Ma'am Angara herself agreed to meet her.

"Hello *po*, Ma'am Angara. Thank you for seeing me, *po*. I need help for my brother-in-law. He has polio and has no caretaker but me. I have five children and cannot care for him as well. I have tried for the last six years to do his laundry and fix his meals. As the years have passed, his condition has become worse and worse. He cannot leave his *bahay* (house) now and is almost blind. I heard that CSWD is who can help my family and that there are programs for us. What can we do Ma'am?"

"I'm so sorry you came so late about Raymond, *po*. It is closing time now and I need to go to church. Please come back in the morning, and we can talk about this, although I don't think we have money to give you. I will pray for you tonight."

We listened to her detailed story, dismayed when she said that Ma'am Angara, the head of CSWD told her simply that the office was closing. She showed her out the back door telling her to come back the following morning and wished her a good evening.

The girls and I were appalled to think that the Social Welfare people shuffled her from the front door through four representatives and finally to the head of the department, who cast her aside. She said that was the last time she tried to get anyone in the government to help them and that she couldn't afford to go back. I asked if she at least had gotten the PWD

(Person With Disability) card that entitled them to a 20% discount on food, transportation, and medication. "No," she said, "what is that?"

All our faces showed shock and embarrassment that no one had even offered her that minimal card. In practice, the card wasn't much help, since, when you had no money, a 20% discount on anything didn't matter much. Her unbelievable story was an introduction to how many provincial government agencies functioned. Not only slowly and ineptly, but without real concern for the human being, whom they supposedly served. No one had even thought to educate her on what was available during the five hours she was at the agency.

"Is there anything we can do for you, Raymond?" the girls asked.

"Yes! I need a wheelchair. That's what I want, so I can get out of here. If I had a wheelchair, I could visit people."

Looking around, I saw the morning rain still lingered in little puddles everywhere. We had slipped in the mud walking from the road up to Raymond's house. There was no way Raymond could navigate a wheelchair through this marshy place, even with assistance. I looked at the girls, and they looked back into my eyes. Taking the Filipino way out, I said,

"We will try to get you a wheelchair, Raymond." *Bahala na.*

This was a hard day for me.

The fourth client we visited was a girl of about 10 who lived with a lot of extended family members in a family compound. We had walked about three miles at this point and were back on larger farm acreage. Everyone was jovial as we approached, with several dirty and happy small children, probably cousins, playing on the swings in the yard. The adults offered us snacks, but we politely refused, and I started my questions to understand the issues. The mother interrupted.

"It's my fault," said the mother. I craved shells when I was pregnant."

My face was as blank as my host father's when I asked questions that were incomprehensible to him. Maybe my ears were lagging again, all-day Tagalog was taxing for me.

"*Pasensya? Paki ulit, po.*" (I'm sorry? Please repeat ma'am).

"I craved shells and her head is wrong. She was born okay, but no one was home, she came out fast and the *hilot* (midwife) helped me with the birth. When she was only a few months old, my husband was on the swing and dropped her on her head. We took her to the doctor at Adventist Hospital. He injected her brain with something and since then she hasn't been right."

Her explanation didn't do much to clear things up for me.

"I'm sorry, what did he inject her with?"

"Something that hurt her brain, I don't know what. He was a bad doctor."

I suspected that the girl had been dehydrated and the doctor hydrated her with an IV, but I couldn't know.

"And then what happened?"

"She had times when her eyes would roll back and all you could see was white. And she would shake and shake. She couldn't talk and sometimes she had foam and saliva coming out of her mouth. We were so afraid and didn't know what to do. We took her to the *albularyo* (faith healer/witch doctor), and another *kwak kwak*, but he couldn't help either."

"Did you go back to the hospital?"

"No. They didn't help the first time and it cost a lot of money."

"Did this happen to her only once? Where she shook like that?"

"No, it happened more and more and got worse and worse. The shaking would last a long time. It was horrible to watch. She stopped walking or talking. She is no trouble now, but she is getting heavy for *Tatay* (Father) to carry. Sometimes for hours she will sit and look at you. She just sits in her chair and smiles."

Like she was doing now, pleasant, but vacant. She could sit in a chair, but her balance was off.

Where was a real doctor when you needed one? This sounded like *grand mal* epilepsy to me. Without intervention, symptoms got worse, the convulsions got stronger, and lasted longer. The result was permanent neurological impairment. If only they knew that an inexpensive pill could control the seizures. The miracle drug, phenobarbital, had been used since the early 1900s, but neither it nor anything else could undo the damage.

This was a hard day for me.

The girls and I exchanged cheerful goodbyes with the family and continued deeper into Golden Valley.

On the long walk, we heard more stories of poverty, malnutrition, ignorance, superstitions...and acceptance of one's lot in life. One boy had severe cerebral malaria as a toddler and almost died. He wasn't able to do much now, and we told his guilty father that it wasn't his fault. Yet, the father insisted that if he had gotten to the hospital sooner, things would not have turned out this way. In Manila, maybe, but the medical care on Palawan was so poor that the outcome would likely have been the same. At that time, Palawan lacked knowledge and had neither adequate facilities nor a consistent supply of medications needed for treatment. Most people with problems needing immediate attention were on their own, perhaps why you heard *bahala na* so much.

The last client we saw that day was back at the highway, we had done a 10-mile loop. Almost dark, it was nearing 6:00 PM, over ten hours since we began. The clouds were threatening rain, but we were hot, sweaty, and dirty from our long walk and wished for a downpour. This last house had no electricity and no water, and the woman lived alone. Another polio victim, this was the older sister of Raymond, who swam with him that same fateful day. Her body was strong enough, but as Raymond had indicated, she had mental problems, although they weren't obvious at first.

"*Magandang hapon, po,*" we greeted her in the late afternoon.

It was fading into dusk as we stood on the steps leading to her shack.

"*Magandang hapon,*" she responded without any energy or curiosity.

"Raymond told us we could come to visit you. He sends his regards to you."

"Ah, Raymond. Yes, he is my brother."

"Sister, this is Ma'am Debs, she is interested in you."

So, it was my time to speak.

"*Mabuhay po.* Nice to meet you. Raymond told me that you swam with him that day when he was six. How old were you po?"

"Raymond is one year younger than me, so if he told you he was six, I would have been seven."

"How old are you now, po?"

193

"Oh, I'm not sure. Whatever age Raymond said he was and add my one year. That's how old I would be now."

"How long have you lived here *po*?"

"Oh, since I was a bride; my husband built it."

Her house was about six feet deep and fifteen feet long and, without electricity, was so dark we could hardly see each other. Sister also was going blind, so it didn't seem to bother her as she began to tell her story.

There had been a baby; she'd wanted a family, but her husband didn't want their firstborn. He found an orphanage up the hill, somewhere, she didn't know where, that paid him money for the infant. That money kept the two of them for some time, but eventually, she got pregnant again. Her husband wanted this child as much as the first, and again took it from her and sold it to the orphanage. But this time, he didn't return. From then on, she had no one and lived alone.

I knew and had worked with two orphanages on Palawan and her story just sounded wrong to me. The orphanages were reputable, and I couldn't believe they would pay to take a child. Perhaps they agreed to take the baby if the parents were going to abandon it? She didn't have much more to say than that, assured us she needed nothing, and thanked us for stopping by.

Her doorstep was two feet from the highway, and we caught the multicab home right there. It stopped about 15 minutes later at the turn for the new *palengke* (market) and I got off the multicab and hailed a tricycle home.

This was a hard day for me.

We saw eight families in ten hours and walked 20 km. Exhausted in heart, mind, and body, I felt overwhelmed. I had been on this island only a few months and was ill-equipped to deal with the issues I had seen. The Golden Valley experience will never leave me.

The best news? Several months later I learned that the deaf teenager who watched me lecture his mother had taken action. I don't know what spurred him on, but he got himself to the National High School in town and registered for classes. That was one of the greatest rewards of my life on Palawan, learning that someone had taken responsibility for his own life.

The girls gained confidence in me and later that month asked me another question.

"Ma'am Debs? We wondered if we might ask for your advice *po.* "

"Of course! What do you need?"

"*Po,* last night a young woman with mental retardation was raped in our *barangay,* and we don't know what to do *po.* "

"Oh my gosh! You need to immediately report it to the *barangay* captain. That is a crime!"

"Yes, *po,* we did that *po.* "

"What? You reported it to the *barangay* captain? What did he say?"

"Yes, *po.* He said, 'Well, what do you expect?' We didn't know what to do next, *po,* so we came to you."

My face flushed and my heart pounded. But I had to put my outrage aside and *think* about what to do next. In the U.S., I would report the incident to the police along with the incriminating fact that the official had not even responded to the crime. However, I was not in California and had to check my prejudices to think this through.

"Let me talk to the social worker at school. She will know what to do."

"Thank you so much, Ma'am Debs. We are just so upset. The woman didn't deserve that, but she just doesn't know things. She wanders the streets and has no one to look after her. *Kawawa babae siya talaga (she really is a pitiful woman).* And we are afraid this will happen again, *po.* Thank you *po* Ma'am Debs."

The sister of Pastor's wife was a veteran social worker, and I knew she would know about this incident and could advise me. She had worked at the CSWD for two decades and would understand both the culture and the law, and what should be done. As I relayed the girls' story, it was obvious she was well aware.

"Good morning po. The social work interns from the school asked me to help them with an issue. I wondered if I could ask you for some advice."

"Of course. Please, sit down, and let's talk. What did they need to know? They can come to me and ask questions; they know that, right?"

"Ah, they took me to visit some of their clients last week. Maybe they just got comfortable asking me questions because of that. I am sure that they know they can come and discuss anything with you."

That seemed to mollify her.

"Oh, good. Well, what is the concern?"

"They told me that last night a woman in this *barangay* was raped and didn't understand what happened to her. They said she had low intelligence. I don't know the woman, so couldn't say much, or really help them".

"Yes, I am aware. The woman you are referring to has the mind of a five-year-old. Her mother has died and her father drinks. She roams the streets most of the day and everyone knows her. The *barangay* captain texted me early yesterday morning. By then, she was in the clinic and had been taken care of. So, you can let the girls know that all is fine and that she is okay."

"They were also concerned that the *barangay* captain didn't take any action against the man who raped her. They asked for my suggestions, and I didn't know how things were handled here. I'm so glad that you are involved. The girls didn't know that you had spoken with the *barangay* captain. So, then, the man will be arrested?"

She looked at me and laughed. "This isn't the first time that this has happened. She doesn't seem to mind, and when men drink, well..."

I gaped at her.

My agitated recounting of the story was as telling of my values as her final response was of hers: "The woman is retarded, what do you expect?"

Saying "Yes" to everything kept me busy day and night. I found that if one project felt *sayang*, I could balance it with one of my other undertakings. This was a valuable life lesson for someone who seemed to get over-involved and put all her eggs in one basket. I had also recovered my confidence rather than walking on eggshells. The constant criticism from the school and my host family wore me down. Getting outside of that insular relationship and helping organize the Chamber and Special Olympics reminded me of who I was. It also reminded me of my past. I was sure they still demeaned me, but I didn't have to be there to watch. Channeling my inner Stevie Wonder, I kept on truckin'.

"...Gonna keep on trying until I reach my highest ground
No one's gonna bring me down
Till I reach my highest ground."

RAYMOND'S HOUSE

THE 10 MILE WALK IN GOLDEN VALLEY

BIBOY CHAINED TO HIS STROLLER

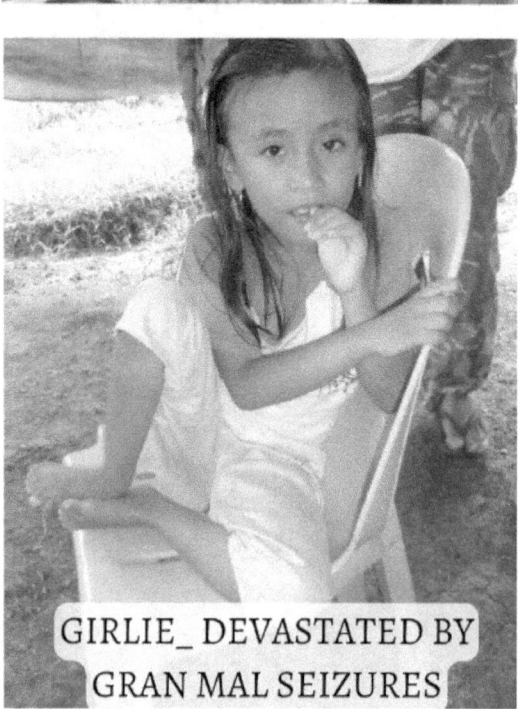

GIRLIE_ DEVASTATED BY GRAN MAL SEIZURES

THE PATH TO RAYMOND'S

Chapter 12

BOUNTIFUL UPS AND DOWNS

Ang buhay ay parang gulong, minsang nasa ibabaw, minsang nasa
ilalim.
Life is like a wheel: Sometimes you're up, and sometimes you're
down.
A Filipino proverb meaning, 'Just be accepting of the ups and downs of life.'

Peace	
Umakyat ng bundok, magpahinga sa lambak, mag-surf sa mga alon	Climb the mountain, rest in the valley, surf the waves
Mabuhay sa panibagong araw na may mas malinaw na mga mata	Live another day with clearer eyes
Umiiyak pa rin ang mga mata	Still crying eyes
Huminga.	Breathe

BEFORE I MOVED INTO MY NEW ABODE IN BOUNTIFUL, I asked Mark Antony if he could paint the walls which were dingy. He was back in Singapore, but texted his agreement, saying his brother would paint. On my move-in day, I arrived to find he had indeed painted, vibrant turquoise and teal walls...at least in the middle. Either he didn't have a ladder or ran out of paint, but the paint stopped in erratic margins about two feet below the ceiling and a foot above the floor. Since he was long gone, and paint was expensive, I knew that the brothers considered the job done. Rummaging through the trash, I found the almost-dry paint cans. After adding water, I eked out enough paint to feather the color to cover the wall. It looked like computer art after you clicked the "gradient" option.

Blue greens were the theme, there were two bedrooms and a living room with pretty stained-glass windows, also in turquoise and teal. The solder was of such low quality that I could easily have shoved the glass inward. It was no wonder that the Peace Corps hesitated for me to live there. The yard was a concrete-block walled disaster, with sharp shards of glass cemented on the top reminiscent of Nairobi 'security spikes.' It was a short walk to the ocean, and coral outcroppings littered the yard, adding to the dirt, weeds, and stumps. Stubbed, bloody toes were common from those sharp old corals when I hung my laundry out to dry.

Landscaping was tough trying to pull out the weeds between the coral outcroppings. Tools were expensive and the sun ferocious. With the rains, the ground softened, and I was able to pull out a couple of the dead bushes and level the earth; it took me hours. The man across the road watched me, laughing at my Western shovel and shears. Without invitation or comment, he brandished his *bolo* (machete) and crossed the street. He made quick work of hacking out my dead bushes. A small herd of children ran back and forth laughing in the weekend's early morning. Sweat rolled down my back as I thanked him profusely.

As the only white person near Bountiful, people stared at me. Every morning I walked two long blocks to the public tricycle stand. Sharp rocks tripped me, and in the rain, I slip-slid through the mud on the unpaved road. The drivers, bunched together waiting for passengers, watched me make my way toward them without any expression. They waited for their trikes to fill up under the shade of the acacia trees. Often you had to wait for a half-hour or more since our area wasn't very populated. Every morning the drivers huddled together waiting for their fares, and I could hear them. "Oh, here she comes. The big one. Maybe we should charge her double, eh?" cackling uproariously at their daily joke.

After the fifth time, I said in Tagalog, "You are so rude. I can understand you!" And, no, they didn't stop.

On the other hand, four to six Filipinos could cram onto one small tricycle. If four couldn't fit because of my bulk, I did pay extra because it seemed fair. One horribly stormy day, I paid two pesos more because it was rainy, and I was thankful to get a ride. The other three occupants glared at me and accused me of driving up prices.... you couldn't win it seemed.

One morning while I was still in bed, I heard a thud and loud mewling. Walking into the yard, I found that someone had tossed a tiny kitten over my glass-shard wall. Allergic to cats, I still loved him immediately and thought he was heaven-sent. Lucky that he wasn't in a sack, drowning at the bottom of the river, he arrived bruised. Black and white with a smudged white nose, he was an indoor cat from the moment I found him. The kitten followed me around the house and onto my keyboard – he could lay in a teacup he was so little. A week later I found him playing with an enormous mole cricket that was flying about. A mole cricket is the ugliest bug I've ever seen and was nearly as big as the kitten. The bug looked on its last legs and the kitten swatted at it. He munched on it before I could grab it away...yuck.

I had arranged for organic gardening training for the teachers the following week. The site was two hours away, so I had to take the kitten with me. At the training center, teachers from the school would learn how to set up organic gardening. Then they could sell their crops to restaurants in town so the school could earn money.

This was one of my many attempts at helping them fund the school. Assembling beads from rolled, then shellacked paper was one of my first projects. Designer necklaces, bracelets, and earrings made from these beads were pretty and everyone loved them. Peace Corps volunteers in other provinces had evolved this into a catalog business that not only made their NGO money but advertised their cause. It was the perfect idea to get in on the tourism trade on Palawan. But explaining how to make money from selling them was more difficult.

"We can give these to people who come to see the school," said Pastor.

"Umm, not many people come here."

"Well, we can give them to our sponsors."

"Another thing we could do is to ask a hotel to sell them. I know a couple of hotels who might do that for us," I said. "That way we could make some money for supplies. I know that the tourism office might do it, tourists would love to buy from the students," I enthused.

"Ha! Our students could never do this. Maybe we can teach the parents."

Sigh.

It was a perfect activity for parents to do since they had to wait three hours for their children to finish school. Sitting on the back benches in the common area, they learned to make the beads. Beads were made from paper torn from magazines, wrapping paper, and newspaper. Such printed paper was common in Western society, but not on Palawan which did not have a printed newspaper at the time, and I never saw a magazine there. Finding the paper was the first step. The Peace Corps had taught volunteers this craft as a way to help our organizations fund themselves. I taught them the simple process, but my technique was clumsy with my big hands. Most of the women had tiny hands and their paper rolling was beautiful and creative. Pastor liked the activity and made some elegant pieces. We 'shellacked' individual beads with glue, dried them, and put them in a big plastic jar that had once held Skittles.

The First Week:

"Ma'am Debs, look how many we have now! When can we string them?"

"Well, how many do we need for a necklace? As soon as you have enough for each person to string, we can begin."

"We have enough to make three. Let's start now!"

"Okay, where is the fishing line? Ah, yes, pick the beads that you think go together best and string them, then tie off the end. Look, Pastor already finished one!"

"Ooh, they are beautiful!"

"Ma'am Debs, do you think you can ask the Tourism Department to sell these? We could make so much money."

"Wow, Ma'am Debs, imagine if we gave each tourist a necklace as they got off the plane in Puerto!"

"Hah! Think of it! There are six planes a day *na*, we could be rich!"

"Let's concentrate on making enough necklaces and earrings to sell here. But yes, I can go to the Tourism office and try to arrange something. Ma'am Angie would help, I'm sure; she works with the Tourism office now. Just think how many beads we would need for even one plane a day, I'm not sure we could make that many."

"We can Ma'am Debs!"

The Second Week:

"Good morning, Ma'am Debs! We want to sell them for 150 pesos each."

"Umm, I'm glad you are thinking of how to sell them. How did you decide the price?"

"We asked our *tita* - she has a necklace someone gave her. She liked this and said she might pay 150 for it."

"That's good to know. Some people think about how to price what they sell by adding up how much it costs to make."

"But it doesn't cost us anything to make."

"Well, like how much we paid for the glue and the fishing wire, I know the paper was free. Then they think about how much time they spent making it."

"What do you mean? The glue goes a long way and we can find fishing wire from the fishermen. We are waiting for our children, so our time doesn't matter. We would make 150 on each necklace - that seems good, *di ba* (right?)?"

"Well, for me, we should think through how to price them. They can't cost too much or no one will buy them, but if you price them too low, you will be losing money."

Blank stares...

"I have an idea to show you what I mean. Let's take a field trip to Puerto. I will pay the *multicab* (public transport van) fee so we all can go. I saw a display of jewelry at the Hibiscus Inn. They had all kinds of jewelry, some round shells and *capiz* (transparent oyster shell), but they didn't have anything like we have done. Maybe they can explain how they price things."

"Oh, my *tita* works there in the resto. A lot of tourists stay there and their pizza is *sarap* (delicious). A lot of locals go there too."

I bet Hibiscus would help us figure out how much our jewelry should cost. Maybe they would buy some from us. What do you think, will you go with me?"

"Okay, Ma'am Debs. Let's do that po."

The Third Week
"Good morning, Ma'am Debs.
"Good morning - where is the jar full of beads?"
"Oh, we made some necklaces and gave them as a thank you to the nuns who visited, and to our *tita* for helping us."
"What! I thought those were for the school to make money?"
"Oh, we can make more."
"But almost half of the jar is gone."
"Don't worry *po*, Ma'am Debs."

The Fourth Week
"Good morning, Ma'am Debs."
"Good Morning, What's going on this morning?"
"Oh - We ran out of paper and are taking a break."

We never went to look at the display at the Hibiscus Inn.
We never made more paper beads.
Need I say, another *sayang*?

After that failure, I figured that it was better to just find them money. One day, I heard a contest advertised on the radio. Jollibee is the McDonald's of the Philippines and everyone I knew loved their hot dogs and burgers. Jollibee had a foundation, and that year started an annual contest. They wanted to recognize family values. This was the first year that they advertised the contest, so most people hadn't heard of it, and I thought I might have a chance. Five organizations throughout the country would be awarded prizes. Each was a family or an organization that epitomized family values and served its community. Nominations had to be submitted by an outsider and I certainly qualified for that.

Applying online was easy and I didn't tell anyone since it was such a long shot. The big award was 300,000 pesos cash ($7,000 which was a huge amount) and 10,000 pesos of Jollibee hamburgers. For all my misgivings of their methods, I thought Pastor and his wife provided a remarkable service to the community. Their endeavors were altruistic. My submission show-cased them with all the details I'd gathered from writing their documents for NGO certification. I was able to cite many examples of the children they had helped and sent photos of our outreach efforts. So, I applied online and forgot about it.

"Ma'am Debs, do you know anything about this?" said Pastor's wife one morning. "I got a message from Manila today from someone at Jollibee. They said we had won a prize and spoke your name. I am supposed to call them back."

"Oh my gosh! We won?" And I had to explain what I had done.

They didn't win the top five but got sixth place in the entire country. That translated to $500 cash, plus 5,000 pesos of Jolibee coupons, and an interview with national media.

We talked about the gift certificates and media and how they could use the prizes. With my marketing head, I said we could use it to market our-selves. We could have a big Open House for the community to understand what we did.

I was out of town for the media visit. They used their prize to give free meals to people in their church and their own family. Intellectually, I understood that this was a treat for people who could not afford Jollibee burgers. But it was morally depressing to me.

So, this organic farming training was another of my attempts to help them fund themselves. This time by growing specialty crops to sell to local restaurants. The Shell agricultural farm was a bucolic setting around a lake stocked with tilapia. Located two hours outside of Puerto in Aborlan, it was a perfect setting for me to enjoy with my kitten.

Marginalized youth competed nationally for the chance to come to one of Shell's training farms to learn organic farming. Pilipinas Shell Foundation helped out-of-school youth, indigenous youth, and indigent high school graduates learn how to farm. Shell set them up with a personal plot and brought in experts to teach the students horticulture and budgeting, supporting them for weeks or months. The price? To commit to return to their home province and farm, and to spread their knowledge. Pay it forward at its finest.

Marvi, the head of Pilipinas Shell Foundation, had kindly funded three days for our teachers and parents to stay at the farm. Shell fed and housed us, and even flew in agricultural instructors from Bicol to teach us. Shell U.S. was my employer for 10 years and I always found their training excellent. The one on Palawan was one of the best I ever attended.

I had convinced Pastor to meet with Marvi the month before. Both he and I sat with our mouths open when she offered us this all-expenses-paid opportunity. We couldn't stop smiling and babbling after our meeting with her. Ecstatic that she did this for the school, I was perplexed as to why Pastor decided not to attend at the last moment. Maybe, like my request of the health officer at the Christmas party, there was *utang* involved? Maybe it was because as head of the school he didn't want anything to appear that someone knew more than he did? Who knew? I never understood those cultural nuances. In any case, he didn't come to the training but did attend the fiesta celebration our last night.

The training was offered to parents, teachers, and church members. It was an all-expenses-paid training and I thought would "sell out." *Sayang* again. Marvi had promised us 15 spots, and after Pastor decided not to attend, we only used half. The extra seven slots went to the local deaf school in Aborlan, including their signing translator.

They were the most excited of all of us. They communicated with expressive eyes, fast sign language, and gestures. But they couldn't hear their unintentional vocalizations, grunts, moans and sighs that were obvious to us who could hear. The husband of one of our teachers kept making loud and obnoxious fun of them. He performed as if on stage, mimicking their noises like a slapstick comedy. The fact that our school served people with disabilities made me furious at his behavior and I finally said something to the leader of our school.

"How can he represent our school that deals with students with disabilities? He is an embarrassment!"

"Yes, I understand, Ma'am Debs. Do you want me to say something?"

"Yes, more than that, I want him to apologize. But I don't even know him, can you talk with him?"

"Yes, I will go discuss this with him."

I watched closely as they talked and was likely glaring at them the whole time. The man, baffled at what I thought he had done wrong, kept darting glances at me. He couldn't figure out why he should apologize, so he didn't.

I apologized to the deaf attendees after class and they looked just as confused as the chastised man.

"Oh, that's just how people treat us. Thank you for your compassion, but please don't worry about it."

Mole crickets might be toxic to cats, or at least kittens, or maybe the mole cricket my kitten ate was diseased. There was no vet for miles around and I had no transportation to get back to the vet in Puerto. My little cat stopped eating and on the third day, he died, with me sobbing over him, feeling like a murderer. The same man laughed out loud at my tears, pointing and mocking me, encouraging others to laugh as well. Allowing for the different ethos of our cultures, I still despised him. We drove home on the bus Marvi provided, in silence.

The following weekend, five of us who had attended the training, along with Pastor and his wife, cleared a sizable area at the school. We were excited about starting a profitable garden for students, families, teachers, and the school. All of us chatted as we worked several hours in the hot sun, burning piles of overgrowth and raking the soil. We talked about how we could eat the vegetables as well as sell them to restaurants and make money to fund projects. Students would learn how to farm and have a livelihood. Which crops would be best? What should we name the garden? So much fun and excitement that day.

That was as far as we got. *Ningas kugon* struck, that flash of interest, lots of personal sweat, a large outlay of effort and cash from a benefactor. All of which died, as they say, on the vine.

Sayang again.

So many opportunities yielded no funding. Most of these ventures required planning and work. People seemed to prefer, and respond to, ways that seemed opportunistic and underhanded.

Once, Special Olympics hosted a free screening by speech pathologist interns from UP Diliman's speech communication school in Manila. Fourteen graduate students and their professor arrived and were set up at the city coliseum. We sent flyers to the *barangays* inviting anyone willing to travel to come to a free speech and hearing screening by professionals.

And they came. It was overwhelming to see families we'd never met and daunting to think that our small group on Palawan could deal with such severe maladies of these 200 families. While Angie and I were discussing what we could do, the UP professor came to us, red-faced and voice shaking.

"Who are those people over there?" she spluttered.

"What? Who? What is wrong, '*miga*?"

"We went to great lengths to make this a FREE clinic!"

"Yes, of course, '*miga* - that is what we are doing."

"No, you aren't! There is a long table set up where people are registering and having to pay 300 pesos to come in."

Needless to say, Angie and I were shocked and walked with the woman to this 'registration' table, where we beheld Pastor, smiling as women from the church took "donations."

Bad things happen if one confronts another outright in this culture, so Angie smiled at the UP professor and said softly that she would handle it. She guided Pastor to a side area, away from others.

"Pastor, these interns came to help those who couldn't pay. UP paid for everything. All of our flyers said this was a free clinic. We cannot charge people."

Ever smooth came his reply.

"Oh, yes, we knew that. We were just collecting donations to give her a thank you present." A laugh-out-loud response.

The UP professor knew exactly what was going on and the money was returned to families who could barely afford the cost of transportation.

Another time, Pastor and his brother were chatting about the bird-egg blue multicab that picked up the children.

"We can't afford a new vehicle," said Pastor, "and it can't be fixed. What will we do?"

"But, can't the mechanic at Petron fix it? He always has before," said the brother.

"No, he said he has done as much as he could for many months now. He said there isn't enough money to make it safe," Pastor laughed.

"I think we should just keep using it."

"Well, I was thinking that we can put a coat of paint on it and make it look nice. Then we could sell it and make some money."

"Oh, that's a better idea. Then we can at least buy a new trike," said the brother.

As I overheard this, my brain was screaming, "But, you can't! How can you sell something that you know is unsafe?"

My ethics and his were so different.

They sold the newly dark blue multicab.

I grappled with ethics from the first week I worked there when I asked lots of questions to get to know everyone.

"Did you attend school here in Puerto?" I asked Pastor one early morning.

"Oh, I got my degree from the Visayas, not here in Puerto. I finished with a degree in Mathematics."

"Wow, that's impressive. And, your wife?"

"Yes, she did go to school here at Palawan State University. She got a degree in Business, but had to take statistics," he snickered.

"Why are you laughing?"

"Well, she has a hard time with Math, and we knew she would fail. So, I had to take the final exam for her. Luckily, no one knew me. Of course, I had to answer several questions wrong, or they would have known it wasn't her."

Again, I was dumbfounded, my face blank with shock. How could this man be a minister?

Outfitting my house in Bountiful and living a routine was a fun and educational outlet for me. I acquired a blender, a small refrigerator, and a fan. A fan was essential for sleeping. So was a cushion for the hard wooden bed. Most people I knew slept on cots or mats, except the wealthy who could afford fabric mattresses and air conditioning. Unattainable for a Peace Corps volunteer.

Electricity cost on Palawan was the highest in the Philippines at the time, and the most unreliable. Residents joked that the electric company got lots of practice for global celebrations; we experienced the annual Earth Hour blackout on a weekly basis.

With year-round heat and humidity and the open structure of most homes, fungus grew overnight. So, while I craved a soft, thick mattress, it was not only expensive, it made no sense. Thus, I went to town to a small shop that claimed they 'manufactured' foam mattresses.

"Good morning *po. Kailangan ang mattress po, pero kaunti lang pera - Magkano po?*" (I need a mattress but have only a little money. How much do they cost?)

"Well, the price of the mattress depends on several things Ma'am."

"I'm sorry, this is the first time that I buy a mattress. Can you explain to me please how it works?" This is how I spoke Tagalog, poorly, even translated into English.

Gesturing so that I would understand her Tagalog, she said, "Come to the back of the shop *po* and I will show you. My husband buys the polyurethane foam from Manila. It ships in slabs that we cut to fit the size of your bed. See here? You can see that each slab is a different thickness. The one-inch is the least expensive and the six-inch is the best quality po."

"And how much is the difference in price?"

"For what size bed *po*?"

"The bed is only for one person, the size of a cot."

"For one-inch it would be 1,000 pesos ($20) only, but for six-inche it would be 6,000 po.

"Gosh, that's a lot of money and it isn't even my bedframe. But I think I would need at least two inches, *di ba*?" as I estimated with my first finger and thumb. "Can I feel how stiff the foam is?"

"Yes, po. They are all the same stiffness, see here." She handed me a small piece and I easily compressed it.

"I think I need at least three-inch foam. And the covering?"

"Yes, po, the covering is included in the cost. We do not charge extra for that. Come over here to the *tela,* the material that you can choose. My mother will sew it into a covering for your mattress."

We took three steps to a space where five bolts of bright material were standing upright. Bright flowers and geometrics were wrapped in plastic to keep the bolts clean.

"Ooh, I like the big red and blue hibiscus flowers, they will make me smile."

"*Opo*, the *gumamela*. We should have that ready in three days since we already have orders today."

Plastic was expensive on Palawan, while labor was cheap. A single-bed-size foam pad, three inches thick, and its loud red and blue hibiscus print cover cost me $60. My bones still bruised on the hardwood frame when I rolled over.

I usually slept in a sarong with a sheet over me to not feel the ants, cockroaches, and spiders crawl on me. It was so hot, even at night, that I ran the table fan (which also helped discourage the flying bugs from taking a rest on me). It became normal to wake up in the middle of the night sweaty and gasping for air during a power outage, sweaty and wondering what had landed on me in the dark.

Laundry was fun in Bountiful. I could do most of it in the spacious, clean, sea-green tiled bathroom that had a screened window vent. While I took my shower, I washed the clothes in one bucket, rinsed them in another, and piled them into a large plastic basket with handles. After finishing my shower, I dried myself, put on a sarong and then toddled off with the basket to hang the clothes outside. There were wires strung across the yard where the clothes dried. Rains were frequent, yet erratic so that you were always running in and out to gather almost-dry clothes before a downpour re-wet them.

There were no frogs in the shower, nor lizards or scorpions in the rooms. Bountiful was decidedly a leg up from my previous abode. The concrete construction and almost-closing windows helped reduce my asthma and bug bites.

The furnishings were also a step up with an antique carved wooden armoire in which to hang some clothes. Lovely, but different from rattan in breathability. I discovered after a week's conference in Manila what that meant. The armoire was effective in sealing out bugs but sealed in moisture. My return revealed furry mold on every piece of clothing in the armoire. It turned blacks to gray and whites to black, encasing even my leather sandals.

There was a small square window in the inside (yahoo!) kitchen above the sink. It faced west and framed the incredible cloud formations that transfixed me. I must have taken 100 photos of clouds framed in that square of glass. I filmed heavy storms with lightning flashes, iridescent sunsets, and the reflected glow of sunrises. The clouds were diverse in form and meaning. Bright white cumulus clouds looked like enormous dense cotton balls piled miles high against the bright blue sky. Wispy, high-altitude cirrus, backlit by the afternoon sun warmed my smile. And the gigantic cumulonimbus, looking like a hydrogen bomb, foretold typhoons. The clouds of the Philippines are one of my top 10 memories.

My fondest memories of Palawan are of its bountiful and wild nature. The monitor lizards that nested in my yard, the brilliant rainforest malkohas, inquisitive coucals, and tiny sunbirds and pittas. The dark shadows of owls flying overhead on brownout nights calling back and forth to each other with expressive guttural noises, sounding nothing like the "Hoo-hoo" of children's books. And my favorite ocean explorations, swimming with octopuses and barracuda, and the ultimate, whale shark, which prompted me to get my first tattoo on my 60th birthday.

Summer saw the move to Bountiful, and in October I experienced the fallout from my conflict at the school. Recalled to Manila, I was to explain my conduct to my manager, the sector director, the country director, and her deputy at a formal proceeding. The purposeful humiliation was like nothing I had ever experienced in all my years at Fortune 500 companies.

"Come in Debra," said the country director, and I walked into her commodious office, where the three others were already seated. I headed for the empty chair. It felt like war.

"We wanted to discuss what happened with you to see what should be done," said Arnel, the sector director. His facial muscles barely moved, and his brown eyes were a wall. This was the man who had finally come to Palawan and smoothed things over.

Details were discussed, and the two men quizzed me, looking very serious while they did so. As they continued in soft and unctuous tones, it was obvious they placed all the blame on me. I replied that I had asked for help in multiple emails, with no response. They criticized my paying the Peace Corps Response expert to come to help the previous year. They criticized that I was trying to improve things. They wanted me to just be helpful and promote events.

The 35-year-old deputy director leaned back in his leather chair and smiled. "The Peace Corps' mission is to promote peace and harmony. It doesn't matter what you do professionally or even if you complete projects, that's not the point."

"Then I guess I joined the wrong organization," I responded.

"Perhaps you were more suited to the Peace Corps Response program."

"Perhaps so, but I'm not in that program. How do I proceed now? I need someone to help me, to give me some guidance on what I did wrong and how to move forward."

Again, the Philippines' deputy director lit up with his smooth smile and said, "No, that's for you to figure out."

I said, "I'm a 60-year-old volunteer with years of experience in the U.S. I know how Special Education and Business work and if I get some support, I can help people. Can't someone help me understand how to translate what I know into a way people will be able to use? Or tell me how something I would normally do might not have the effect I want due to culture? Isn't that what a manager is to help with?"

The serene smile again had me thinking he would make a good priest and made me want to slap him. "Each volunteer finds his way forward."

I was beyond frustrated and near tears.

At this point, the only other non-Filipino in the room spoke up. The country director had been doing paperwork at her desk, and I didn't think was even paying attention. She said, "Okay, I've heard enough. Debra will be fine returning to her site. Thank you all for coming."

And that was that. I returned to Palawan.

A month later in late November, the Peace Corps brought all volunteers to training in Manila. I had a decision to make: to stay at the school on Palawan or move to another assignment, like on another island. That was the ultimatum the Peace Corps had given me when they flew me to headquarters for the reprimand. I didn't want to leave, especially because of my rewarding work with the Chamber and Special Olympics. Born under the sign of Taurus, and known for perseverance...or bullheadedness, I knew my answer.

After the scheduled three-day training, I visited the famous Cartimar pet market with another PCV. It was fate, she was a devout animal lover like me. Fascinated with acres of live animals, we wandered through rainforest birds, hedgehogs, and puppies.

"Ooh, Deb - look at these! You HAVE to get them!"

"Them?"

"Yes," said the proprietor, "they are litter mates."

215

And so, with a nudge of encouragement, and for $40, I bought two fluffy puppies. They were a mix of Japanese Spitz and Labrador (so they claimed). A big travel cage fit the two pups easily, and I stashed them at the Peace Corps headquarters with the guard. When Arnel, my sector manager, asked for my decision, I walked him to the puppies, who would return with me to Palawan. Thus, he had his answer about where I would spend my service with little need for further explanation. He didn't seem all that pleased.

Yet, my impetuous purchase had consequences – how to get the puppies back to Palawan? My foolish foreigner assumptions always tripped me up. Another pet shop told me, after the pups were mine, that airlines would only take animals over three months old. And they had to be vaccinated. The vendor I bought the pups from laughed when I returned to him panicky.

"In the Philippines, everything is negotiable, *po*. Come, I will help you find a veterinarian."

He took us to a vet who was doing surgery and we waited.

On Palawan, I once saw a spaying operation on a wooden table in the parking lot in front of the vet's office. Did they need a brighter light? Was there a brownout? Why in the dirty parking lot right on the main highway? The dog was splayed open on the table and looked dead. It was a small white, curly-haired dog, limp from anesthesia. The scalpel and knives lay next to gauze stained with blood that was congealing in the hot sun. Those conditions seemed commonplace on Palawan.

At least here in Manila's Cartimar, they had indoor surgery and we didn't have to watch the pitiful, bloodied animal. We sat for only 30 minutes before the vet emerged. The vendor explained the situation and the vet said, yes, he would write an official letter. It would state that my two-month-old pups were three months and vaccinated. He also told me to be sure to get them vaccinated when I got home because rabies is endemic and rampant in Palawan.

My idealistic winged self on one shoulder was talking to my devilish pragmatic one on the other.

"How can you succumb to this lack of ethics, lying to get the puppies home?" said the angel on my shoulder.

Logically, I couldn't leave them behind. But it was a major conundrum in my idealistic mind. Our PCV Thanksgiving travel north put off the decision for a while. I left the pups with the vet and told him I would return in ten days.

"*Walang problema po.* Have a good trip."

What was I thinking?

JOLLIBEE AND ME

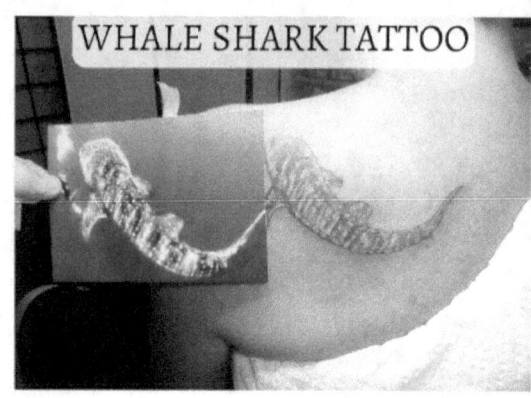

WHALE SHARK TATTOO

STICK BUG IN MY SINK

THE KITTEN

MY TURQUOISE WALLS AT BOUNTIFUL

Chapter 13

RICE, TURKEY AND POLITICS

Mahirap mamatay ang masamang damo
Weeds are difficult to kill.
A Filipino proverb meaning, 'It can be hard to rid yourself of bad things
or people.'

Di napapagal	
It doesn't slow down, excerpt	
Maria Elena Sadang Develos	
Naging mabuti ako, oo naging mabuting tao ako,	I had been good, yes I was a good person,
Pero bakit hindi sapat, nasaan ang halaga ko?	But why is it not enough, where is my value?
Sa walang katiyakan at mapaglarong mungong ito	In this uncertain and playful world
Bakit mas napapalad ang masasamang damo?	Why do bad weeds get more fortunate?

LEAVING THE PUPS WITH THE VET, I took off with 20 other volunteers on an overnight bus leaving Manila at night. Our first 'dinner' stop was scheduled about three hours into the 12-hour trip, around Tarlac. We would make a quick stop at Benguet around midnight, a shame since Benguet was the Salad Bowl of the Philippines, famed for its cool weather, vegetables, flowers, strawberries, and mountain tea; nothing would be open at that time of night. Another five hours past Benguet, we would arrive at the bus destination of Banaue, the world's oldest rice terraces.

We left the Cubao station at 8:00 PM and the bus aircon was intense without the sun's heat. By the time we got to the high country, most of us were freezing. The Cordilleras Mountains showed us a whole different world and temperature from our tropical beaches.

For months on Palawan, I had not felt temperatures below 77F. Even now in the rainy season, our 'winter,' it was regularly 80F. People on Palawan walked around in woolen beanies, wearing long sleeves and gloves. "*Malamig*!" (it's cold!) they would shiver.

But, on this bus, wearing my shorts and flip-flops, and using my thin cotton sarong as a blanket, the 55F (13C) temperature felt frigid. When we stopped in the middle of the night, somewhere around Bokod in Benguet (at over 4,000 feet elevation), several of us hopped out and quickly rummaged through heavy clothing at the all-night secondhand, or *ukay ukay* shop.

"*Meron ang parka? Sobra malamig dito*!" (Do you have a parka? It is so cold here!) we chatted with the sleepy shop clerks. The girls giggled in response, "*Oo nga - malamig dito*!" (Yes, truth - it's cold here!), as they probably said 20 times a day to silly tourists who expected all parts of the Philippines to be balmy.

Translated from Cebuano, *ukay ukay* means dig dig. They obviously thrived on tourists digging through their clothes for 3:00 AM purchases. Back on the bus, we snuggled in our parkas and slept.

Around 8:00 AM we got to Banaue, the gateway to the rice terraces, freshly flowered and green after a heavy rain the night before. Half of us tried to wake up with caffeine and breakfast at a small hotel overlooking the Banaue terraces, a World Heritage site, the terraces 2,000-6,000 years old. Others of us wandered the steep city streets, asking where we could hire a jeepney to take us up the mountain to the drop-off point for the hike into the renowned rice terraces of Batad.

Many of the young volunteers had an aptitude for Tagalog that evaded my old brain and they easily discussed details and schedules with helpful townsfolk they encountered. They found a driver for the eight of us interested in going to Batad, where spectacular terraces were rumored to be. We threw our luggage on the benches and piled into the jeepney, about twice as big as a Palawan multicab.

The drive was supposed to take about two hours and the hike to Batad another hour. Forty minutes into the drive, we nearly peed in our pants as the driver navigated the muddy and slippery one-lane mountain road. The track was rocky; new construction was attempting to turn it into a tourist highway, hence the loosened and slippery mud from last night's rain. You could feel the jeepney hydroplane as the wheels slid sideways.

The precipitous cliff on the right side had most of us huddled as far to the left as we could get. The hour trip up that treacherous mountain took nearly two since it was slow-going after the rain. There was little conversation, and we scarcely breathed when we had to stop on the edge to allow a construction truck coming down the hill to pass. The view was incredible, but our hearts were in our throats, our white-knuckled hands gripping the ceiling straps, and no one appreciated the scenery.

At the top, the jeepney negotiated the tight turn-around and the driver gestured to the hiking path. We piled out, calling out our thanks for getting us there safely. Our fear and sleepiness forgotten, we thanked the driver again with our payment and assembled our gear.

The path descended steeply into Batad, another hour's hike, where we would spend the night overlooking the rice terraces tended for millennia by the Ifugao people. Hefting our backpacks, we started the rocky descent. This was the main thoroughfare for villagers and hoteliers, men passed us carrying cases of beer on their heads, some barefoot, the rest in old flip-flops. Just the daily courier service. The path was narrow enough that we had to step to the side to let caravans of young delivery men through.

What an awesome sight about 50 minutes down, an amphitheater of bright green terraces of sprouting rice, built 2,000 years ago by the Batad, an Ifugao tribe.

We continued down to the rustic hostel where we dumped our packs. My young friends went with a guide on a three-hour hike around the amphitheater and swam in chilly Tappiya Falls. I chose to stay atop, on the open deck to view the panorama and thought what a fascinating country of contradictions this was.

The peaked geography and fertile fields differed from Palawan's lethargic beaches and heat. The history here felt more complex, rich, valued, and colorfully alive, people seemed tuned into the larger world, educated and multi-faceted...a world away from insular Palawan.

I zoned out with my feet propped against the open wooden rail that overlooked the sculpted valley 200 feet below. I watched the hikers, who looked like ants, treading on the foot-wide margins of hard mud outlining the hundreds of rice plots.

That evening, we bought pizza and San Mig beer from a tiny restaurant farther down the hill. We were treated to a native dance with the bright geometrics of red, yellow, and black woven fabrics, Ifugao's traditional clothing. Feathers of the endemic Great Hornbill, called the Kalaw, adorned the headdress. Our host urged us to try it on.

Only one petite girl in our party was small enough to fit into the man's costume and ornate headdress. The hostel owner's daughter demonstrated some traditional Ifugao dances, and told us the Kalaw is considered the messenger of the gods from their ancestors, the *anitos*. We sat and listened as the family shared their stories of old traditions, like chewing betelnut and headhunting, successfully outlawed only in the 1930s.

They also recounted the recent present. "I found her, you know. She was in the stream down there, hidden under the rocks," said the hostel owner in the settling dusk. "I was head of the search party for her because I know the area. U.S. soldiers were with us as we searched. She went missing and we didn't find her body for ten days. It was in the creek down below us."

He was talking about the Peace Corps volunteer who went missing three years before and was found murdered. We listened, spellbound.

"The man who killed her did not grow up here but had lived here a long time with his wife's family. He had mental problems and people avoided him. We tried to help his wife and asked him to leave, he was not a good man. But some things just aren't meant to be. He stayed and became even stranger.

"I think he saw the blonde woman and wanted her. He told the police that he was angry when she bumped into him as he was leaving a fight with his neighbor. But that doesn't make sense. I think she rejected him and he killed her for it. If only she had not been so independent and had someone with her, this would not have happened. Our community was shamed and saddened."

In the dark that night, I felt his pain and shame and understood better why the Peace Corps kept such a tight rein on us, telling us to always travel in groups. We were not in Kansas anymore living under U.S. rules. This was a reminder to accept the way that people thought and acted here, and to prepare to deal with it, not discount it.

I wondered if, in some way, this region's ability to speak fluent English may have prompted "familiarity breeds contempt." So that people were more emboldened to show and act on their feelings. It might explain at least a part of what I felt in the cities, that mixture of love and hate toward Americans.

In 1898 the U.S. acquired the Philippines. In 1901 a group of 600 American teachers arrived in Manila on the U.S. Army transport ship, "Thomas." Representing 192 educational institutions, their mission was to promote public education, that is, Western education.

These "Thomasites" were assigned throughout the country to teach, much like the Peace Corps works today. They were a debatable positive since the result of learning Western-centric teachings like Shakespeare and lauding achievements like the Egyptian pyramids unintentionally discounted their own culture. Ifugao narrative literature and the incredible, sculpted rice terraces that can be seen from space are just as laudable, if not more so.

Without taking a stance on how the Thomasites contributed to a devaluation of indigenous knowledge, there was no doubt that the missionaries had made our visit smooth. Because the Thomasites had been in this area for over 100 years, our hosts' English was impeccable, and even nuanced communication was easy.

After their folk and horror stories, we ordered two big pizzas and relaxed. Some of the PCVs asked me to smoke with them, fun after a 30-year hiatus, but way too powerful for me and I slept heavily.

We woke, ate breakfast and as the old lady of the group, I extravagantly hired a porter to carry my backpack on the hike out of the valley. Having packed for our Thanksgiving dinner as well, all of our packs were abnormally heavy. A bit embarrassed when we started the climb, I was grateful by the time we got to the top. Even the porter seemed winded, I didn't pack lightly. An industrious trek for a 60-year-old used to walks on the beach, but an indelible memory.

Back in Banaue, we reconnected with the others and caught a jeepney on its way to Sagada in the Mountain province where we would spend Thanksgiving. Filipinos are masters of repurposing items and the GI Joe jeeps left over from WWII cleverly morphed into the vivacious public transportation of the Philippines today. Jeepneys were the way locals got around and each jeepney was decorated flamboyantly to reflect either the family, the country, the province, or religion, sometimes all four.

This was a Sunday, and a few of the men passengers held one or two roosters, feet tied with a thin rope. The birds were blindfolded with a kerchief to keep them calm and silent. The men were on their way to a local weekly cock fight to gamble their money, betting that their cock would kill the others and be alive at the end of the fight for them to collect.

Racing pigeons was one thing, cocks fitted with sharp blades attached to their legs fighting to the death quite another. And, on a Sunday? Really? I refused to go to a cockfight but heard they were exciting bloody messes, with many birds dead at the end of the day. Animal cruelty was accepted to the point of it being blood sport, but difficult for some Americans like me to stomach.

People crammed into the inside seating area of the jeepney and a potpourri of items could be found topside (once I saw an entire tricycle on top, held down by heavy bags of rice). Today it was mainly sacks of rice and people. Top-riding was forbidden by the Peace Corps administrators, but it seemed everyone did it, who was I to protest?

"Come on up, Deb!" yelled my Peace Corps sons and daughters. The jeepney was moving again as I acrophobically climbed up the outside ladder and then crawled over sacks of rice and clumps of luggage to a stable-ish position, holding onto a cargo rope my entire crawl.

"Yay! *Tita* Deb! You did it!" They cheered.

The curlicue mountain roads and chill air were invigorating, and the 360-degree scenery was spectacular. We munched on barbecue-flavored Piattos as we passed the high Cordilleras mountains, the granite crags that reminded me of Yosemite. What a different world from Palawan.

Four hours later we arrived in the late afternoon at the outskirts of Sagada, which looked like a Swiss alpine village with its wood chalets, smoke rising from each as we looked down the chilly valley. Hefting our packs again, we headed down the road to find which chalet was ours. Our alpine lodge had a huge fireplace in the great room with views of the valley of pine trees. We doubled- and tripled-up in the seven bedrooms with a variety of beds and some sleeping on the living room couches.

A group went to town to the *palengke* to buy what we needed for a typical American Thanksgiving. After a brisk walk the next morning, we set about preparing the feast. Someone had purchased a chicken at the market, and we kept it tethered until we would kill and pluck it. I wasn't sure I wanted to do this to the poor fowl and often considered becoming vegetarian in the Philippines, not just due to sanitation concerns.

Not only was the coveted lechon fatty, but people slaughtered pigs so inhumanely that my skin crawled. The pig's throat was cut, but it was not killed outright, it would bleed out, slowly. Hours of horrendous squealing, the sound like nails being screwed into sheet metal or dozens of human nails scraped across a chalkboard.

At least chopping off a fowl's head should be quick with a hatchet. Did chickens in the Philippines run amok without their heads like U.S. chickens? At one point it was moot since the creature slipped its tether and we spread out on the hillside looking for it. By this time I felt awful for the poor thing and hoped it escaped, but someone did catch it. My friend Aja dispatched it with considerable difficulty since the hatchet was not sharp, it was more sawn than whacked. Escaped once, we didn't let it run amok, it was still tied up when its head was finally severed. Aja still does penance for that kill.

Two of the men placed it on the outside fire they had made, complete with a branch for a spit. The man in charge was the Filipino lover of one of the volunteers and I assumed he knew what he was doing.

I have never tasted a tougher bird in my life and stuck to the mashed potatoes, carrots, and delicious Hmong egg rolls made by my friend Paj.

By this time, I had a fever and a cough. I was a tropical body now, not a mountain queen. So I stayed in bed while the rest went to the famous Sagada caves with the hanging coffins. They told me later that they had to wade through knee-deep water in parts of the cavern, sad I missed it, but glad I did not go.

The 12-hour ($10) bus trip back to Manila was cold and long, but we had warm clothes now and we arrived in the eerily deserted streets of Cubao at 2:00 AM. We were well-known since most Peace Corps Volunteers had been housed over the years at Pension Natividad, in the Malate area. The guards let us in at any hour, and that night we slept well.

PCVs loved to come to the Manila pension in part because the showers were warm. You never know how comforting a warm shower feels, spraying out of a showerhead until you don't have that option. Bucket showers were okay, but were cold, and nothing like those showers at Natividad which reminded us of home.

Malate was also known as the red-light district of Manila where tourists, especially men, could find whatever kind of sex their hearts desired. Convenient for the hostel to be both our lodging and our training ground. Our instructors took us out at night to show us what we would be working against during our time in the Peace Corps: trafficking of children and women, prostitution of children, pollution, and trash 100 feet deep at Smoky Mountain, and horrendous poverty.

We could see the poverty huddled against the gates of the pension, which had tall heavy spires and posted security guards. The guards protected us, and if we hailed a taxi there, they wrote down the license number and the driver's name. Just outside the gates, families slept, half-clothed and ill-fed, babies crying. Around 8:00 PM, the pension opened its gates and fed some of the people on the street. More and more families took up residence in the streets outside. It was the reality of this city and both disturbing and painful to watch. Most upsetting was to watch your own reaction recede over time.

My first task after my shower at the pension was to pick up my pups from the veterinarian. They were unrecognizable, covered in fleas, and miserable. My industrialized-nation expectation that a vet would actually take care of animals was crushed. He wrote out the airline permission form, vowing that they were three months old and that he had vaccinated them and I left to debug them.

I stuffed my ethics and returned with the pups to the pension where puppy-starved volunteers fawned over them. We named the male "Rambutan" for the sweet red and green fruit because he was chestnut-colored with spiky hair. The female became Chika Chika, which means 'gossip' in Tagalog. Chika loved to be cuddled while we gossiped.

The first thing I did back on Palawan was to take the pups to the vet, at the time there was only one, apart from the government veterinarian. She was Patty Ortega, whose husband Gerry, also a DVM, was murdered in broad daylight two months after I arrived on Palawan. Brazenly, this happened around 10 AM at one of my favorite *ukay ukay* stores just down from the police station on the main drag.

Gerry's radio program had harangued the governor for years about environmental degradation and accused him of embezzling a multi-million-dollar energy fund. I guess (by this time ex-) governor Reyes finally got tired of hearing negative comments and hired [oops, 'allegedly' hired] a gunman to kill the beloved veterinarian/radio commentator.

For the next several years we followed the manhunt drama of said governor and his brother escaping to live in Thailand. Such a Filipino tale, the fugitive governor, tired of running away, wanted to run for office again, but he had to live in the Philippines to qualify. No problem, he allowed himself to be apprehended in Phuket, extradited to Puerto and put in the squalid city jail to await trial for murder.

Many of the guards were his former followers and were obsequious, affording him unique benefits to the point that the jail warden was finally fired. In the Philippines, the way to riches is through politics, and even though in jail, Reyes wielded power. The ex-governor's estate, which I frequently passed in Santa Monica, underwent enormous beautification during this time. His political intentions and confidence that he would beat the rap were obvious.

Apparently, you can run for office even if you are jailed. His name and that of his brother were added to the list of candidates running for mayor and vice-mayor of Coron, a municipality in the north; they were the only two candidates incarcerated. I felt a breath of fresh air when contrary to predictions and historical results here, they were both defeated while in their jail cells, but only narrowly. Allegiance in politics is understood, and he had a large following on Palawan, as well as high name recognition, which is always an indicator of success.

At some point, a judge ruled that there wasn't enough evidence to proceed to trial, which most of Doc Gerry's friends scoffed at, there was plenty. Yet, only recently, the judiciary reversed that ruling and issued a new warrant of arrest, now ten years and counting. But, with money and power to buy lawyers and judges, Reyes was in and out of jail on technicalities. Amazingly, he ran again for governor of Palawan in 2022 and didn't lose by all that much, capturing over 40% of the vote. It seems that murder is a publicly acceptable method of political power on the island.

However, Doc Gerry's supporters were also fierce and continued their fight to have Reyes arrested. Well-placed family and friends with laudable ethics and values, they were highly educated and would not let this go. They fought on principle against a corrupt system and dangerous men who kill remotely by making a phone call.

The more I learned of people in power, the more I wanted to stay far away from them. I felt safe with the few friends I knew, but scared when I thought of how nonchalantly a life could be snuffed, without any impunity.

BATAD OVERLOOK

ME RIDING ON TOP TO SAGADA

POOR CHICKEN_ READY FOR THE AX

LEAVING RAMBI AND CHIKA

READING THE NEWS IN MANILA

SCARY ROAD TO BATAD

Chapter 14

NEIGHBORS AND FRIENDS

Pulutin ang mabuti, ang masama ay iwaksi.
Emulate what is good; ignore what is bad.
A Philippine proverb meaning, 'Do good.'

Takdang-aralin sa mesa sa kusina
Homework on the kitchen table
Ashley C. Lanuza

Kung ang init ay may amoy
Ito ay rolyo ng sariwang-tinapay.
Gamit ang maliksi na daliri ay hinihila ko
ang loob ng pan de sal,
igulong ang inihurnong kuwarta sa isang bola at
patagin ito sa bubong ng aking bibig.

If warmth has a smell
It is bakery-fresh bread rolls.
With deft fingers I pull
the insides of the *pan de sal*,
roll the baked dough into a ball and
flatten it against the roof of my mouth.

Sa likod ko, ang kahoy mong kutsara ay tumama sa bakal na kawali
Nagiging sanhi ng pagsirit ng bawang at sibuyas.

Behind me, your wooden spoon hits the iron pan
Causing garlic and onions to sizzle.

Kinakanta nila ang aking puso
Gamit ang lyrics ng la la la
Mahal kita.

They sing songs to my heart
With lyrics of la la la
I love you.

So, we settled in, my new little family and I. Training two puppies was tough, they could be unruly. Rambutan (Rambi) was the explorer/wanderer while Chika Chika had a loving, homebody temperament - until you put food in front of her.

My pups were tiny but vicious when it came to feeding, something I observed with many dogs in the Philippines, probably because food was scarce. They growled protectively over their bowl, and if another attempted to steal a morsel, they would attack with snarls, teeth snapping. Aggressive enough that I never got in their way and situated their bowls far from each other. Chika was smaller but nastier than Rambi who rarely got any of her leftovers and kept his distance.

The three of us had a merry little Christmas at Bountiful. It has been said that Filipinos love two things the most: eating and Christmas. Starting in September, the Christmas season lasts through at least the Day of the Three Kings, and much of January, until the Feast of the Santo Niño. That is, for five months, nearly half of an entire year.

You can hear Christmas music playing in malls on September 1st, except at noon Sundays, when Catholic Mass played over the mall sound system. I always felt slightly sacrilegious as the priest intoned the benediction and I handed over cash for my groceries at NCCC, the only department store when I first got to Puerto.

Christmas in the Philippines was notably different, far less commercial than in the U.S., and deeply religious, with church and food the primary attractions.

About 80% of the Philippines is Catholic, but neither of my host families was. One was Mormon, at about 1% of the population, and the other was Born Again evangelical which is supposedly growing in popularity but is still lumped into the 'other' statistical category.

It fascinated me that regardless of the foundation in the belief of Jesus as the Christ child, there could be such animosity between Christian sects. Neither my Catholic nor Mormon friends seemed to harbor ill will about other religions, at least vocally. But my host family on Palawan identified as Born Again, in their minds the only true Christians. They decried Catholics as idol worshippers, while Mormons seemed to be lumped with

Muslims as being polygamous, no matter how I tried to argue differently. For them it was a fact.

Whatever your faith, most of December in the Philippines was devoted in one way or another to Christmas. Every business, faith, government- and non-government organization had at least one party for employees; many had several, one for each division and region.

Catholicism had cultural rituals, like *Simbang Gabi*, with people up at 2:30 AM to make the 4:00 AM Mass at the cathedral before they went to work for the nine consecutive days preceding Christmas. They also had a custom of *Panunuluyan* on Christmas Eve, a symbolic reenactment of Joseph and Mary seeking shelter. Processions of neighbors walked from home to home, where they might receive refreshments before going on to the next home.

During the holidays, masses of people went into debt to be hospitable and provide food and drink to relatives and friends and paid for it months into the New Year. The big day in the Philippines is not Christmas Day, but the night before, known as Noche Buena. Plateloads of delicacies were heaped on the table, the centerpiece lechon, with the crispy *bato* (skin) the choicest part. I never liked chicharrónes, and baked pig skin was pretty similar, but as a foreigner, I was always offered first dibs and I couldn't refuse.

There were many 'treats' that I had difficulty viewing as appealing. *Puto bumbong*, basically, pulverized rice mixed with sugar, was formed into a cylinder and dyed purple. Regular *puto* was rice-based but formed into a round ball, a few had a drop of food coloring. People moaned with pleasure when they ate these. They tasted like sweet, mashed rice to me. *Bibingka*, heavy rice cakes cooked in clay pots, were cherished, and not made any other time of year. I couldn't finish even a half because it sat so heavily in my stomach, but I bought them as treats for others. *Pancit* was plentiful, and long-life noodles, for obvious reasons. I was thankful that my favorite, *leche flan* was popular at Christmas and I clogged many an artery.

I never guessed that Filipinos were such heavy drinkers, but Christmas brought out not only the ubiquitous San Mig beer but also the Tanduay rum and the more cosmopolitan liquors, especially scotch at the more affluent affairs. I left parties before people (mostly men) got falling down drunk. Street gutters were littered with overturned tricycles that hadn't quite executed their turns.

Christmas Day dawned late for most revelers, and the day progressed slowly, with families eating leftovers from the night before, and opening a small present or two. The day was slow, with no public transportation to be found, and no businesses open. I had been invited to Angie's house on Christmas Day and finally had to call and cancel, there were just no multicabs or tricycles out near Bountiful.

Within a week, families purchased buckets of fireworks for New Year's Eve and had gotten their houses in order. To ensure a prosperous year ahead, people stocked their pantries, to show both mythical folk and neighbors that they were primed for riches. Cupboards, windows, and doors were left open to encourage bounty to come into their lives but quickly shut at the end of the day to make sure the wealth did not escape. And you did not sweep on New Year's Day; otherwise, you might sweep all of your good fortune right out the door.

New Year's Eve was the hardest day of the year for all the dogs. Superstition was that evil spirits could be warded off with loud noise, and the sounds were terrifyingly loud. For most people, the idea of a 'pet' was not common, and dogs were badly neglected, mistreated, and abused. I had to compartmentalize my love of animals. It was hard to watch dogs massively chained to the porch for their entire lives to function as guard dogs, never being walked. Or being eaten alive by untreated mange, walking without fur and with skin cracked and bloody. Early on, I saw what I thought was a pink dog, but coming closer, saw that it had advanced mange and its skin had a violent allergic reaction to the mites' bites. But the worst to witness were dogs that survived inhumane attacks by humans.

My neighbor's dog had a two-inch deep wound, it looked like a sharp cut from an ax to the neck, although I suppose it could have been from another dog. I called the new vet (making three on the whole island) and told him where I had seen the animal last and asked him to help it. But apparently, it belonged to one of my neighbors, they left milk and scraps out for it but did nothing else.

These situations were hard for me; observing things that my home culture would object to, like mistreatment of animals or the disabled. The amazing thing was that the ax-wounded animal lived, and its wound healed; it took months, but the old dog survived against all odds. So, with that as a backdrop, it wasn't shocking to me that animals were cruelly targeted on New Year's and fireworks were thrown at them.

Starting before dark you could hear the "ffst" of firecrackers being lit, and on homes like mine with tin roofs, those missiles hit the roof and exploded loudly. Some were deliberately aimed at the street dogs who scattered as fast they could. Both Rambi and Chika were terrified and shivered in my lap, as scared as I was of the outside war. Amazingly, no fires caught, and the partyers lived through it, some with fewer digits than the night before.

Witnessing the animal abuse, I again recalled the cultural assumption several people had voiced that the bible gave man power above all animals and could do as he wished with them. My objections were viewed with something akin to suspicion, and I left it alone. Sensitive soldiers might feel as I felt when fighting a war they didn't believe in, that no amount of arguing with superiors or peers would change the stream of destruction and that they were swept along with the tide.

Rambi and Chika were treated as family and we went for leashed walks through the Bountiful neighborhood with trails of children giggling behind us, me feeling like the Pied Piper. Here, my neighbors helped each other, and youth rambled from house to house without knocking. I couldn't tell which children went with which parents, it was just a community. Everyone smiled at me, but I was definitely an outsider and I'm sure there was *chika chika* about me, just not to my face. I felt an affinity with my across-the-road neighbor who was Muslim, nothing more than both being outsiders, but it's funny what unites people.

* * * * * * * *

Some mornings, before 7:00 AM, two small boys walked through the neighborhood calling something that I couldn't decipher. It sounded like they were singing, but it was only one word with each syllable elongated. Finally, I caught them at my gate, and they showed me the delicious warm yeast buns their mother made – *pan de sal*. They called "Pan-desaal, Paan-desal" in their choir-boy voices, lugging the covered baskets secured with a diagonal strap to their bodies. Now that I understood, I bought six pieces from them every morning for two pesos each. Infrequently, *taho* vendors sold that warm, silky tofu with tapioca, slathered with evaporated milk and syrup. Coupled with hot Milo, those were my favorite breakfasts.

Like most neighborhoods, we had *sari sari* stores where you could buy small packets of Milo if you ran out. *Sari saris* were attached to the front of a normal home, maybe four feet deep, partitioned off from the living room. Just enough room for a body to maneuver and for storage. Like my host family who sold hotdogs, industrious people saw a need and made money by being a distribution site for the neighborhood. The town was a long distance for people who had no money for transportation or had to walk, so *sari sari* owners would go to the department store and load up on groceries and whatnot. In town, you saw tricycles filled to the brim, cases of Ding Dongs or Topps cupcakes on top of the roof, precarious crates of eggs, and jugs of cooking oil balancing as the trike transported everything home to their family store. The store owners broke apart the cases, separating them into individual items, and marked up the price by only a couple of pesos. It was a lifesaver for the neighbors and made the family extra income.

Sari sari translates to "variety" in Tagalog and each *sari sari* store had a little different inventory. You could buy refrigerated meats from one, RC Cola from another, and *uling* or charcoal from another, or all from one, it just depended on what the owner wanted to sell and what the residents would pay for. Because soda bottles were returnable for refund, the store owners didn't give them to the customer, instead, the soda was poured into a plastic bag and a straw inserted at the top, and the purchaser walked away sipping the soda from a plastic bag.

It seemed they all sold cigarettes, called "sticks," as in cancer sticks. People purchased one stick at a time; one was affordable, but an entire pack of cigarettes simply was not. Similarly, laundry soap, shampoo, lotion, and such were sold in individual sachets. Cookies came in packs of two or four cookies, and all those millions and millions of plastic sachets and wraps went into the rivers and ocean.

When we first arrived, we Peace Corps volunteers were shocked to see the motto on big placards: 'Segregation is good.' We laughed to find it wasn't referring to racial segregation, but garbage. They've now changed the wording to recycle, but still have waste management signs printed that read,

"No segregation = No pickup." Filipino English didn't always make sense to me.

Learning Tagalog was hard enough for an oldie, but learning Tagalog texting shorthand was stupefying. It looked something like: "Gd dy d van com 20 c u." I had to read it out loud to try to decipher if the van was coming to pick me up, or if I was supposed to pick someone up. I could usually text a question, but couldn't understand the reply. I ran to my kind neighbor once and called through his gate, "Can you help me? I think the driver said he is on his way, is that right?" My neighbor came to his gate, took my phone, chuckled, and said, "Yes, he wants to know if he can come in 20 minutes and says to meet him at the end of the street. Let me text him back for you."

I recall only a couple of times when I felt threatened or unsafe. People were kind, accepting, and tolerant of my Western ways; they truly looked out for me.

Only once did I feel hostility as a foreigner in Puerto. I had just dropped off Angie and a carful of dignitaries and doctors from Manila who would spend the day at Share A Life School, far from the city proper. I wasn't feeling well and didn't stay; they would take public transportation back.

Turning left back onto the highway, I saw a big dump truck approaching but there was plenty of time to execute the turn. I saw a motorcycle to my right but didn't gauge its speed. The motorcycle was coming a lot faster than I thought and it didn't slow at all. My car at the time was a tank, an old red Toyota 4Runner purchased from a friend. We called the car *Pula* ('red' in Tagalog). Big and bright red, you couldn't miss it. And the motorcycle didn't.

Time slowed as I watched the two men without helmets hit Pula's side, barely making a dent or a sound. They went flying and I stopped in the middle of the road, threw open the door, and ran out to help them. The dump truck didn't slow and continued north.

The father yelled Tagalog epithets at me that I didn't understand, but I was more worried about his son who was in pain. They hobbled to a bench at the Rotary-sponsored bus shelter, while villagers began swarming from their homes. I started to move my car from the middle of the highway but the father harshly commanded me to leave it exactly where it was.

He proceeded to text on his cellphone, calling everyone from his wife to the police to the hospital to the fire station, and as icing on the cake, the television news. This big, white-haired white lady started to panic in a sea of angry residents who were staccato speaking in a language she was ill-equipped to follow.

I was only meters from the school and texted my friends frantically, with shaking fingers. They immediately ran down the road, knowing I needed help. By this time it was quite the scene and I felt like a big white Gulliver awash in a flood of brown people who came up to my collarbone. None of them had smiles, and many had scowls, looking ready to tie me down like Gulliver. It was scary and I was still concerned about the two men.

The road was now blocked by two police cars, a fire engine with rotating red lights, and a news van complete with a live camera, a real scoop for the news. I could see the headlines and hear the announcer, "Stupid old foreigner mauls Father and Son." People looked at me hostilely and gathered in increasing numbers mumbling to each other, shielding their mouths with their hands as though I could lip-read Tagalog. *Chika chika* was plentiful, the story embellished with every new rapid responder.

Lucky for me, *Pula* was a tall car that I could hide behind if I stooped a bit. The reporter with a camera dogged me, trying to get a good shot, but I circled the car to block my nightly-news cameo. We circled at least twice with him hissing at me and angling for a mug shot. I thwarted him but was nearly crying with fright and gratitude when I saw Angie crossing the highway.

As with many things in life, it was more important to have the right support rather than to be right. My friend, Angie, patted my arm when she saw my pale face and smiled reassuringly, "It's okay Deb, don't worry."

She chatted and laughed easily with everyone. Angie was the wife of City Councilor, Matt, and they were beloved. As her presence became known, tension lessened and smiling faces surrounded her. By the time she left the scene, the motorcycle victims were posing for selfies with her and thanking both of us. Angie also arranged with a contact at the news station to not show my picture or say anything more than there was an accident. She returned to the school and the Special Olympics' mission, asking our friend, Joven, to stay with me as my companion. He began to usher me through the logistics, as the hospital ambulance drove away with my victims.

The police told us to follow them to the central station, the same place Gerry Ortegas' murderer had been taken, and I recorded my statement. The officer noted that my California license was out of date and that I needed to get a Filipino license. I was mortified. He also divulged that the motorcycle owner had neither a license nor registration. He released me to go to the hospital where it was understood and documented with my signature, that I would pay for whatever medical attention the two men required, and that would be the end of it. I know none of this could have happened without Angie's intercession.

When Joven and I arrived at the hospital, there was a small crowd of friends and extended family outside, a common occurrence. When you check into the hospital, you have a *kasama,* someone who can help you with everything from filling out paperwork to taking you to the bathroom. And, even when *kasamas* aren't needed, all sorts of relatives and friends appear to show support. I spoke to the motorcyclist's wife and said I was sorry. I didn't feel any animosity from her as I had from the crowds at the scene, so I felt a bit better.

We waited with the family for several hours to get the x-rays and for both men to be seen by doctors. The atmosphere was relaxed with children scampering outside in the dirt driveway and people were more curious than anything. Interaction with people like me was still rare on Palawan and as Joven chatted with them, he made me less a threat and more acceptable. Thankfully, the men were fine, just a bit banged up. We apologized to each other, and I gently shook the father's hand. I paid all the bills, said I would pay to repair the motorcycle, and everyone filed out of the emergency room. We looked more like the aftermath of a party than a traffic accident.

Feeling terribly guilty, although the fault was shared, I asked Angie a couple of weeks later if I should do anything more.

"Oh, you want to send them more money?" she responded in a gale of tinkling laughter.

Angie was like a daughter to me and taught me about local culture through my never-ending questions.

"What should I buy as a thank you for helping me?" was one of my frequent questions, the answer almost always food, especially cookies and cakes.

"Should I trust him that he will do as he promised?" Angie gave people the benefit of the doubt and said yes.

"Is this a safe neighborhood to live in?" – she told me that there had been a body found in the ditch last year. It was rare for me to disregard anything she said.

Her great-great-grandfather was a Visayan hero, celebrated on National Heroes Day for his role in fighting the country's revolution against Spain back in 1896. She married a man who had ties to Palawan. His grandfather was governor of Palawan during WWII and tried to thwart the Japanese takeover, but unfortunately was beheaded by them and died a martyr. Her husband, Matt, had been a heartthrob actor until he decided to go into politics. When he told me his decision, I frowned.

"Why are you going into politics?" I nearly wailed. "You are a good guy. I like you and you will change into a politician!" Always so smooth.

Matt looked at me in shock. "Deb! I'm going to help Palawan, I won't change."

They were a power couple on Palawan. Angie had attended the prestigious National Science High School and gone on to get a degree in chemical engineering at UP Diliman in Manila, an elite profession, exceptional for a woman. Angie notably braved a man's world as an engineer at an industrial cement plant. After the birth of her oldest daughter with Down syndrome, she helped start an NGO in Manila that provided services to children with disabilities. She was a force.

Angie and I are probably both ADHD, but we are the opposite in how we plan things. I was usually the odd man out seeking strategy, organization, and accountability. Most big events were planned at the last minute which frustrated me. Our homeland cultures seemed to decide our approach to things and we clashed, me planning for the future, her celebrating the present. But we were a great team, building Special Olympics from scratch.

She and I could vex each other with our idiosyncrasies, but she said she loved having me around to nag her. I, on the other hand, found it stressful to argue and demotivating to be doing flurries of activities and see not much forward movement. Angie laughed at my dislike of "little-by-little."

It felt similar to how I viewed the Peace Corps in the Philippines: lots of fun events but little strategy or concern as to why they were being done. I've always wanted to change things systematically, refusing to see that doing things incrementally also had worth. Additionally, I had a visceral reaction to disagreement. Of course, over time, I saw the merits of little-by-little, but my vantage point at 60 years of age was different from a 35-year-old who had many years in front of her.

Still, as a team, and along with the president of Special Olympics, we made things happen. From weekly bocce ball competitions and tennis clinics to Sports Days at the coliseum and Christmas performances at the mall, we showcased the children and brought them out into the open. I dressed up as Mrs. Claus every year and Jesuit Brother Virginio with his long white beard played Santa. Pilipinas Shell Foundation provided presents and Mr. Donut gave us hundreds of donuts as children sang and danced on the central stage at Robinson's Mall. Because Special children were misunderstood and often shunned, just exposing the community to them was a step forward. With all our efforts and seeming national progress forward, it is hard to hear that the new Marcos government has zero funds allocated to Special education in 2023.

Angie, like her name, was kind and considerate of everyone. She also knew how to work the system, and worked it well, witness my car accident. She was smooth and flexible and light-hearted whereas I was blunt, skeptical, and serious.

Morals felt different in this country. The end in some ways justified the means, and rules seemed made to be broken or severely bent, often by the same people who made them. Maybe the whole point of life was to do good, little by little, while you tried to change the system. Angie was modifying my American views and I owe her so much. But even Angie had limitations on intervening in what would happen to me.

CHRISTMAS PAROL

SARI SARI STORE

PULA AND THE MOTORCYCLE

RICE DRYING ON SIDE OF ROAD

PUERTO FOUNDER'S DAY

THE PINK DOG

Chapter 15

MOMENTOUS THAILAND

Ang kalusugan ay kayamanan
Health is wealth.
A Filipino and American proverb advising that Health is one of the most valuable possessions. Treasure and protect it.

Grace

Habang idinaragdag mo ang iyong mga nagawa,	As you add up your accomplishments,
Idagdag ang mga buwan na naramdaman mong masigla at malusog, ang regalo ng buhay,	Add the months you felt vibrant and healthy, the gift of life,
Idagdag ang mga buwan na minahal mo ang iba nang hindi nangangailangan ng pagsamba o pagsunod.	Add the months you loved others without demanding adoration or subservience,
Idagdag pa ang mga buwan na naramdaman mo ang kagandahan ng mundo · ang kanyang kabuhayan at kagandahan,	Add the months you felt the bounty of the earth, her sustenance, and beauty,
Idagdag mo pa ang mga buwang puno ka ng buhay at ibinigay ang lahat ng mayroon ka, kahit na hindi ito naisip ng iba,	Add the months you were full of life and gave all you had, even if others didn't think it enough,
Idagdag ang mga buwan ng pagtrato sa bawat buhay na bagay gaya ng pakikitungo mo sa iyong sarili.	Add the months of treating every living thing as you would treat yourself.
Nagdadagdag ng biyaya.	Your sum is Grace.

IN MY SECOND FEBRUARY ON PALAWAN, I traveled to Thailand mainly to visit my daughter in Bangkok who was a Rotary scholar attending Chulalongkorn University's master's program in international policy. Angie kept the pups. I didn't know at that point that her dog had killed four cobras in their yard or I'm not sure I would have left them. Only a year later her dog died defending her three children, its sixth cobra. Another *bahala na.*

I first visited the islands, Koh Samui and Koh Pha Ngan, snorkeling and sunning as huge monitor lizards undulated within inches of me on their way down the sand hill into the ocean. Bright blue corals blanketed the shallows on the quiet side, far from the Full Moon parties. Then it was on to the temples, culture, and night market of Chiang Mai, finishing with a bus to Chiang Rai to tour the White Temple. Templed out, I arrived in the late afternoon at my hostel, where I thought I would spend the night.

The manager, however, had arranged a stay for me to visit some of the Hill Tribes. I was delighted.

"What is the transportation?" I asked the hostel owner, who promoted not only accommodations but his travel agency as well.

"There is only one of you. You will join two other foreign women who are already there." Not an answer, but I didn't worry...then.

"Sakda will take you there. Here is a refreshment before you leave."

"What? We are leaving now? He is my driver?"

We walked outside, and as usual, when confronting someone, my instinct was to passively go with the flow.

I kept my eyes closed on the dusk motorcycle ride, holding my duffle bag between me and the tiny Thai driver. True to his name, he was powerful, balancing both of us as he weaved through city traffic and up and down mountains. After about 90 minutes, the last 30 on dirt, we arrived well after dark at my two-day stay. Two other solo women travelers, one from Korea and one from Japan, had their sleeping mats already spread out on the floor. I have fond memories of the lovely village with free-roaming pigs shaded under the houses, and diaperless children running with the pigs. After preparing a dinner of rice and pork, the woman of the house offered us intricate and vibrantly colored weavings and I bought several.

The two travelers told me they were going hiking the next morning and they and the hosts insisted I go with them. I had not planned on any trekking or packed for it. I had only sandals and no backpack, but they assured me that was fine, and they made me a knapsack of sorts with my duffel and tied it to my back. Off we went on our 30km trek with the prospect of lunch near the top of a mountain with the head of the Akha tribe. We set out in the warm morning, hiking the ridge of the burnished hills, carpeted with leaves from the golden shower trees blowing in the wind.

At about 10km, the woman in front of me suddenly slipped on a blanket of leaves covering the downhill path but recovered. The next instant, I also slipped, right over the edge and slid down the mountain, stopped by a rock that impaled my left leg in the middle of the tibia. The guide silently slip-tripped down the precipice and frantically tried to pull me up.

"No!" I waved him away, dazed, but knowing I needed to get up on my own. My body went into shock and I calmly observed white bone at the site of the impact. My shin immediately swelled up like a baseball with only small dribbles of blood. I felt nothing and said, "How far do we have to go?"

"Maybe 15km," said the nervous guide, "then we will be at our lunch, and you can rest. I am sorry there is no other place from here to there." He couldn't look me in the eye and fretted with his fingers, his face crumpled to cry.

It wasn't his fault that I had fallen and I didn't want him to feel bad. So, we walked on. After another ten minutes, the shock wore off and the leg began to throb with shooting pains as I broke out in a sweat. I wondered how I would possibly make it to transportation. We boarded a boat to cross the Kok River and the guide spied a small group of tourists in the distance. He sprinted toward them and begged their guide to take me back with them. They were a tour of three, two men and one woman. I didn't register language or nationality, and remember nothing of the drive back to Chiang Rai and the hostel. I limped to the front desk and told the owner what happened. He looked at my leg and said, "Oh, not so bad."

I wondered if he was worried about his reputation and was downplaying it. Then I remembered my encounter with young people in Cambodia who had missing limbs amputated from stepping on landmines, and I felt guilty. There were far worse things than a hurt, not even broken, leg and I chastised myself, "What a privileged wimp you are, Debra!"

I limped upstairs to elevate my distended leg and rest. I was the only person in the dorm room, which had heavy drapes that darkened the room to keep out the heat. The cots were simply thin cotton mattresses on the floor and it was very difficult with the swollen leg to squat down or get back up off the mat. The lack of elevation had the leg throbbing. The pain intensified, I cried most of the night without sleeping, and by 3:00 AM I hobbled downstairs to hail a cab to go to the hospital, any hospital.

The poor driver I flagged down couldn't understand where I wanted to go, so after miming for several minutes, I pulled up my skirt and pointed to my leg. He started violently, whether from my immodesty or the wound, I don't know. He got me to the hospital in five minutes.

Chiang Rai was less than a fourth the size of Puerto Princesa, yet the Kasemrad Sriburin Hospital was modern, huge, and spotlessly clean, such a difference from the two in Puerto. I hobbled in and woke up two sleeping interns who blearily asked what my problem was. I had figured out the language and pulled up my skirt again, pointing to ask in slow English, "Is it okay to walk on? What If there are blood clots?"

"What? Do you have problems with blood clots?"

"No, but look at my leg!" I shrilled, looking at the black, blue, and bloody baseball lump on my bloated shin.

"No problem, Ma'am. We will clean, and it will be okay."

They took an x-ray, showing no fractures, cleaned the wound, and gave me pain medication.

"So, is it possible for me to go on my tour of the Mekong Delta tomorrow?" (said skeptically).

"No problem Ma'am."

"And I can fly to Bangkok on Sunday?" (in a challenging tone)

"Why not?"

And so I did. I enjoyed the tour the following day immensely, the painkillers were great.

At the Golden Triangle, we crossed the Mekong River to Laos and were offered whiskey bottled with either a cobra or scorpion, I passed. We visited the Opium Museum with a dark history that most Americans can't imagine. The day ended with a newly opened tourist stop highlighting the culture of several of the hill tribes, who would never live in such proximity. Tourists laughed and pointed at women of the Karen tribe, the Padaung 'long necked' women whose heavy brass rings stretch their necks and compress their shoulders. Our guide explained that if the women took off the neck rings, it could result in paralysis or even be fatal because their muscles were so weak. The longest neck ever measured was of a woman 5 feet, 4 inches tall whose neck was nearly eight inches long. The Padaung women were gracious, but the overt exploitation made me uncomfortable as if we were in a zoo watching the caged animals, or at a circus showing off the bearded lady. I slept fitfully for many reasons that night.

The next morning, I flew to Bangkok and positioned myself awkwardly on my daughter's couch, with my leg extended in pain. Her schoolmate was a doctor and told me I should elevate and ice the bruise, and that it was not an insignificant wound. I toured Bangkok on my own the next day and before I boarded the plane for Manila, ate some delicious street meat, a serendipitous mistake.

The typical several-hour layover in Manila and hour flight to Palawan saw me with not just leg pain; my stomach had begun rumbling. For two days I was sick in bed and toilet, before giving up and going to the emergency room at Adventist Hospital.

"Oh, sorry, *po*, all of our doctors are at a conference in Manila. You will have to wait to get a blood test."

It boggled my mind that all doctors were allowed to leave the island with no backup, but as with many things, one just accepted it. They sent me home and I called the Peace Corps doctor who told me that the upset would probably go away. It didn't, and I returned to the hospital emergency room against the Peace Corps medical advice. Finally, a phlebotomist came who took my blood and bustled back quickly to say perfunctorily,

"You have dysentery. Come with me and we will admit you and get an IV started."

I expected to stay overnight and asked my friends to feed the pups. And I immediately asked the doctors to look at my leg.

"No need," they said, "It's just a bump, doctors in Thailand took x-rays and it is not broken. You will be fine."

On the third day, they got tired of my nagging and finally did a sonogram.

"Oh, you have many blood clots in your leg." No shit.

"Do you want to do surgery now or wait?"

"Now!" I said in amazement. Why on earth would I wait to get rid of blood clots that had been there for over a week and were likely aggravated by all the air travel?

"I have friends visiting from America who arrive in four days," I said. "I have to be ready to take them snorkeling. Do the surgery now so I can heal."

What a lonely operation that was. One of the lowest times of my life. The one-bed, circular operating room had chips of paint peeling from the high white walls and the anesthesiologist noticed my desolation. He took my hand and asked how I was. A tear rolled down the side of my face.

"No one even knows that I'm here. What if I die?"

He was empathetic and assured me that wouldn't happen. He held my hand until the anesthesia took hold. I didn't have any *kasama* or companion with me and felt utterly alone in the world. My Puerto friends were working and taking care of my dogs and my family was half a world away. I woke up alone in my hospital room. My daughter tracked me down through Angie and we talked, which made me feel better, at least someone cared that I was alive. Some friends visited after work, although I was hardly cognizant that they were even there.

My U.S. visitors arrived three days later and were horrified both at my condition and the hospital itself. From the outside, Adventist Hospital had expanded and was several stories high, but the inside wasn't finished at all. Beds lined the corridors with moaning patients who had no rooms, shocking my U.S. friends who cringed away from the sounds and smells.

They had brought U.S. string cheese with them, which Bryce and Krystal fought over, having not seen dairy products in months. We had a bit of a party with their edible gifts and local condiments when local friends stopped by. Filipino hospitals were usually jovial places with entire families bringing in special feasts for the patients. Like most patients, I slept while they laughed and carried on around me.

My family members in the U.S. had said, "hang on a couple more days, the cavalry is coming and will help you."

But it wasn't like that in the Philippine provinces. Contrary to what many believe, Filipinos are not fluent in English, and in a hospital, you need to communicate precisely. Foreigners didn't know how to speak common Tagalog and didn't know how or what to ask for, the whole system was foreign. They didn't understand how the system worked, and that they were responsible for tending to the patient rather than the nurses. In some ways, my friends made it more difficult, compounded by my guilt that they'd come so far for a vacation, and I couldn't do anything, although I was still expecting a quick recovery.

They stayed at a nearby hotel since I wasn't home, and they wouldn't have a clue about how to get to my place using the local transportation. Angie again rescued me and offered to take them to Sabang and the Underground River with her family so that they weren't stuck in a hotel room. She also arranged for them to get to El Nido which relieved my guilt about ruining their vacation, even though I was going to join them in a couple of days.

In the wee hours of the morning, I complained that I was having problems breathing and the nurse called my doctor. I drifted in and out of sleep but woke once to see him standing silently staring at me, his face pale with alarm. An industrial tank of oxygen was wheeled into my room by a nurse shorter than the tank. She hooked it up and put the mask over my face. Another doctor came in to consult and agreed that I was passing a blood clot, although no one told me that. The next morning, my Peace Corps friend, Krystal, got on the phone to the Peace Corps in Manila and demanded they get me to Manila ASAP. The move to Manila saved my life.

After nine days in Palawan's provincial hospital, I was going to a modern hospital in Manila. Petra came from Aborlan to ride with me in the ambulance to the Puerto airport and flew with me to Manila. A Peace Corps doctor met us at the airport and whisked me away for admission to Makati Medical Center. The Peace Corps doctor accompanying me ordered me a Burger King Whopper as a treat for dinner. You have to wonder what she was thinking, ordering such a meal for a person with blood clots, but it tasted great.

Makati was night and day from Palawan Adventist, with medical technology everywhere. They were horrified that I had eaten a hamburger, and it was my last for quite a while. Still, the food I was allowed to eat was so much better than my previous hospital fare of vegetarian mystery food that I didn't mind.

Under the care of cardiologist Jeffrey Chua, they re-operated on the leg and got the rest of the clots out. I credit Jeffrey Chua for truly saving my life and thanked him many times. As many times, he humbly replied, "I didn't save your life, the Lord did. I am but an instrument of Him."

I thanked him for being such a good instrument.

My friends were mostly oblivious to the drama, enjoyed El Nido on Palawan, and finished their three-week visit, *sans* the person they were visiting. They returned to Manila just in time for my release from Makati Medical Center. I had been in hospital for over three weeks, was exhausted, and couldn't walk, but at least I was out. We Ubered to Greenhills Mall and they pushed me around in a wheelchair, I felt like a wet rag. We all stayed at an apartment near the hospital where I had to remain another two weeks for observation.

On our last day together, I was convincingly ambulatory and led them to a shawarma shop in Malate that the Peace Corps volunteers frequented while in Manila. The sights walking through the streets were familiar to me now and I concentrated on recalling the route to the restaurant through some back alleys. But, for my visitors it was dreadful, the poverty, children without clothes, beggars, and overall human suffering *en masse* were monstrous to them.

"Okay Deb, that's enough. We don't need to see this."

In less than two years, my life had veered far away from the people I had lived with most of my life. What did she mean by "We don't need to see this"? This was exactly what privileged people needed to see. And I hadn't intended to show them anything, I was just walking, leading the way to shawarma sandwiches. Sigh, with a bit of outrage.

The Peace Corps paid close to a million pesos for my treatment, a fact they repeated to me during my Makati stay. My U.S. friends said goodbye and took off back to California. They have since reminded me what a horribly memorable vacation it was for them. They had spent a lot of money and were not world travelers, at least to developing countries. It was frightening for them to be alone in a dramatically foreign place and to see me so ill in such a dismal hospital. I suppose on their vacation, they wanted the tourist view of the country that I was immersed in, not to see how the masses lived. They hadn't planned on visits to a hospital with gurneys of critically ill patients parked in dim halls because there were no rooms available. They especially didn't want to see me in that situation.

Again, the Filipino spirit of care and hospitality saved them and me through my miraculous friend, Angie. I have no idea what my friends or I would have done without her. But even Angie couldn't divert a governmental agency like the Peace Corps. My gig was up.

LAOS COBRA WHISKEY

THE SLIPPERY LEAVES JUST BEFORE MY FALL

KIDS PLAY

THAILAND WOULD BITE ME

HOME STAY IN THE HILL COUNTRY

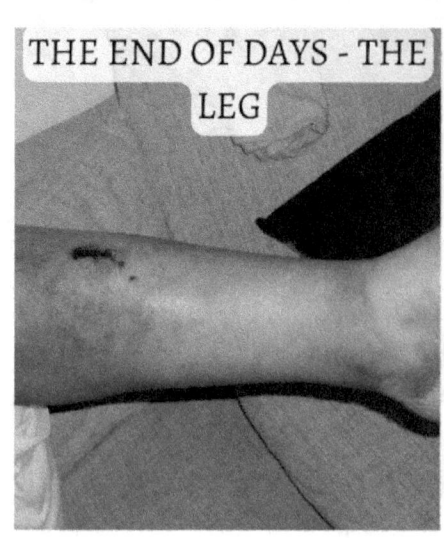

THE END OF DAYS - THE LEG

Chapter 16

THE END OF DAYS

All good things must end
Lahat ng magagandang bagay ay dapat wakasan
An American proverb meaning, "Nothing lasts forever."

A Chill
The changeable seasons reflect
our unpredictable lives,
Life can change on the slip of a leaf,
Becoming cold and snowy for a while.
Yet even harsh snows thaw
Allowing spring buds
to emerge in unimaginable ways.

I WAS RELEASED FROM THE HOSPITAL the first week in April, Holy Week in the Philippines, and I got a taste of how Easter differed in our two countries. In California, parents ordered chocolate rabbits from See's Candies and dyed hard-boiled eggs to decorate with their children. Put into woven baskets that also held jellybeans, the treats were hidden to find when the family awakened on Easter morning. Easter egg hunts were popular at country clubs and there were prizes for the youngster who found the most colored eggs.

In the Philippines, Maundy Thursday began the solemn recognition of the Last Supper. Many Catholics honored the *Visita Iglesias* when they visited seven churches in one day. Good Friday was a national day of mourning, contemplation, and prayer. In the provinces, people stayed inside their homes, quietly reflecting on Jesus' death. In cities, there were prayer parks with the Stations of the Cross for families to walk through.

That particular Holy Week, nearly everything in Manila shut down from Thursday to Monday, even the mega malls. In the capitalistic U.S., a store might close for a day, but not for four or five days. Nothing here in Manila was open, and transportation was scarce. The first time I needed a cab to get to the medical center, it arrived 90 minutes after I called.

The only place I saw for food service was McDonald's on Thursday, and I had no interest. So, I read books in the apartment, bought hot noodles and tuna sandwiches at 7-Eleven, and waited for Manila to come back to life.

It seemed that churches were the only welcoming buildings. On Easter Sunday, church bells rang, and families filed in for Communion, emerging with huge smiles on their faces. They returned home where friends and neighbors gathered for a meal. As somber as Good Friday was, Easter was light and gay.

That week in Manila, I learned that the Peace Corps was sending me home and would 'medically separate' me. I discussed returning to my post with the director, who was vague in how or when that would happen, but I didn't understand that they meant all along to separate me permanently. The Peace Corps also informed me that I would not be allowed to return to Palawan before being sent back to the U.S. Palawan, where all my belongings were, including my dogs. No goodbyes for me to the community I served. I was too exhausted to be furious; that came later.

Worn out from 18 days in the hospital and a month of bodily trauma, I frantically tried to find how to legally transport my pups back to the U.S. I asked people if anyone could adopt them and got no takers, except someone who wanted them as meat. Krystal and Bryce had been going to the house to feed them, but that was a lot to ask. I was arranging to have them shipped to Manila with proper immigration papers when my dear friend Susan said she would take them. She already had two big hounds and her husband balked at two more, but she wore him down, saving me and the pups a lot of stress.

Now, how to get my belongings to the U.S., and who would pack everything up on Palawan and get rid of things I could not take back? How would I even remember what I had in the house? Camaraderie is strong between Peace Corps volunteers. The Peace Corps was doing nothing to help me, but fellow PCVs on Palawan saved me again.

"Hi Deb, how are you feeling today? Are you ready to figure out what we should pack up for you? What do you think about this?" said Petra, holding her phone camera over the dress as we Skyped.

"Hmm...I think that one has a big tear in the back, so, no."

"How about these figurines - they look like they are from Thailand."

"Oh my gosh, yes, I bought those with my daughter at Chatuchak Market in Bangkok. Do you also see the singing bowl next to them? Yes, I want those. And the carved wooden sea creatures from Asiano."

Piece by piece, we decided that my bookshelves stuffed with books should go to the school and that the second-hand *ukay-ukay* stores could have my stretched-out clothes and other small stuff.

"You know, some people came by from your school. They wanted to know if they could have some things. What should I tell them?"

Folks were even then huddled outside my turquoise and teal Bountiful home waiting to claim anything of value. I asked Petra to only let people in the house after the big things had been distributed. First dibs were placed on my $300 bicycle and my books, as long as they were free. Since only a few things would be sold, I wanted to decide who got the expensive items. I disappointed several people.

My brand new refrigerator was claimed by a colleague who arranged to pay installments through a mutual friend (she never paid one) and my other appliances and belongings were parsed out, a windfall.

Coordinating my Palawan exit from my Manila hospital bed, I tried to figure out what I would do when I got back to California. My PCV friends helped me exit my Palawan life, although I wasn't able to say goodbye. But the Peace Corps wasn't worried about where I would land back in the U.S., they seemed more concerned about having me leave. The Peace Corps did take responsibility for the surgeries and medical treatment in the Philippines but said I was on my own when I got home. They arranged nothing for me, no one to meet me, no place to live, and no doctor to take over my care.

Five weeks after first being diagnosed with dysentery on Palawan, I injected myself with a syringe of blood thinner and boarded a plane for San Francisco.

LOVE_ SPECIAL OLYMPICS

ANGIE, BEA, AND MRS. CLAUS

1ST OLYMPIC GAMES

COACH PET'S SPORTS

CHAMPIONS

MEDALISTS

Epilogue

Pag binato ka ng bato, batuhin mo ng tinapay.
If someone throws a rock at you, throw him bread.
A Filipino proverb that best captures the Filipino spirit. It means be forgiving, accept life, and move on from the thing you felt wronged you.

Thank You

Salamat	Thank You
Dahil sa tiwala mo na wala sa akin,	For the trust you didn't have in me,
Tinuruan ako nitong magtiwala sa sarili ko	It taught me to trust myself
Para sa mga hadlang na inihagis mo sa akin	For the obstacles you threw my way
Tinuruan ako nitong magtiyaga	It taught me to persevere
Para sa mga patakaran na ikinadena mo sa akin	For the rules you chained me with
Tinuruan ako nitong gumawa ng sarili kong mga patakaran	It taught me to make my own rules
Para sirain ang reputasyon ko	For undermining my reputation
Tinuruan ako nitong maging totoo sa sarili ko	It taught me to be true to myself
At, Salamat sa tulay sa isa ng bagong pananaw	And, thank you for the bridge to a new. perspective
Binago nito ang buhay ko.	It changed my life.

The Peace Corps did not help me navigate my abrupt re-entry to the U.S., and it was not easy to figure out the insurance and doctor referrals without support. I didn't even have a home to return to, I had rented that out and sold my car when I went to the Philippines.

Ironically, a Phil-Am doctor handled my case, releasing me from care within a couple of months. She wondered why the Peace Corps sent me home at all, saying I could have been treated in the Philippines.

It was as though I had been erased. I had served 18 months, yet never received even a piece of paper recognizing that. Everyone else in my cohort has a beautiful commendation signed by President Obama. The Peace Corps washed their hands of me as though I never existed.

I arrived, exhausted, in San Francisco and stayed with one of the friends that Angie had rescued during my hospitalization. She helped me find insurance and a doctor to monitor my platelets. I sequestered myself from even lifelong chums as I landed back in U.S. society which felt alien to me now. Most returned volunteers experienced this reverse culture shock, but most didn't have my additional trauma. I needed time and space.

Dear friends let me borrow their extra car so that I could get around. Other friends welcomed me into their homes to stay for a few weeks at a time and let me heal at my own pace. It was lovely and weird. I was a vagabond.

After three months, and a formal medical release, I was told I could return to the Philippines. Surprise, the Peace Corps didn't want me and let me know roughly, the way a dog is kicked to the curb.

With my home in California rented out for another six months and no place to live, I had to make some decisions. Why not return to Palawan for that time, to finish some of the projects I had started with Bart? I was excited that the timing meshed with my cohort's end of service, so I could at least make that event with my PCV friends.

The new Country Director contacted me personally to make it clear that I was not welcome at the ceremonies. He said I would be turned away.

While my dream of the Peace Corps feels ignoble now, it afforded me an introduction to the incredible life I would live for the next many years. Some would say still a life of service, and it was. But for me, my return to Palawan would become a fulfilling personal journey and an often-unintended education. On Palawan, my version of Paradise, where I became an adopted Palaweña.

I returned on my own dollar, *sans* any link to the Peace Corps, to begin a deeper journey with the people and geography I had come to love. I worked on several projects that Bart and I had started and one of the Chamber members gave me a job that evolved into a treasure.

I would work there nine years as the only foreigner working for a regional financial company and help them grow to national prominence. Special Olympics also grew in size and recognition, and a section of the Palawan State University library houses the first SPED library with my collection of books. All because of a woman's perseverance.

I found a lovely place to live in the jungle, with a younger woman and her child, and my little dachshund Happy. We did see cobras and monitor lizards in the yard but no pit vipers, and we had multiple geckos happily keeping the mosquitoes at bay.

It was my version of paradise, although my U.S. friends couldn't comprehend living without clean or heated water, air conditioning, or cheese. Medical care was not of paradise quality, and my daughter asked me to return so that I could live a few more years.

I returned to California just in time for COVID lockdown and began writing this book. As they say, time heals wounds, and the pain and shame I felt with my dismissal have dulled. I have chosen to concentrate on how the Peace Corps unintentionally built a bridge for a decade of my life. They gave me the basics, the language and cultural training a foreigner needs in a new country. They afforded me medical care when I needed it most. Their policies allowed me to survive with a secondary project when the first didn't work out. Those new projects allowed me to work with people who had similar interests to mine and wanted to improve things in Puerto Princesa, in business, tourism, and community efforts. People became my lifelong friends and colleagues on the incredible island of Palawan. A life-changing adventure, full of escapades and rewards.

I have always wished that instead of Military service, the United States required service in the interest of Peace, and the Peace Corps offers that to young graduates and older professionals.

Today, I spoke with a book publisher and at the end of our conversation she said, "You've painted quite the picture of how you grew as a result of your experience. I can see the possibilities - emotional expansion and gaining a whole new perspective. And then there's the idea of discovering Truth. Wow. Can I have my sister call you - she just retired and needs something new. Can she call you to find out more about the Peace Corps?"

So, it seems that even with my somewhat dismal experience, I am still an ambassador for them, for Peace, and for the Philippines.

Deb Pritchard, 2024

The Characters Now

I ALWAYS WONDER IN books, what happened to the other characters?

My Peace Corps friends

★ **Bryce** and **Krystal** live in central Oregon with their two children.

★ **Petra** lives with her husband and child in Oregon as well.

★ **Aja** lives in Hawaii doing work to prevent trafficking and was an immense help to me in editing this book.

★ **Chris** runs Parks and Rec in San Rafael and has adopted a son.

My Olongapo Family

★ **Tess** went on to help raise the daughter of her younger son (the son whose belongings were in that cardboard box in my room). She still makes *chika chika* with Manang Ester next door.

★ **Joseph** made many upgrades to his mother's house and she is comfortable. He quit Subic Water and started his own company, with Joie as his partner, and he now has pigeon condos and his own three-story home..

★ **Gelo** has done all the IT work for his father's company and entered college in Baguio in 2022.

★ **Oliver**, the son who wanted to go to the U.S., arrived with his six family members in San Jose, California in 2019. Never underestimate dreams.

The Palawan crew

★ **Angie** and her husband, City Councilor **Matt**, visited me in California and continue to help Palaweños in both political and community efforts. Angie still runs Special Olympics on Palawan, as well as other ventures like a zipline and canopy walk in El Nido. Their oldest daughter, Bea, is in her 20s and is an ambassador for Special Olympics and a teaching assistant at Salve Regina School.

★ **Pastor**, his family, and the church members still live on Palawan. The school now concentrates more on community teachings rather than on individual students.

★ **Bart** passed in 2016, and I have a wonderful relationship with his son who lives in Washington state. Thank you for everything, Bart.

The Peace Corps continues as it has.

Acknowledgements

Great appreciation to my now-defunct writer's group here in San Luis Obispo. Covid did us in, but your brilliant critiques over several months made this a very different book than its beginning.

Thank you to my friends, Julie, HR, and Jim who read the early version and gave me invaluable feedback on the content, format, and design.

Thanks, Laurie of LMW designs for capturing in green graphic form the impact that vipers and geckos had on my thinking and cultural understanding. And to the incredibly patient and talented owner of Sienna Designs for the beautiful interior.

To my Peace Corps daughter, Aja, your line-by-line critique and our arguments over nits made the book better, especially for your age group. I'm always surprised by how old I am and that younger generations have no knowledge of momentous events that were 'current' in my youth.

A reverent thank you to the Philippine poets who allowed me to use their work. The notable Marjorie Evasco for allowing me to use your lovely poem as my epigraph. I feel as though the sunbird in the thirst-quenching fruit tree is me, relishing the sound and scent of my beloved Palawan. Ashley Lanuza for her reflections on her Filipino ancestry in her delightful book, *The Heart of Rice*. Maria Elena Sadang Develos for her contemplative verse about the illogic of good and bad in the world . And thank you to the brother of the late Diana Gamalinda for allowing me to include her lyrical musings on the elusiveness of Truth. To me you poets are the heart of the Filipino and what I love so much about the true culture of the archipelago.

To my friends on the magical island of Palawan - whether you were Viper or Gecko, you gave me the richest experience an alien could ask for. *Salamat sa inyong lahat.*

And, to Ami, who knows my transformation best, thank you for your lovely Foreword. You captured my intention, my foibles, and the fact that acceptance can transcend language and customs. My journey is one I wish every American could make toward understanding that there is no one Truth and that we are all interconnected.

Understanding Filipino Cultural Traits

Filipino sociologists and philosophers have studied Philippine society for decades and have named the basic tenets and norms that underpin and drive the culture. I studied their books to try to understand the mores that were so different from mine so that I would blend in better (wishful thinking).

Some are impossible for outsiders to grasp, and even a decade of experience was insufficient for me to fully understand the rules. This list defines a few traits, but there are nuances and incongruities within them that I will never understand. And, while Filipino scholars have studied these, most Filipinos are oblivious to them, because, as in all cultures, they are ingrained from birth.

Amor Priopio - Translated as "Self-love" but more like Pride. In the Philippines, where appearances trump reality, this trait is less about self-esteem than promoting yourself to be more than you are. A man is not a store guard, he is a criminologist; a trike driver promotes himself as a transportation engineer. This trait is linked with *Hiya* and can be tricky to navigate, especially with perceived personal affront. If there is a conflict with another person that might offend him, it is best to ask an intermediary to help you negotiate. You will save face and not infringe on the *Amor Propio* of another.

Bayanihan - This spirit of kinship, camaraderie, and working for the common good is joyous. Cooperative endeavors help a collective society. This trait offers reciprocal labor and people give help without being paid. Relatives and neighbors get together and feed an elderly woman's dog, or repair the roof on their neighbor's home.

Crab Mentality - Routinely pulling down anyone who achieves or is about to achieve success greater than yours. This behavior takes its name from how crabs scramble to get out of a boiling pot by clambering on top of the others. A lot of the *chika chika* (gossip) that is spread is for this purpose. Even in everyday conversation, it is common to make fun of others to make yourself look better, often unconsciously. You can see how it is linked with *Amor Prioprio* so that you try to appear better than your neighbor, and make sure of that by pulling him down.

Galang - Showing respect is an underpinning of society; respect for elders, those in authority, and those with business or educational accomplishments. Showing familiarity with those in power is also disrespectful. The language demonstrates this with the appellations that each person is given like *Attorney* Castro or *Engineer* Mendoza. Elders are esteemed for their life wisdom and on Palawan were given an additional title of respect: *Manang* or *Manong*. And youngsters demonstrate respect by the *mano po* ("your hand, *po*"), placing an elder's hand on their forehead as a manner of greeting and asking for their blessing.

Hiya - The big one: Shame; the underlying motivator of most behavior. The ultimate disgrace is being shamed by anyone, and it has been said that "face is more important than truth or justice" - especially in public. In a Gallup poll, Filipinos were ranked as the most emotional people in the world and they are sensitive to perceived personal affronts. And Hiya is reciprocal - Filipinos want to save face for you, the foreigner. Therefore, people save face by telling you what they think you want to hear, even though to Western foreigners it might feel like people are lying to you. Similarly, people refuse to lose face by accepting any blame - even if they were obviously the reason for a problem. It is always someone else's fault - or God's - *bahala na!*

Kapwa The Philippines is a 'collective' society and this is a crucial concept, although it can conflict with other concepts like *Galang*. It means the unity of 'self' and 'others.' It is that recognition of shared identity and that we are all one and reflects our obligation to our fellow humans. The act of treating everyone equally and of doing something for the sake of others is pre-colonial and pre-20th century *kapwa*. If only my country had this.

Pakikiramay - Having compassion for others and going out of one's way to help another is obvious in daily life. Putting yourself in the other person's shoes is what Filipinos try to do. They are empathetic, even when their sensitivity misinterprets another's wishes. A tradition like bringing back *pasalubong* (souvenir) from a trip to show someone you were thinking of them is a practical demonstration. The language reflects this by being other-focused. The object (the other) matters more than the subject in Tagalog - the opposite of American English which is subject-driven.

Pakikisama - The "togetherness" that maintains smooth interpersonal relations; that it is better for everyone to feel good rather than for anyone to feel bad. This means going along with someone's views, whether agreeing with them or not. Overall, this enhances the camaraderie, trust, confidence, and loyalty crucial to a collective society. *Pakikisama* is the opposite of individualism, which is frowned on. Doing something as a group, even if done badly, is always better than doing anything individually, no matter how well the individual might do it. It is also very confusing to a foreigner from Western culture because she cannot figure out what someone's true feelings are. A response of 'Sure,' 'Yes,' or 'Maybe' can easily mean 'No!' because the word no is rarely, if ever, spoken so as not to offend anyone.

Utang Na Loob - Translated as a "debt of one's inner self, "debt of honor," or "debt of gratitude," this is the most moral obligation of society. It is a system of reciprocal obligation that can last a lifetime, or in fact, carry on into the next generation. If someone has done something for you, you are expected in turn, to do something of equal or greater value for them. It has been related to "gratitude" but as shown in this memoir, it carries a much heavier weight and one needs to be careful what he accepts as "a favor."

Tagalog Glossary

My friend Julie asked for a quick glossary to remind herself.
So, here it is.

Abularyo - Traditional folk-medicine practitioner; sometimes called a *kwak kwak*

Aircon - Air conditioning

Amor Prioprio - Self-love, but more like pride

Anay - Termite

Apo - Gandchild

Asawa - Spouse

Askal - Street dog; also the name of the national football team, The Askals

Aswang - Evil, shape-shifting beings of folklore

Ate - Oldest daughter; also a term of respect for a woman

Bahala na - "Come what may" or "It's up to God" Accepting adversity...or laziness

Bahay - House or home

Bahay kubo - House made of nipa palms

Balikbayan box - A cardboard box shipped "back to the homeland" by Filipinos overseas

Bangka - A native boat, usually a double outrigger dugout canoe

Barangay - Historically known as a barrio, it is a recognized neighborhood of town

Barkada - A close-knit and trusted peer group you frequently hang out with

Bayad - Fee for something like transport

Bayan - The nation or country.

Bunso - The youngest child in the family

Carabao - Water buffalo that you see everywhere in the farming fields; also *Kalabaw*

Chika chika - Gossip

Duwende - Usually a little person in fantasy - an elf, fairy, dwarf

Dynasty - A Family whose relatives have attained, and maintain economic and political power in a province Proclaimed by law to be illegal, there are over 100 dynasties.

Gagamba - Spider

Hay Naku! - An exclamation meaning, My goodness!

Hilot - A folk-medicine practitioner using massage and invocation

Ipil - A hardwood tree used for furniture and construction

Itim - The color black

Kalabaw - Filipino name for the carabao, or water buffalo, that plows the fields

Kalapati - Pigeon

Kanin - Rice

Kapwa - Treating each other as one humanity in society

Karaoke - Singing along with recorded songs - Filipinos love to sing together.

Kilig - A feeling where your heart is fluttering with excitement - usually for your crush.

Kulambo - Mosquito net

Kubo - A shack or hut

Kuya - Older brother; also a term of respect given to a man

Lamayo - dried fish

Lang - only

Lechon - Roasted pig

Leche plan - Also *leche flan* (there is no 'f' in Filipino) - A rich pudding dessert

Little by little - things take time; one step at a time

Lola - Grandmother

Lolo - Grandfather

Longganisa - a spicy sausage

Mabalahibo - Hairy

Mabuhay - Similar to Aloha! This is a general greeting meaning Live Long! (pre-Spock)

Magandang Gabi - Good Evening

Magandang Umaga - Good Morning

Makulit - Stubborn

Malaki - Big

Manang - Term of respect for an older woman

Manong - Term of respect for an older man

Mano po - Same as *pagmamano*, the blessing asked from an elder

Merienda - A snack - usually one in the morning and one in the afternoon

Multicab - A small truck, covered with bench seats used for public transport. They have fixed routes.

Nanay - Mother

Ngiti - Smile

Ningas kugon - The trait of becoming enthusiastic about something, then quickly ignoring it. From "flaming cogon grass" when a farmer clears his field for planting.

OFW - Overseas Foreign Worker. 11% of the population are OFW in 100 countries.

Opo - Yes, ma'am (or sir)

Pagmamano - Blessing asked for from an elder by touching an elder's hand to their forehead

Paki - Please

Pakikiramay - Compassion

Pakikisama - A core value of getting along with others; Comradeship

Palengke - Marketplace, commonly open air, outdoors

Pambahay - House clothes that you would never wear outside the house

Pandesal - White, yeast rolls

Para po - Stop please - used when you want to get off of a multicab.

Pasaway - a shade worse than *makulit* - Disobedient

Pasensiya - Sorry

Pasma - a "folk illness" of the Philippines due to cold and hot confrontation

Po - A 'filler word' to denote respect. The higher the respect, the more 'po' in the sentence.

Pula - The color red

Purok - Not an official government unit, a small neighborhood within a barangay with a leader who helps the barangay manage his neighborhood.

Puwet - The derriere, or buttocks

Rambutan - A delicious lychee-like fruit with a spikey bright red exterior

Salamat - Thank you

Sari Sari - Small neighborhood variety store

Sayang - Oh how sad; what a lost opportunity

Shabu - Slang for the street-drug Methamphetamine

Spag - Spaghetti

Sylvanna – a caloric frozen cookie of cashew/meringue wafers filled with whipped cream

Tabo - A small bucket to pour water on yourself to bathe

Tamilok - A woodworm 'delicacy' only on Palawan

Tao po - Greeting called when arriving outside a person's home

Tatay - Father

Tita - Auntie

Tito - Uncle

Tsinelas - Flip flops; slippers

Tuko - Tokay gecko

Ube - Purple yam/sweet potato of the Philippines

Ulam - The entree, or main dish

Uling - Charcoal used to start a cooking fire

Ulit - Again

Utang na loob - The idea that if you take a favor, you will owe the other person forever

Wallis tambo - A broom made of soft tiger grass for indoor sweeping

Wallis tingting - A stiff broom made of the thin ribs of palm leaves - for yard cleaning

White lady - Female ghost who lives in the weeping fig trees - think The Grunge

Reading Guide
Questions

1. Did you know about the US Peace Corps before this book? What did you think about it before you read the book? Did the book change that view?

2. What do you think Deb's reason for joining the Peace Corps at her age really was?

3. How do you think Deb feels about the Peace Corps now – specifically, at the end of her Postscript? Write a timeline of her ups and downs during her journey.

4. What was the author's purpose of writing this book? What questions would you ask Deb?

5. Who were your favorite characters? Why did you like them? What did they show you or teach you?

6. Did you get a feel for the culture? Did you place judgments on the culture? What sort of judgments? Do you think your culture and values are "Truth" – why or why not?

7. Did the book provoke you to think more about the values that you were raised with? Did you question those values like Deb did during her service?

8. Do you think someone can really belong to a dramatically different culture after being encultured in their birth culture?

9. What do you think about The Ugly American? Can you think of Americans you know like that? How does "Pinoy Pride" or "amor propio" relate to this?
10. Discuss ways that US culture differs from the Philippines' culture as recounted in the book. Hints: attitudes toward work/life balance, food, time, marriage, employment, family.
11. Who would you recommend this book to? Why them?
12. What songs would you put in the movie score to this book? Who would play the characters?
13. Thinking of The Heroes Journey, did the protagonist win or lose in the end? Did she reach her goal, or fail? Was this a triumph or a disaster?
14. If this was your journey in the Peace Corps, what would you have done differently? How would you have approached the challenges?
15. Is the book an Inspiration for you to seek the unknown even if there is risk? Or does it do the opposite and scare off the reader from new things?
16. Were you angry at the author for making you question things? How did you respond to her 'voice'?

About the Author

A native Californian, Deb loves adventure and taking risks. She began her career at Shell Chemical as the first woman promoted to management, then took a break to raise two daughters.

She returned for degrees in Special Education and Educational Therapy and joined the Peace Corps at 59.

Sent to the Philippines, she remained after service and helped start major community projects on the remote island of Palawan. A blissful 10 years later, she returned 'home.'

Deb has had various careers: corporate sales and marketing director, Special Education teacher, Educational therapist, management consultant specializing in organizational development, and now, Author.

She lives in beautiful Avila Beach with her dog, "Twix."

I welcome you to Like my Facebook author page to keep up with me and see exclusive photos from my journey.

Click the following link to head over right away! **Facebook Page** or search it this way. https://www.facebook.com/debra.pritchard.author

www.ingramcontent.com/pod-product-compliance
Lightning Source LLC
Chambersburg PA
CBHW071143130626
46553CB00004B/1493